By THOMAS KUNKEL

MAN IN PROFILE

MAN IN PROFILE

JOSEPH MITCHELL
OF *THE NEW YORKER*

THOMAS KUNKEL

RANDOM HOUSE | NEW YORK

Published in the United States by Random House,
an imprint and division of Random House LLC,
a Penguin Random House Company, New York.

RANDOM HOUSE and the HOUSE colophon are
registered trademarks of Random House LLC.

Grateful acknowledgment is made to Simon & Schuster Publishing Group
for permission to reprint a telegram from M. Lincoln Schuster to Joseph
Mitchell dated November 24, 1944 (New York: Simon & Schuster, Inc.).
All rights reserved. Used with the permission of Simon & Schuster
Publishing Group.

LIBRARY OF CONGRESS CATALOGING-IN-PUBLICATION DATA
Kunkel, Thomas
Man in Profile: Joseph Mitchell of *The New Yorker*/Thomas Kunkel.
pages   cm
Includes bibliographical references and index.
ISBN 978-0-375-50890-5
eBook ISBN 978-0-8129-9752-1
1. Mitchell, Joseph, 1908–1996. 2. Authors, American—Biography.
3. Journalists—United States—Biography. 4. New Yorker
(New York, N.Y.: 1925) I. Title.
PS3525.I9714Z69 2015
818'.54—dc23
[B]   2014024105

Printed in the United States of America on acid-free paper

www.atrandom.com

9 8 7 6 5 4 3 2 1

FIRST EDITION

Frontispiece: Photo by Therese Mitchell
Book design by Barbara M. Bachman

For Deb,
more than ever

Every portrait that is painted with feeling
is a portrait of the artist, not of the sitter.

—Oscar Wilde, *The Picture of Dorian Gray*

CONTENTS

MAN IN PROFILE

CHAPTER 1

THE WONDERFUL SALOON

THROUGHOUT HIS LIFE BILL's principal concern was to keep
McSorley's exactly as it had been in his father's time. When anything had to be changed or repaired, it appeared to pain him physically. For twenty years the bar had a deepening sag. A carpenter
warned him repeatedly that it was about to collapse; finally, in 1933,
he told the carpenter to go ahead and prop it up. While the work was
in progress he sat at a table in the back room with his head in his
hands and got so upset he could not eat for several days. In the same
year the smoke- and cobweb-encrusted paint on the ceiling began
to flake off and float to the floor. After customers complained that
they were afraid the flakes they found in their ale might strangle
them to death, he grudgingly had the ceiling repainted. In 1925 he
had to switch to earthenware mugs; most of the pewter ones had
been stolen by souvenir hunters. In the same year a coin-box
telephone, which he would never answer himself, was installed in
the back room. These were about the only major changes he ever
allowed.

—From "The Old House at Home," 1940

. .

THE LOW, LATE-AFTERNOON SUN FILLS THE FRONT OF McSORLEY'S
wonderful saloon with light the same color as the ale they've
been dispensing here since before the Civil War. Even at this quiet
hour, laborers from the East Village, NYU students, and a few stray
sightseers fill most of the tables and the stools along the (again) sag-
ging bar, across the top of which is carved the legend BE GOOD OR BE

GONE. About half the patrons are women, a fact that would have dismayed "Old John" McSorley, the tavern's founder and namesake, who enthusiastically enforced his male-only policy, to the point of personally showing bolder offenders the door. But progress nudges even landmarks, and McSorley's Old Ale House is one of New York's most venerable. It has been operating here, on East 7th Street just off Cooper Square, longer than any other tavern in the city.

Now a trim, erect man walks in to the tavern, bringing with him a bit of the season's chill air. He removes his coat to reveal a smartly tailored Brooks Brothers suit, white shirt, and dark tie, all topped with a handsome fedora. He hangs the coat on a hook and takes a seat at a table near the back wall. At age seventy, he has the look of a much younger man, made all the more attractive by a small smile that he usually gets when he is back at McSorley's. He is, in a word, exactly what people have in mind when they call a man "dapper."

The elegant patron is the writer Joseph Mitchell, who has lived just a few short blocks from McSorley's since he moved to Greenwich Village in the early forties. It is late autumn of 1978, although because this is McSorley's it might just as well be 1878. He orders a tall mug of ale—at McSorley's you can have light or dark, your only two choices of the house specialty, although they also have porter and stout. McSorley's has never been big on choice, or change. The presence of women, in fact, is about the only accommodation the place has made to a postmodern age (and to its court rulings frowning on gender discrimination, even in quirky saloons). Certainly McSorley's is much as it was in 1940, when Mitchell immortalized it in the pages of *The New Yorker* magazine. The same wavy plank floors are still slick with sawdust. Generations of names are carved into the same oaken tabletops. The same dust, only thicker, coats the same gaslight fixtures and firemen's helmets and stopped clocks. Crowding the walls above the wainscoting are photographs of the same cops and pols and sports heroes, mostly Irish, all as dead as the New York they belonged to.

Mitchell watches the young man at the bar expertly draw another mug of ale, and he considers the establishment's unbroken chain of Irish ownership. Old John McSorley opened it back in 1854 and was its sole proprietor until 1890, when he made his son, Bill, the head bartender. Bill took over in 1910 when the old man died. In 1936, Bill sold McSorley's to a friend, Daniel O'Connell, and it would remain in O'Connell's extended family for several generations until just the past year, when it was sold to Matthew Maher, yet another Irish immigrant who had worked at McSorley's for fourteen years before taking it over. On this lazy afternoon Mitchell appears to be nursing a drink, but what he really is doing is watching, and listening—always listening. He overhears snippets of conversation off to one side or another, and once in a while, maybe catching a well-turned phrase, he removes a folded piece of paper from his jacket and makes note of it. (His note-taking regimen has never changed: Before he goes out for the day, he takes a piece of *New Yorker* copy paper, folds it in half, then neatly folds it again into thirds—the perfect size to slide in and out of a coat pocket, where he also keeps his ever-ready pencil.) In other words, Mitchell is doing precisely what he did back in 1940—hanging out, becoming a McSorley's fixture himself, until the language, rhythms, and lore of the place are second nature and ready to be carried to the page.

Though Mitchell comes here often, on this particular afternoon he has a kind of mission. A friend has asked him to produce an essay in an effort to have the New York City Council proclaim a special day honoring McSorley's when it reaches its soon-approaching one hundred twenty-fifth birthday. To his immense satisfaction, Mitchell's appraisal is that McSorley's not only has changed little since he profiled it almost four decades earlier, but it has changed little since Old John first opened the doors in the middle of the nineteenth century. "It is a landmark that has never had to depend on the Landmarks Preservation Commission or any other commission for its preservation," Mitchell would write. "Its owners and bartenders and pot-boys and waiters and customers have preserved it without any outside help at all." In his fifteen-hundred-word essay, which he apparently never intended for publication, Mitchell testified to the remarkable fact that McSorley's somehow had managed to retain its crusty character even after becoming one of the most famous bars in the world. It did that, Mitchell said, by resolutely clinging to the tried and true:

As in [Old John's] time, fresh sawdust is spread on the floor every morning. And, as in his time, the place is heated by a big potbelly stove. Some days in the dead of winter the coal in the stove is punched up so often that the belly turns cherry red. Several overfed cats sleep in corners or roam around under the chairs and tables, and they are reputed to be descendants of cats owned by John McSorley, who was a cat lover. The old man was especially fond of a cat named Minnie—a picture of her is on one of the walls—and to this day all cats in McSorley's male or female are called Minnie.

At this point in his life, Mitchell finds the saloon's resistance to change particularly gratifying, and it's one of the reasons he keeps coming back. As he recorded in a kind of journal he kept sporadically in his later years, he liked to "find a chair at one of the round tables up near the front window and sit there and look out on the street and drink a few mugs of ale and meditate on times gone by." In subsequent journal notes he would write that "most of the NYC that I knew has disappeared—the Red Devil, the Pantheon, the Villanova, the Blue Ribbon, Perry's Pharmacy in the World Building: coffee urns, counter stools." The Red Devil, Pantheon, and Villanova were but a few of the restaurants Mitchell used to frequent with his great friend and eating companion A. J. Liebling, as well as other *New Yorker* colleagues. The Blue Ribbon was the restaurant where *New Yorker* founding editor Harold Ross recruited Mitchell, back in 1938. Now the Blue Ribbon, like Liebling—like the immortal Ross himself—was gone. McSorley's was one of the few places left where Mitchell could "escape for a while from the feeling that the world is out of control and about to come to an end."

His gloom is understandable. Outside these smoke-infused walls, inflation is galloping and America is stuck in its post-Watergate, post-Vietnam miasma of frustration and cynicism. And New Yorkers have things even worse. Their city is basically broke (only three years earlier, the *Daily News* published its infamous FORD TO CITY: DROP DEAD headline), a crime-ridden punch line, a living symbol of despair and

Joseph Mitchell in the seventies, a time he spent struggling to settle on the subject of his next story.

dysfunction. It's dirty and dangerous, with rampant crime and an army of panhandling homeless. Perhaps worse for Mitchell, a champion of New York's historic preservation, the city has been knocking down its architectural patrimony, including such magnificent examples as McKim, Mead & White's original Pennsylvania Station. The combined circumstances have helped put Mitchell in a discouraged frame of mind, more or less permanently.

Yet Mitchell's discouragement goes a good deal deeper than watching the atrophy of his adopted home, a place he has come to know as intimately as the swamps and tobacco fields of his native North Carolina. By his own admission he has been "living in the past," carrying around a heavy melancholy, for years. He has waged a fierce but worsening battle with depression, or what he would call "the black dog." Just a few years earlier he lost his father, whose approval he sought his entire life and who cultivated in him a still-raw guilt about having left the family homestead half a century ago. His long-term employer, *The New Yorker,* is no longer America's uncontested arbiter of culture, and under its eccentrically brilliant editor, William Shawn, there are now times when it seems to almost parody itself. Then there is the deepest cut: It has been fourteen years since Mitchell has published a piece in the magazine. A man who for decades had been an avatar of literary nonfiction, a role model for a generation of journalistic acolytes, is becoming something of a punch line himself, to jokes about the world's longest case of writer's block. Whispers are turning to outright questioning: What is Joe Mitchell *doing*?

That, alas, is rather hard to answer, especially since, in all those intervening years, Mitchell hasn't exactly been suffering from writer's block; indeed, he has been writing quite steadily throughout. It's just that he isn't *finishing* anything. Some who are close to Mitchell and have watched him become ever more deliberate over the years feel he has turned into such a perfectionist that nothing he produces is good enough for him—and there is at least some truth to that. In his anxious, unsettled state, he is moving from one ambiguous subject to another. Even now, besides the short McSorley's essay, he is hard at work on a book project that is attempting to merge autobiography with an overarching mosaic of his beloved New York City—a kind of Gotham version of what the writer he most reveres, James Joyce, had done with *Dubliners.* But will he be able to do it? By this point he has absolutely no confidence that he can.

LITERARY JOURNALISM IS THE CONVERGENCE of superior reportage and writing that manages to be both penetrating and transcendent. Put another way, it is everyday life transported to the realm of art. It is a union that occurs rarely. Joseph Mitchell was the greatest literary journalist of his time—some would have it of all time. With prodigious

skills of observation, with curiosity and empathy, with prose as unforced as it was precise, Mitchell crafted some of the most memorable
characters in the nonfiction canon. Other *New Yorker* writers, like his
stablemate Liebling, would travel the world or turn to politics or business or war to find compelling subjects; Mitchell found his around the
corner, virtually without leaving the city limits of New York, which as
a young newspaperman he came to know intimately by walking neighborhood by neighborhood, block by block. To say that Mitchell wrote
about New York, however, is to say that his hero wrote about Dublin.
Mitchell, like Joyce, simply used his city as the canvas for stories that
went to the heart of the human condition. So it is that we have Mazie,
the tough Bowery ticket-taker with the heart of gold. And Commodore Dutch, who gave an annual ball to benefit himself. And Ellery
Thompson, world-wise captain of a Connecticut trawler. And the
bearded circus performer, Lady Olga. There are the oystermen and
clam-diggers and fishmongers of Mitchell's treasured waterfront
haunts, as well as the courageous Mohawks who worked in high steel.
There is the strange, mesmerizing figure of Joe Gould, who was com-
piling a massive *Oral History of Our Time*. And there is George Hunter,
who oversaw a remote cemetery on Staten Island and who perfectly
channeled Mitchell's own pervasive sense of melancholy and mortality.

Mitchell seemed to prove the journalist's adage that there is a story
in *anyone* if only you take the time to listen. That's not really true, of
course; everyone may have a story, but it takes a connoisseur to ascertain the handful worth telling. In Mitchell's hands, outwardly unremarkable people yielded remarkable tales, all conveyed with novelistic
detail and the explorer's sense of delight. "He is a reporter only in the
sense that Defoe is a reporter, a humorist only in the sense that
Faulkner is a humorist," said the critic Stanley Edgar Hyman.

Malcolm Cowley was the first significant critic to point out that
Mitchell's work was rising to the level of art. His characters "might
have come straight out of Dickens," Cowley wrote in the early forties.
As it happens, some who knew him well viewed Mitchell himself as a
kind of Dickensian character, idiosyncratic enough to rival his own

colorful subjects. Whether in pursuit of good stories, good talk, or good food, Mitchell walked the city incessantly, and little escaped his notice. He was fascinated by architecture and building materials, and it wasn't uncommon for him to return to the tiny Greenwich Village apartment he shared with his wife and two daughters with bricks (all the manufacturers had their distinctive signatures), or discarded posters from the Fulton Fish Market, or pickle forks from hotel dining rooms (Mitchell wound up accumulating nearly three hundred), or the colorful glass insulators from telephone and electric lines. He saved restaurant menus and matchbook covers and the tiniest of receipts, and he was a faithful member of both the James Joyce Society and the Gypsy Lore Society. He was fastidious to the point of mild eccentricity. He never went outside without his hat, even if he was taking out the trash. If that trash included discarded razor blades or the lids of opened tin cans, he wrapped these carefully and then put them into Mason jars to protect the garbage collectors from accidental cuts. He routinely dusted his extensive book collection. He also enjoyed vacuuming, so much so that, later in life, he was known to turn up at his daughter's apartment having lugged his own Hoover onto the train.

Mitchell was an iconoclast who sought out other iconoclasts, especially if they could talk. Indeed, he was a world-class listener. He could, and did, listen to these talkers for hours without end, long after they would exhaust courtiers with less stamina or imagination. Mitchell would fix his sparkling blue eyes on his subjects, and he would emit an enthusiastic, multisyllabic "*Ye-e-e-ssss!* Yes in-*deed!*" when he thought they'd hit some point squarely on the head. But when so inclined, he was an equally good talker. With his soft Carolina drawl, Mitchell would launch into long, looping monologues, flights often punctuated and further drawn out by his semi-stutter and a vivid memory that kept reminding him of new details to mention as he went along. His discourses threatened to trail off into dead ends until, at the last possible moment, he doubled back onto the subject at hand.

Which is to say, Mitchell had a genius for both unearthing people and then paying attention to them until, in time, they unlocked their own secrets. He also had a playwright's ear for speech and the way language defines character. One reason his subjects are so real is because Mitchell lets them talk, often in lengthy speeches.

Some literary critics have maintained that Mitchell became invisible in his stories, but in fact his is a palpable presence in most of them, be it as narrator or commentator, and the reader learns much about the writer—his appetites, his encyclopedic knowledge of flora and fauna, his Southern roots, his preying mind, his propensity for wandering cemeteries. But more than this, Mitchell often seems almost to inhabit his characters. Like him, they are rooted in the past, they are stubborn but compassionate, and they have scant use for the changes and acceleration of modernity. Certainly he saw a good deal of himself in the figure of John McSorley, who died two years after Joseph Mitchell was born. But Mitchell's reporting—and doubtless that personal connection—brings Old John back to life so vividly that the great man might as well be looking over your shoulder as you read his story. "Except for a few experimental months in 1905 or 1906, no spirits ever have been sold in McSorley's," wrote Mitchell, continuing:

> Old John maintained that the man never lived who needed a stronger drink than a mug of ale warmed on the hob of a stove. He was a big eater. Customarily, just before locking up for the night, he would grill himself a three-pound T-bone, placing it on a coal shovel and holding it over a bed of oak coals in the back-room fireplace. He liked to fit a whole onion into the hollowed-out heel of a loaf of French bread and eat it as if it were an apple. He had an extraordinary appetite for onions, the stronger the better, and said that "Good ale, raw onions, and no ladies" was the motto of his saloon.

Now on this chill autumn afternoon Mitchell finds himself back at McSorley's, where he came so often when seeking to quell some restlessness. Ostensibly here to assess how the saloon was managing its later years, the writer almost certainly was asking the same question of himself. In the fall of 1964, when Mitchell was fifty-six, *The New Yorker* published "Joe Gould's Secret," the surprising sequel to the Profile of the Greenwich Village vagabond he had written two decades earlier. And then … nothing. A naturally private person—his father had taught him it was best not to let people know too much about your business—Mitchell had never been inclined to discuss works in progress. So as year followed year and no new work appeared, and as a kind of stasis settled in on Mitchell, co-workers and readers alike were left to ponder the mystery of a gifted writer who was trapped by his own expectations.

Or maybe he was simply starting to live out the great themes of his best work—stories about earth and sky, time and tide, the serendipity of life and loss, unavoidable sorrow and ultimately death, and, not infrequently, the triumph of the human spirit. He had profiled dozens and dozens of other people, yes, most of whom in some way, cursorily or profoundly, resonated with the writer. Now here he was, literally trying to write about himself—and he was stuck.

CHAPTER 2

THE CENTER OF GRAVITY

TREE-CLIMBING WAS EXHILARATING TO me, and I discovered that I
had a natural aptitude for it, and I got to be quite good at it; it is one
of the few things I have ever been genuinely good at. Barefooted,
and using a throw rope to draw myself up from one limb to another
if the limbs were too widely spaced, I could climb some of the tallest
trees in the branch. . . . Sometimes, up in a tree in one of the thickly
wooded parts of the branch, I would look for some overlapping
limbs from a neighboring tree or for a connecting vine, and I would
cross over to the neighboring tree on the strongest of these limbs or
vines, risking my neck as often as not. . . . It was part of the game to
go from tree to tree as rapidly as possible. Sometimes I was Daniel
Boone pursuing a hostile Indian chief and sometimes I was the hostile Indian chief; sometimes I was the sheriff of Robeson County
pursuing a convict who had escaped from the chain gang and sometimes I was the convict; sometimes I was a slave fleeing on the Underground Railroad and making a gap in my tracks to throw off the
bloodhounds; sometimes I was Jan Ridd, the farmboy hero of my
favorite novel, *Lorna Doone,* fleeing from Lorna's brothers, the out-
laws of the Doone Valley in Exmoor in England. . . .

—From Joseph Mitchell's unfinished memoir

. .

NORTH CAROLINIANS LIKE TO SAY THEIR STATE REPRESENTS THE
nation in microcosm, and at least geographically it does, its
five-hundred-mile expanse reaching from the beaches of the Atlantic
Ocean to the Piedmont to the misty Appalachians. In the state's un-

derbelly, just above the South Carolina border, lies Robeson County, where rivers, swamps, ancient cypress and pine stands, and rich black farmland converge in a natural wonderland for adventurous and imaginative children. Here are places where vine-wrapped trees create a canopy so dense it's always like dusk, and in the pools below, mud sliders crowd the trunks of fallen tulip poplars. In the lower part of the county is the small community of Fairmont, and in Fairmont the Pitman Mill Branch of the Old Field Swamp.

"I spent a large part of my childhood and youth in Pitman Mill Branch," Joseph Mitchell would remember years later, writing in what was intended to be a kind of memoir but was never finished. Land and water—these elements were part of Mitchell from his earliest memories, and they were such powerful forces in his experience they became motifs he would return to again and again in his writing career.

"From the time I was old enough to wander around by myself—old enough, that is, to be trusted to shut gates and to watch out for snakes—until I went away to college, I spent every moment in it that I possibly could," he said of the swamp that abutted the Mitchell family farm. "Quite often, in the winter, I went into the branch as soon as I got home from school and stayed in it the rest of the day. Quite often, in the summer, if I had no work to do for my father, I went into it early in the morning, right after breakfast, and stayed in it until dinner, which we had in the middle of the day, and then I went back and stayed in it until supper. Some days, I kept pretty close to the stream. I would walk beside it, climbing over the fence that marked the western boundary line of my father's land when I reached it and following the stream across other people's lands for several miles. I would walk slowly and keep looking into the water, studying it. The water mesmerized me; everything in it interested me, still or moving, dead or alive. . . ."

By the time young Joseph was frolicking in those trees and swamps, his family had become as much a fixture in Fairmont as Pitman Mill Branch. The Mitchells traced their Robeson County roots to Nazareth Mitchell, a Revolutionary War veteran who was born in the northern reaches of the North Carolina colony in 1758, and who as a twenty-year-old joined the militia in the War of Independence. Nazareth first saw Robeson County during the war, and in 1787 he moved there and started a family. The last of Nazareth's children—born when he was seventy-three years old—was Hugh G. Mitchell, who in turn would have twelve children of his own. One of these, Quince Bostic Mitchell, married Catherine Nance, and in 1881 they had a son, Averette Nance (or A.N., as he was often called later in life). When A.N. took over the family homestead, he became the fourth generation of Mitchells to earn his living from the rich land in and around Fairmont.

Fairmont, Joseph Mitchell observed, "happens to be a remarkably inexact name. The town's original name was Ashpole and this was changed to Union City and this was changed to Fairmont. There are no *monts* in or around it or anywhere near it." At the turn of the century, Fairmont was a village of several hundred people, the small hub of an agrarian region focused on cotton and tobacco. Farms were worked by both poor whites and poor blacks (both often tenant farmers), as well as by Native Americans of the Lumbee tribe, who called this region home and provided much of the backbreaking labor. Indeed, this was one of those parts of the South where race was more than a binary issue; public facilities, for instance, often had three separate sections—labeled WHITES, NEGROES, and INDIANS.

"I used to climb a tremendous white oak high up on the hill of the branch," Mitchell would write, "from one of whose topmost limbs, hidden by leaves, I could look out on a wide panorama of small farms on the southern side of the branch mostly owned by Negro farmers and watch people at work in cotton and tobacco fields who were entirely oblivious of course to the fact that they were being watched and being watched secretly and from aloft and from afar, a situation that made me feel Olympian but at the same time curiously lonely and alien and uneasy and cut off from the rest of the human race, the way a spy might feel, or a Peeping Tom."

Such a tableau would have been equally familiar to A. N. Mitchell when *he* was a boy—though his own childhood was considerably more compressed. When Averette was just fourteen, his father died unexpectedly, suddenly turning the boy into the man of a household that included his mother and six sisters. If that prospect intimidated him, young Averette didn't show it. Confronted with adversity that would buckle many an adult, he simply set out to do what had to be done. On a North Carolina cotton farm in the late nineteenth century, that meant, first and foremost, getting out the crop.

David Britt, who served as North Carolina's Speaker of the House of Representatives and a Supreme Court justice, knew A. N. Mitchell as a law client and family friend. He related a legend about the steely boy who would grow to become one of the most influential men in all of Robeson County.

In early spring of 1896, the first planting season after Quince Mitchell's death, Averette hitched up the family's wagon and rode off to the county seat of Lumberton, a fifteen-mile journey from his small farm outside Fairmont. He planned to get his seed and other supplies from a purveyor his father had used for years, a man named McNeill. The merchant sized up the boy and the situation, then told him, "I'm afraid I've already taken on all I can handle this year." So Averette walked in to the store of another supplier in town. There he found the owner, a man named Caldwell, busily moving around the aisles, and the boy hesitated several times before working up the nerve to interrupt him and make a fourteen-year-old's case for credit. Caldwell listened to his story, which Averette concluded by saying, "If you let me have enough supplies to get started this year, I'll never forget you." The owner decided he would take a chance on this determined if desperate young cotton farmer. Caldwell asked for a list of his seed and supply needs, which the boy had carefully calculated and handed over. After reviewing it, Caldwell said he didn't need any money at the moment; they would settle what was owed when the cotton crop came in.

Some years later, A. N. Mitchell was not only running his own successful farm but was starting to buy up nearby properties and acquiring a name for himself as an up-and-comer in the southeastern part of Robeson County. Back in Lumberton one day, he ran into the merchant McNeill.

"Aren't you Mr. Mitchell's son?" McNeill asked. A.N. said he was.

"Well, I sure would like to do business with you," the merchant said. "Your father did business here with us for I don't know how long."

"Mr. McNeill," A.N. replied, "when I needed you, you wouldn't listen to me. I don't need you anymore."

In 1907, when he was twenty-six, A. N. Mitchell transplanted his mother and his siblings to a new, larger spread in Fairmont proper. He was beginning to make the transition from just another cotton farmer to one who also bought the commodity from others in Robeson County and nearby South Carolina and then resold it to exporters based in Charleston, Norfolk, and other regional ports. A grower was important, but a buyer was a person of greater influence in a farm community.

Young man in a hurry:
A. N. Mitchell in his
twenties.

By this time he was also courting a keen young woman who, while rather traditional in most of her views and carriage, had enough of an independent streak to set her apart. Elizabeth Amanda Parker, born in 1886, was five years younger than the wiry and ambitious A. N. Mitchell. Like many residents of the region, she descended from Scots lineage on both sides. She, too, had grown up on a family farm in Robeson County. Unusually for a girl of that time and place, Betty Parker was a college graduate, having attended Southern Presbyterian College in Red Springs, North Carolina, which later became Flora MacDonald College. "I don't know if she expected to have a career," wrote Joseph Mitchell's daughter Nora Mitchell Sanborn, in a family history, "but she never did."

Indeed, despite her education, she was soon destined for the conventional path of a farm wife, if one with more amenities at her disposal than most. A. N. Mitchell and Betty Parker were married on November 3, 1907. Early on they built a new home, at 305 Church Street in Fairmont, for the large family they anticipated. It was an inviting and comfortable Southern residence, big and breezy and surrounded by screened porches. One side porch, with a row of wicker rocking chairs, would become a favorite gathering spot before and after meals. The home cost seven hundred and fifty dollars; A.N. later built a twin to it next door, for his mother and sisters.

Almost nine months from their wedding day—on July 27, 1908—Elizabeth and A.N. had their first child, a son. He was christened Joseph Quincy Mitchell, the middle name after A.N.'s father. When it came time for his wife to deliver, A.N. was in the hospital, recovering from a contagious fever then circulating in the area, so Joseph was born on the Parker family farm. A Lumbee woman served as the midwife. As it turned out, Joseph would be the first of a passel of Mitchell children—a common-enough occurrence in agrarian families—and the young couple wasted little time. Next came Jack, in 1911, followed by Elizabeth, in 1913; Linda, in 1915; Harry, in 1919; and finally Laura, in 1922. Betty Mitchell spent most of her first two decades of married life chasing around someone in diapers.

By the time Joseph was born, A.N. was well on his way to becoming one of the largest and most influential landowners in the region. Over time he would accumulate upward of six thousand acres, individual farms that the Mitchells continued to reference by their historic names—the Butler Place, Fox Bay, the Townsend Place—and that ultimately would require more than fifty tenant farmers (white, black, and Lumbee) to keep under cultivation. A.N.'s business savvy and intense focus resulted in a remarkable, Horatio Alger type success story. The Mitchells were not wealthy, exactly, but financially they were more than comfortable, especially for that time in that part of America. For instance, when Joseph was young, his family was one of the few in the Fairmont area to own an automobile (though in the beginning its utility was confined to fair weather, as a good rain would turn the country roads to mud). A cook and a cleaning woman helped Joseph's mother with the growing household, while other hired hands were always busy around the Mitchell properties.

So Joseph and his siblings were raised wanting for little. Yet at that time the area was one of the poorest corners of the South, and Mitchell's early grasp of this dichotomy would profoundly affect him and shape his life's work. Pictures of Robeson County taken in the Depression years depict a gritty reality: the dirt roads, the barefoot children in tatty clothing, the swayback clapboard shacks of the Mitchell tenant farmers.

Though A.N.'s formal schooling ended with his father's death, his agile mind never rested. He had a knack for doing complicated mathematics in his head, a useful gift for a man in commodities markets who had to make snap decisions with a great deal of money on the line. He was also quietly observant. A.N. understood not only the natural world, where he made his living, but also a fair amount of human psychology; he had come to learn how both a man's strengths and flaws could be turned to one's advantage if you were shrewd. Yet he played fair; by all accounts he was highly principled and respected, a man whose word was as good as any contract. Later in his life, he would twice be elected mayor of Fairmont.

On the other hand, life had suppressed any youthful frivolity A.N. might once have had; taking on so much responsibility at such a ten-

*The house in Fairmont that A. N. Mitchell built
anticipating a large farm family.*

Young Joseph reads to his siblings, from left, Elizabeth, Jack, and Linda.

der age would give him a stern, emotionally remote mien that marked him for the rest of his life. Though not an unpleasant man, people would say, A. N. Mitchell was certainly not one to be trifled with. Joseph Mitchell often related a story from his early childhood to make that point. Halfheartedly studying arithmetic one afternoon, he saw his father enter the next room, calmly pull a revolver from the bureau drawer, load it, then leave. From an overheard conversation, Joseph knew his father was in a boundary dispute with a violence-prone neighbor. Now A.N. meant to walk the property line with the man, and he wasn't taking any chances. "I wasn't worried about my father in the least," Joseph wrote years later in his journal. A.N. had "a quality of no-nonsense about him. . . . If necessary, he would shoot."

A.N. "was very smart and a good businessman," recalled Nora Mitchell Sanborn in her family memoir, "but . . . he was very dour and intimidating. . . . He called all girls and women 'sister' and all boys and young men 'son' or 'buddy,' and he expected to be called 'sir,' as did . . . most Southern men." To his few intimates he was A.N., or Averette; to most others he was "Mr. Averette" or simply "Mr. Mitchell." To Joseph and his five siblings he was always "Daddy," even when the children had become middle-aged or older themselves. He was, in other words, a formidable figure to most everyone he encountered— including his firstborn son.

THE MITCHELL HOUSEHOLD MOVED to the rhythms of the farming and business cycles, punctuated by the cotton crop (harvested in the fall and sold through the winter) and the tobacco crop (harvested and cured in summer, for sale through early fall). For much of its history, Robeson County was unquestionably "cotton country." Tobacco certainly was grown, and it was important. But cotton was king, and A. N. Mitchell was a cotton man. Having first established himself as a successful grower, then as a buyer, of the Southern staple, A.N. went on to build his own cotton warehouse next to Fairmont's railroad tracks. But with the eventual arrival of boll weevils and the devastation of the cotton industry, tobacco suddenly became the county's cash crop, and A.N. would transition to that commodity as his primary focus—growing it as well as storing it in another warehouse he built for that purpose. In later years the Mitchells, like other farmers in the region, tried their hand at commercial corn and soybean crops. But they couldn't really compete with the big Midwest operations, and in any case they considered those crops considerably less dignified. Cotton and tobacco built the South, they shaped the fate of the nation, they changed how Americans lived. Joseph Mitchell would say that his father could scarcely utter the word "soybean" without an inflection of disgust.

As A.N. rode his properties or visited with other farmers in the county, he often took along young Joseph in the family buggy. It didn't take the boy long to appreciate that life on a farm was hard at best and backbreaking at worst, as experienced by the laborers tending to cotton fields in the oppressively damp Southern summer. ("A lot of men made their career decision during the heat of the day," said David Britt.) Passing by certain farmsteads and houses, A.N. would comment on difficulties those owners had encountered, perhaps recently but as often as not in the distant past. Maybe a hailstorm had ruined a crop, or an estate had been divided up acrimoniously, or a mortgage couldn't be met. Some of the people he discussed were distant relatives of the Mitchells themselves. It astonished the boy how much his father knew about these people, and all of it at ready command. "Know a little something that will be to your advantage," A.N. would tell him. "If you know how some of these people did in the past you'll know how they'll most likely do in the future."

At the same time he advised Joseph not to let anyone know what *he* knew, or what he was thinking. Put this information in the back of your mind, he would say, and don't mention it to anyone else. Never give another man that advantage over you. The father asserted this idea so often that it became almost a mantra to the boy. Joseph understood what his father meant by the admonition; many times he had noted A.N.'s inscrutable face at the seasonal tobacco auctions, which had helped make him a successful broker. But Joseph would adopt this lesson for different purposes. All his life he was remarkably circumspect about himself and especially about his work. Even fellow writers who were close friends didn't know what Mitchell was working on most of the time, and eventually they learned not to ask. On the other hand, Mitchell himself was forever observing others, deriving information from them or about them. It underlay his endless sense of curiosity. Know a little something that will be to your advantage, said the voice in his head.

The boy didn't realize it at first, of course, but these father–son transactions were all part of an implicit apprenticeship, a tradition centuries old. It was assumed Joseph, as scion of a family that had been tied to the land for generations, would make his career there in Fairmont, first working with his father and brothers, then eventually taking over as the head man. In the rural South of the time, this was so evident it scarcely needed saying.

At home, Betty Mitchell ran things as efficiently as A.N. ran his business, and family life revolved around her. She was "one of the finest women you would see," said Britt, who was Joseph's contemporary growing up in Fairmont. She was friendly if not especially outgoing. She preferred simple dresses and wore her hair in a long braid down her back or wrapped about her head. She doted on her children and didn't often leave her comfortable house, except for trips to the local stores, where she exchanged gossip with the merchants and her neighbors. She was nearly puritanical about the use of bad language in her presence.

As in many farm families, the day's routine centered on a main meal. In the Mitchell home this was the noontime repast, called dinner (the evening meal being supper), an opportunity for the men to come in from the fields, eat, and get some rest before returning to the day's labors. This tended to be a capacious spread, featuring the bounty of their farms and extensive gardens. According to Nora Mitchell Sanborn, a typical dinner from her father's childhood might include fried chicken, biscuits, a variety of beans (all prepared with fatback), tomatoes, onions, cucumbers, corn, and iced tea. And the feast was always followed by some kind of homemade dessert. In summer this might be a fresh pie that the family cook, a black woman named Anna

McNair, made from huckleberries that young Joseph had picked while out in the swamp.

Though Betty Mitchell had few material wants, her life was not a placid one. A.N. loved his family but he was not the easiest man to please or be married to. Betty worked hard to put across the image of a perfect family, as her neighbors' impressions were important to her—her own father had been a bit of a ne'er-do-well—and to her husband, given their position in the community. Her granddaughter suggested that "she must have had a pretty hard life, raising six children, close in age, with a distant, silent husband who was destined from childhood to be as obsessed by work as she was destined to be insecure about what would happen next."

Still, she had more than enough spirit to challenge her husband, if need be—as is evident from an anecdote Mitchell enjoyed telling friends. Sunday was supposed to be a day of rest, church, and a big dinner. At certain times of the year, however, A.N. spent part of his Sunday on the telephone to Texas—long-distance, that is, when such calls were a nearly unheard-of extravagance—talking to fellow cotton dealers about market conditions. Midday one Sunday, the family was gathered at the table, ready for the meal, but waited and waited while A.N. carried on his business. The children saw their mother becoming increasingly irritated with her husband's priorities. At last he joined them in the dining room. As he did, Betty said sharply, in what would be as close as she would come to reproaching him in front of others, "Averette, did your ox fall in the ditch?"

As a girl, Betty likely didn't venture beyond the county line much more than young Averette Mitchell had. Yet as the first person on either side of Joseph Mitchell's family to attend college, she had a much more visceral sense of the world than her husband did, at least until business caused him to travel occasionally. According to her grandson Jack Mitchell, Betty subscribed to dozens of magazines and devoured them, and she always had them around the house for her children—especially Joseph—to devour, as well. Thanks to her formal education, Betty also had a highly developed cultural appreciation, and she particularly loved books. She ingrained in her first child a passion for reading and a taste for literary variety. Joseph read constantly; even when he was "doing his homework," he often had a novel slipped inside the textbook, taking pains not to let his father see it. Betty ensured that once Joseph outgrew children's books he became familiar with Mark Twain (who would remain a lifelong favorite) and the action stories of Jack London. As an adolescent reader, Joseph was particularly enamored of Francis Parkman's *The Oregon Trail*, a romantic and popular recounting of a young man's adventures in the American West. While it's doubtful that Betty Mitchell's intent was to plant the notion that her son's future lay elsewhere, she wanted him to know there was life beyond the fields and swamps of Fairmont, North Carolina.

Though A.N. didn't travel all that often—he didn't enjoy it much, frankly—when he did he sometimes took family along. As a boy, Joseph, unlike most of his Fairmont friends, was exposed to the excitements of actual cities—Wilmington, Charleston, Savannah, and beyond—and these excursions were thrilling to him. For a lad already transported by literature, one of the highlights was visiting honest-to-goodness bookstores. (Mitchell specifically recalled buying copies of *Winesburg, Ohio* and *Madame Bovary* during one visit.) But one trip easily trumped all the others: the time A.N. took Joseph with him to New York City. The boy was all of ten years old, and the impact of *that* journey on Joseph Mitchell, who later in life would chronicle the great metropolis like few others, was never doubted by his family. According to Mitchell lore, the first time he saw the skyscrapers and hurly-burly of Gotham, Joseph declared to his father, "This is for me."

THAT TRIP ALSO WOULD have marked one of Joseph's earliest opportunities to see firsthand the divergent social structures of North and South. While discrimination was a fact of life in both regions, it was fixed in Southern law and woven throughout Southern life. On the other hand, everyday interaction between whites and blacks was much more routine and natural in the South than in the North, where often the races were physically segregated from each other. Certainly Joseph had the typical Southern farm child's exposure to, and familiarity with, people of color. He was at ease with them because he literally grew up with them.

But for anyone living in Robeson County just after the turn of the century, there was an additional element in his or her racial consciousness—the population of Native Americans. In fact, the county traditionally had been divided into roughly one-third of each group. Many of the Native Americans were members of the Lumbee tribe. For the most part they lived along the Lumber River, which in its meandering from northwest to southeast roughly bisects Robeson County. Post-emancipation, the three groups coexisted uneasily at best. Blacks faced the same kinds of discrimination that their brothers and sisters did throughout the South; in fact, some chroniclers of the civil-rights movement consider the prejudice rooted around Robeson County to have been among the most virulent in the nation. And as for the Lumbees, well, in the eyes of many whites they were inferior even to blacks. The upshot is that Joseph Mitchell, while completely comfortable interacting with all his neighbors, witnessed what it was like for many of them to live as second-class, or even third-class, citizens.

Born into a family that had farmed North Carolina's coastal plain for well over a century, Joseph knew from an early age that his ancestors included slaveholders; later in life he would discover that his Nance forebears might have owned as many as one hundred. But whenever the inquisitive boy raised the subject, he found it was not one A.N. was especially interested in discussing. Mitchell would recall the "irritation in his voice" while rebuffing his son's curiosity. Of course, this was not an uncommon reticence, or even one confined to whites. When Mitchell was getting acquainted with George Hunter, the African American son of an escaped slave and the protagonist of Mitchell's 1956 story "Mr. Hunter's Grave," the two men were talking about their respective family histories. Hunter asked Mitchell whether his family had owned slaves. He reluctantly acknowledged that they had. "Mr. Hunter," he said, "I've thought about it a lot. It's just all history. I can't even visualize it. I'm sorry." George Hunter said he understood. He told the writer that he often asked his mother to talk about her slave experiences as a girl in Virginia, but she was disinclined to rake up those memories. She would simply say, "Let the dead bury the dead."

It would be hard to find a more "Southern man" than A. N. Mitchell, circumspect and proud. A product of his times and temperaments, he fully embraced the planter's lifestyle. Yet when it came to race, it seems his judgment of a person had much more to do with what he did and how he comported himself than with what ethnicity he happened to be. Part of this owed to A.N.'s being an unsentimental businessman who had various men of color working for him as tenant farmers and whose capabilities contributed to his own prosperity. A.N. knew well which farmers could be relied upon and which couldn't, who warranted credit and who didn't, who drank to excess and who didn't, who respected his wife and who didn't—and none of that had anything to do with skin color. But the consistency of A.N.'s outlook suggests it went beyond mere self-interest to a deeper level of tolerance. For instance, in an environment where whites routinely referred to blacks as "niggers," A.N. and Betty considered this an offensive term. Mitchell related an episode that occurred when he was small and accompanying his father to a country store. A drunken white man in the store was carrying on at length about "niggers." On their way home, A.N. became increasingly upset about the man's tirade, and he reinforced his objection to that "ugly way of talking." He told Joseph, "I never heard my own father use the word nigger and I never heard my own mother use it, and you never heard me use it, and you certainly never heard your mother use it, and don't you ever let me hear you use it."

Nor was A.N. enamored of the Ku Klux Klan vigilantes then spreading fear in the Carolinas. "I'm not in favor of people taking the law in their own hands," he said. This attitude indirectly led to one of Mitchell's better-known early contributions to *The New Yorker:* "The Downfall of Fascism in Black Ankle County," a short story he wrote in 1939 during his first year at the magazine. Mitchell's fictional Black Ankle County is a sparsely populated North Carolina region of cotton fields, tobacco barns, plain white churches, moonshine stills, slow-moving rivers—not to mention the gooey, tarry flats that give the county its name. It's a place, in other words, much like Mitchell's native Robeson County. (Not far from Fairmont, in fact, is an actual swamp known as Black Ankle, one of many interconnected swamps that permeate the county.)

"Downfall of Fascism" is a comic telling of the brief history of the local Klan chapter. The group is populated exclusively by local eccentrics, no-accounts, and drunks, headed up by one Mr. Catfish Giddy, who leads his sheet-wearing cohorts on B-grade night rides and cross burnings more as an excuse to get out of the house than to provoke real terror. They are finally brought to heel when the three moonshine-manufacturing Kidney brothers, having been tipped off to the fact that they are to be targeted, lie in wait for the Klansmen—and in their own state of inebriation set off dynamite charges so fearsome that they rattle half the county. No one is actually hurt, but the next day a clearly shaken Mr. Giddy, having contemplated the fate he narrowly escaped, tells everyone he encounters, "Friend, I have resigned." Resigned from what? they ask. "Don't make no difference what I resigned from," Mr. Giddy replies. "I just want you to know I resigned."

What Mitchell's readers could not have known is that "Downfall" was based on one frightening evening the writer himself experienced, probably when he was the same age—about fifteen—as his narrator in the story. According to family accounts, Klansmen had made it known around the county that they were going to stage a ride to the Mitchell home after A.N. had refused their request to use his cotton warehouse for a meeting. Taking the threat seriously, A.N. readied himself with a shotgun—and likewise armed Joseph and his younger brother Jack. They sat on the front porch and waited into the evening. At last the sheet-wearing riders materialized from out of the darkness. As they neared the house, A.N. calmly stood, raised his gun, and fired a blast over their heads. The Klansmen retreated, and that was the end of the trouble.

It doesn't take much imagination to appreciate what an indelibly terrifying experience that must have been for a teenage boy. But the episode provided Joseph Mitchell with more than fodder for a good story. It reinforced a notion about tolerance, not to mention about right and wrong, that he repeatedly saw in the example of his parents. Due in great part to their enlightened perspectives, Mitchell developed his own acute sense of social justice and a deep appreciation for the underdog—values that went on to inform a lifetime of storytelling.

CONSIDERING HOW SMALL AND OUT of the way Fairmont was—think Andy Griffith's Mayberry, if Mayberry had slave descendants, Native Americans, tenant farmers, and tobacco—it's hardly surprising that some of Mitchell's most vivid childhood memories centered on the annual arrival of the traveling circus. This highly anticipated event was a commotion of lights, foods, music, and people quite different—including exotic gypsies and sideshow acts—from those he was exposed to the other fifty-one weeks of the year. "They were just little one-ring circuses, you know," he would recall. "There'd be an elephant and a camel and a half dozen other animals—that would be enough for Fairmont. It was just a little town. But that was such an exciting time. They'd be playing those 'race records,' don't you know, and those fish cafés would be open just about all night. My God, you never saw such a time." Then he added slyly: "Course, the rest of the year was pretty dull."

In fact, about the only other excitement sleepy Fairmont experienced coincided with the tobacco auctions. On these days, when the corporate buyers converged on the town to assess and bid on that year's crops, Fairmont took on a charged atmosphere that was a bit like the circus in miniature. Mitchell's daughter Nora called the auction days of Joseph's youth "a veritable carnival, with medicine men and blues singers and entertainment and scam artists of every kind." People of all classes and colors crowded the town, mingling and gorging themselves on fried foods, grilled meat, and sweet, succulent melons. More than a business, the auction was an entertainment—a fact hardly lost on Mitchell. "My father was very proud of running a tobacco warehouse," he said. "The kid whose father was an auctioneer, Christ,

Tobacco farmers bring their product to market in Fairmont,
just after the turn of the century.

your father could be the ringmaster in the circus and he wouldn't be
any better. He was in show business."

Of course, in Mitchell's culture, raucous Saturday nights inevitably
gave way to sober Sunday mornings. Like the majority of their neighbors, generations of Mitchells were raised as Southern Baptists. But
with her deep Scots roots, Betty was an observant Presbyterian. Thus,
when the family headed off for Sunday services, Betty went to her
church with her daughters, and A.N. took the boys to the main establishment in town, the First Baptist Church. Joseph publicly professed
his Christian belief in the fall of 1923, at age fifteen, and was baptized.
But what he seems to have most carried away from those early religious experiences, as animatedly practiced in the rural South early in
the century, was the fear and the trauma they could, and indeed were
intended to, provoke.

This is clear from notes he made for his unfinished autobiography.
Summoning memories more than half a century after the fact, he
could still smell the brimstone and would shudder. His was "an old-
line fundamentalist Southern Baptist church," he wrote, "a kind that

identified itself in those days with a line in gold letters across the top of the announcement-box in the yard in front of it: WE PREACH JESUS CHRIST CRUCIFIED RISEN AND COMING AGAIN." Each week Mitchell attended both Sunday school and the regular service, occasionally returning Sunday night for yet more worship. "By the time I was an adolescent I was so familiar with hell that I began to have nightmares," he said, going on to recall riveting, if at times terrifying, preachers at revival. He remembered one in particular who dropped to his knees in front of the congregation as he impersonated a hapless sinner consigned to hell and begging for a drop of water. Then the preacher was suddenly on his feet again and playing the role of Satan, jabbing at the wretch with his imaginary pitchfork and reminding him that he didn't think about the consequences "when you spent entire Sundays lying on the riverbank drunk, did you?"

For young Mitchell, hell was no abstract concept but a real place of eternal torment and cruelty. It's hardly unusual for weighty matters of belief to occupy an intelligent child, but evidence suggests they really preyed on Mitchell's mind. He recalled in particular one childhood discussion with his mother, prompted by the emotional funeral of a family friend. Afterward, the son quizzed his mother on heaven and hell—what they were, where they were—in a colloquy that segued into the larger concept of God. Betty Mitchell patiently tried to answer his questions, until he had her mildly exasperated, in the way that only astutely inquisitive children can exasperate a parent. Finally she moved to foreclose further discussion, declaring flatly, "God is everywhere. He has always been everywhere. He was here before He created here. He was always here."

Wrote Mitchell, in his sixties: "Her answer confused me then and confuses me now."

Still, his fundamentalist upbringing formed a baseline of belief and took a firm hold on him—one he spent much of the rest of his life trying to shake. But he never really could, no matter what the rest of his life's experience, his intellect, or his copious reading was telling him. The Baptist ministers of his youth had insinuated themselves too deeply into his psyche to scrub, and it is no coincidence that later in life Mitchell would write about countless preachers, some of them truly inspirational, others little more than grifters. He was alternately bemused and in awe of them, and in any case they were Proustian connections to his childhood.

Which is not to say Joseph was a sober mope. On the contrary, he was a highly energetic child who mostly spent his days doing what all kids did—he played, dreamed, socialized, explored. As he looked back on it, this part of his childhood was idyllic. A collector from his earliest days, he liked to roam the nearby fields after a hard rain to see what kinds of arrowheads and Indian pottery shards had been dislodged. He and his friends played on a rope swing that hung from a massive white oak on the property. Then there were those many happy hours spent in the swamp trees, where he used an ingenious "climbing rope" of his own design, which had knots for handholds and rag-loop footholds tied into it and a brickbat at the end to return the rope to him when he slung it over the next branch up. High above the ground, moving from tree to tree, the boy's vivid imagination also took flight. Naturally, many other Fairmont kids could be found cavorting in those same trees and swamps. But it's a good bet the only one who was well read enough to pretend to be dashing Jan Ridd of Exmoor was Joseph Mitchell.

Literally everything about the swamp environment fascinated him, as passages from his draft memoir make clear.

> I was just as interested in a streak of a kind of algae known locally as frog snot or in a cluster of old dead cypress roots covered with snails as I was in the fish and the crawfish and the water bugs and the water snakes. The water was the color of whiskey or tea—from some substance in the leaves and pine needles and cypress needles rotting in it, I was always told. You weren't supposed to drink it—people said you could get chills and fevers, by which they meant malaria, from drinking branch water—but it looked clean enough to drink. . . . There were no well-defined paths in the branch and walking along beside the stream not watching where I was going, I would brush against some of the

plants with my pants legs or step on them, bruising them, whereupon their various and sometimes quite surprising fragrances would suddenly fill the air. And occasionally I would reach down and pull a handful of leaves from some aromatic plant—a kind that I especially liked, such as wild ginger or wax myrtle or dog fennel, or a kind that might be unfamiliar to me and, for all I knew, poisonous—and crush them in my hand and smell them. Hours later, sometimes, the smell would still be on my fingers. And quite often, at night, taking off my clothes and hanging them up before going to bed, I would smell the fragrances of aromatic plants on my pants legs.

Such recollections do more than convey the unfettered joy of a rural childhood; they underscore the boy's inborn powers of observation. Mitchell grew up knowing all these things in real time, as it were—what the plants were, the names of the trees, the flight patterns of red-tailed hawks and great horned owls, which reptiles were dangerous and which harmless, what was lurking in those tea-colored pools. He grasped "the significance and provenance of every arrowhead and pottery shard, the names of every native weed, flower, snake, bird and fish," his daughter Nora would write. This acuity was due not only to Joseph's prodigious curiosity but also to both parents, who took pains to educate their children about the natural world surrounding them—if for no other reason than safety's sake. Beyond that, however, Betty in particular brought an aesthetic appreciation to these lessons. Just as she had with Joseph's reading, for instance, she cultivated in her young son a passion for wildflowers.

The boy's curiosity extended to the county's families and their collective history. Many of these families were interwoven with the Mitchells and Parkers, and, as Joseph noted himself, he "developed an interest in it long before I was ten years old; the more attenuated the relationship, the more interesting it was."

This part of his education also sprang from his parents, as well as from various aunts and uncles. Instead of the swamps, here Mitchell's "classrooms" were the myriad little cemeteries that are as much a part of the North Carolina landscape as are the piney woods. Mitchell often addressed the emotional and intellectual significance of cemeteries in his life. They were not eerie or sad places but vibrant extensions of everyday life, to be used by the living to remain connected to kin who had "gone on." When Joseph was a boy, for instance, his Baptist church routinely held Easter-egg hunts in its cemetery, the prizes hidden in the tall grass and weeds in and around the tombstones. "How wonderful it was to find them in the graveyard," he recalled, "right where my grandmothers and grandfathers were buried." Sunday rides in the country often included stops at cemeteries, where his father and mother would find the plots of their relatives and explain who they were to the children. At other times, Betty and her sisters would get together for a picnic behind their church after Sunday service, and once the fresh-picked watermelon was sliced and consumed, the group would stroll over to the adjacent cemetery. Mitchell's Aunt Annie in particular could be counted on for some no-nonsense commentary on the graveyard denizens. "Here and there she would pause at a grave and tell us about the man or woman down below," he wrote. "'This man buried here,' she would say, 'was a cousin of ours, and he was so *mean* I don't know how his family stood him. And this man here,' she would continue, moving along a few steps, 'was so *good* I don't know how his family stood him.'"

Still, the person who figured most prominently in young Joseph's life, far and away, was Daddy. Like so many sons throughout history, Joseph Mitchell would spend his entire life endeavoring to win his father's approval. Even as a boy, he somehow sensed that their bond was destined to be an emotionally complicated one. In his journal notes, written some six decades after the fact, Mitchell recorded an especially harrowing childhood memory. Like all farmers who owned land in and around the swamps, A.N. often was out clearing dead trees or removing stumps—the latter usually involving dynamite. Joseph was fascinated by this process, so calculated and yet so violent. A.N. was an "expert dynamiter," his son recalled; he had tried to train others to do it, but they would displace too much earth with the explosion or set up the charges so that they achieved more noise than results. But

A.N. seemed to know exactly how to do it. He approached the task carefully, like an engineer. He would circle the stump repeatedly, studying it, almost trying to "understand" it, before deciding how much dynamite to use and where to put it. "It was the first time I ever heard the phrase 'center of gravity,' which I love," Joseph wrote.

Yet the boy, already well steeped in his Bible studies, also read a dark metaphor into the inherent danger of this father–son moment. "It reminds me somehow of the story of Abraham and Isaac and other stories about sacrifice that I had heard," he wrote. The very thought, he said, "horrified me."

More prosaically, of course, stump-dynamiting represented another of the essential lessons in a farmer's education. "He never said so in so many words," Mitchell recalled, "but I knew he expected me to follow in his footsteps." Yet as he got older, Joseph privately was feeling much less sanguine about the idea. He loved Fairmont, loved the country life, and genuinely admired his father. But the prospect of one day taking A.N.'s place thoroughly intimidated him.

Each passing year introduced more reasons for doubt. His love of literature was showing him there was a wider, more interesting world beyond Robeson County, and the sporadic travel he'd already done with his family only whetted his desire to experience more of it. It would be a lot of pressure, trying to replicate his father's accomplishments and stature; hundreds of people relied on him for everything from small loans to planting advice to their very livelihoods. But a more acute, and practical, reason for Joseph's apprehension was simply this: He was terrible at math. Quick as he was in every other way, for Joseph the sort of rote addition, subtraction, and multiplication that most children master by fifth grade was sheer misery. It wasn't for lack of effort. He did the same kinds of memorization drills as his schoolmates, and he could grasp the underlying concepts. But for some inexplicable reason, the computational mental process that quickly becomes second nature for most people simply froze him. It was an organic condition that never really improved for the rest of his life.

The boy understood how such an obstacle would thwart someone in his father's line of work. "You have to be extremely good at arithmetic" at commodities auctions, he told the literary critic Norman Sims in a wide-ranging interview conducted when Mitchell was eighty. "You have to be able to figure, as my father said, to deal with cotton futures, and to buy cotton. You're in competition with a group of men who will cut your throat at any moment, if they can see the value of a bale of cotton closer than you. I couldn't do it, so I had to leave. . . . Millions have come to New York City who didn't quite fit in somewhere."

The situation made the boy miserable. It embarrassed him, and classmates, as they will, teased him. Much worse, he constantly feared his father would bring up the math issue—"deliberately or inadvertently." His daughter Nora said it often *was* deliberate—and not infrequently this played out at the dinner table, with the entire family there to watch. It's unlikely that cruelty was A.N.'s intent; he surely believed this "tough love" would help crack what he assumed was merely a mental block for his intelligent son. Then again, he wouldn't have been especially concerned if it *did* seem cruel. According to Nora, he "tortured" Joseph with quizzes: "He would ruin meals by shooting arithmetic problems at [him]—'8 times 6?' '30 minus 7?' '200 times 15?' '13 squared?' I'm sure this was the beginning of his ulcer and his terrible headaches."

In later years, Mitchell tried to compensate for the disability by keeping almost obsessive numbers-oriented records and lists. These were not just the basic ones many people maintain, such as stock holdings or important dates (though he kept those, too), but lists of things most people don't think twice about. Mitchell's files are full of handwritten tallies of amounts he'd paid for dry cleaning, books, movies, cab fare, lunches, even tips. Going over them, one imagines a man who felt that if he committed everything to paper, where the numbers couldn't shift around on him, he might just wrest some control over his frustrating condition.

Tellingly, as an older man, Mitchell would sometimes refer to his math disability as a kind of dyslexia, the reading disability that didn't really enter popular consciousness until the seventies. In retrospect, it's quite possible that Mitchell suffered from a related condition called dyscalculia, which is the inability to perform basic mathematic functions. Just as dyslexics have a fundamental problem perceiving, say, the correct letter order in a word, people afflicted with dyscalculia might transpose numbers in their head, or confuse symbols, or otherwise jumble the components of the math equation in front of them. And they often come from parents who are exceedingly good at math, which only fuels their sense of anxiety or inadequacy. On the other hand, many sufferers are gifted with words; it's not unusual for them to become writers and journalists. Although Mitchell is not known to have been so diagnosed, or even to have known of the existence of dyscalculia, he clearly experienced many of the condition's symptoms.

This shortcoming created a stigma for Mitchell that went to the bone. The extent of his anxiety is most vividly illustrated in a vignette Mitchell produced in his journal in 1986. It was prompted by a recent

*Mitchell (in the middle of the third row)
amid his classmates at Fairmont High School.*

visit back to North Carolina, where he learned of the death of a woman named Ruth Page Magnin. Ruth, whom Mitchell describes as a "consumptive-looking but appealing" girl, was in Mitchell's high school class, and her father was one of the growers who sold cotton to A. N. Mitchell. In the scene, Ruth—presumably also math-challenged—resolutely refuses her teacher's directive to go to the blackboard to work problems in front of the class. Mitchell expresses a grateful admiration for a frail girl's courage—a courage one infers he had difficulty summoning in himself.

Go to the board, meaning the blackboard. God bless you, Ruth: You were delicate, but you outlived almost everybody in the class, and you never went to the board. Self sufficient. I'll take the consequences, but I won't go to the board.

When you went to the board, you put yourself entirely in the hands of the teacher: She could make a fool of you in front of everybody. A way of putting a rebellious student in his place, cutting a pupil down to size.

Long division, algebra. Some people, standing up there with a piece of chalk in their hand, if I did know it when I was sitting down, I didn't know it when I stood up.

What I learned from her, if you are willing to take the consequences, all you have to do is say no. If the bastards get you into a corner, all you have to do is say no.

Go to the board, Ruth.

I don't go to the board. . . .

Given that the episode occurred more than sixty years prior, the scene is noteworthy for Mitchell's still-raw ire, even rage. But one sees as well the small-town provincialism and petty tyranny that, even at a tender age, chafed him. After four generations, a Mitchell son was determining that the future awaited somewhere other than in Robeson County, North Carolina.

CHAPTER 3

CHAPEL HILL

I DIMLY RECOLLECT ONE DAY long ago at the university hearing you or Jack Crow or one of the other Spanish buffs or maybe it was one of the campus intellectuals at *The Tar Heel* or *The Carolina Magazine* say something about the enigmatic quality or the mysteriousness of the Spanish proverbs that were the inspiration for many of Goya's *Caprichos* and that he used as titles for some of them. It is more than likely that I had never even heard of Goya before, but for some rea-son that aroused my curiosity and I went right over to the art de-partment in the old library and got out whatever they had on the *Caprichos*, and my lifelong admiration for Goya began that after-noon.

—*From a letter to a University of North Carolina classmate, 1985*

. .

I N THE SPRING OF 1925, JUST SHY OF HIS SEVENTEENTH BIRTHDAY, Jo-seph Mitchell graduated from Fairmont High School. A.N. had not entirely given up the hope that his eldest might yet follow in his foot-steps, but he was a pragmatist and for now he knew Joseph needed to continue his explorations. The young man had lately expressed a desire to study medicine, and even for A.N. that was an acceptable career alternative. He acceded to his son's wish to attend the University of North Carolina at Chapel Hill. Founded in 1789, Chapel Hill had a long-established reputation for academic excellence and was one of a handful of more "worldly" outposts available to the state's brighter students. Situated in the middle of North Carolina, one hundred miles north of Fairmont and just west of the capital, Raleigh, it was (and remains) an exceedingly beautiful campus, its colonial-style brick buildings tucked amid ancient stands of Southern pine.

Socially, Mitchell thoroughly enjoyed his first extended time away from home, and he was a popular student. By now he had grown to his full height, a trim five feet ten inches. He had acquired a handsome, almost pretty face accentuated by penetrating blue eyes and a prominent but aquiline nose. A farm boy accustomed to hard labor and roughhousing with friends, he nonetheless carried himself with a physical grace surprising for a product of swamps and cotton fields.

In his first year, Mitchell, like all Tar Heel freshmen, plunged into his general coursework, with a particular emphasis on subjects he most loved—English, history, and geology (in fact, Mitchell would wind up taking enough geology courses to earn nearly the equivalent of a minor in it). But it seems that early on at Chapel Hill, his medical ambitions were scuttled by "his paralysis over mathematics," in the words of his daughter Nora; doctors needed to be able to perform mental calculations as adroitly as tobacco buyers. More than that, because math proficiency was a requirement for graduation, Mitchell quickly realized that his "block" would likely preclude his earning a degree. He explained the situation years later, during World War II, when he was applying for a position with the Writers' War Board: "It became obvious, after my freshman year, that I could not cope with college mathematics and would never be able to get a degree, so I was given permission by the dean of the college of liberal arts to become what was called a special student. Thereafter, I studied much as I chose, taking courses in journalism, history, philosophy, geology and biology."

It's not clear when he conveyed this setback to his parents, though he may well have waited lest A.N. immediately reel him back to Fairmont. Nor is it known exactly how Mitchell's math disability came to the attention of the university's administrators in the first place, as his transcript doesn't show him being enrolled in *any* kind of math class at Chapel Hill. No matter; Mitchell was now free to pursue a self-selected liberal arts portfolio, which, beyond the subjects he mentioned in his letter, would include courses in Spanish, French, sociology, and music.

DILLARD S. GARDNER
Editor-in-Chief

GARLAND McPHERSON
Business Manager

The Carolina Magazine

EDITORIAL STAFF

JOHN O. MARSHALL	*Assistant Editor*
J. Q. MITCHELL	*Associate Editor*
SHEPPERD STRUDWICK	*Associate Editor*

BUSINESS STAFF

T. J. GOLD	*Assistant Business Manager*
GORDON GRAY	*Assistant Business Manager*
J. E. MARSHALL	*Auditor*

Following his muse: Mitchell wrote and edited stories for
The Carolina Magazine *while a student at Chapel Hill.*

His record reveals a solid if not superior student, one earning A's, B's, and C's more or less equally throughout his four years there.

Though disappointed that he would never earn a degree, Mitchell understood that his academic dilemma was, in a perverse way, a gift. He used his latitude to pursue subjects that he liked and needed and that expanded his cultural awareness; the result was a unique education that ran from the discovery of artists (such as Goya) to new literary inspirations (Crane, Dostoevsky, Turgenev, and others). Mitchell was like a hungry field hand sitting down to a yawning meal. He found himself especially drawn to the emerging modernists—most significantly the early work of James Joyce. It was at Chapel Hill that he first read *Ulysses;* a fellow student who had been abroad smuggled it back (considered obscene, it was still effectively banned in America at the time) and shared it with Mitchell. But later in his life Mitchell would say it was an unexpectedly compelling course on Chaucer that left the most enduring mark on him. "I probably learned more about writing in that course than I did working on newspapers," he said.

Fairly early in his time at Chapel Hill, he fell in with the campus's circle of student writers, and he was appointed one of the editors of *The Carolina Magazine,* the student literary publication. Mitchell and his colleagues wrote as well as edited, swapping story drafts for feedback. His own writing tended to be set in the rural world he knew so well, but its themes were moving into more expansive explorations of the human condition. Yet he was still a Fairmont boy and a Baptist in good standing, as is clear from an amusing exchange of letters, late in Mitchell's life, with one of his best friends and classmates at Chapel Hill, John Armstrong Crow. After university, Crow would go on to become a distinguished writer himself and a respected Latin American scholar. Reminiscing about their college years, Crow told Mitchell, "I remember our meetings with Parson Moss . . . with nostalgia, especially the time Lionel Stander asked [him] if he thought Jesus had ever had intercourse, and as I recall things the question aroused an angry response from you, who evidently considered it not appropriate."

By junior year, Mitchell had found another outlet for his writing and expanding curiosities: journalism. Mitchell had carried around the writing bug for a number of years—at least as far back as the fifth grade, when he entered an essay contest and won a five-dollar prize. A few years later, one of the magazines he was reading religiously was *Lone Scout,* published by the Boy Scouts of America specifically for kids like him, whose homes were so remote that troops were unavailable to them. Early in 1925 the magazine reported in a small news item that "Joseph Mitchell of Fairmont, North Carolina" was intending to publish an "Amateur Journalism Annual" that will be sixteen pages, in color, and cost ten cents. (*Lone Scout* apparently encouraged such self-publications, which it called "tribe papers.") It's not known if Mitchell, just sixteen at the time, actually published the annual, but his early seriousness of purpose was evident.

At Chapel Hill he took at least seven journalism courses, the closest subject to a major had he graduated. Just as important, North Carolina's journalism school maintained intimate ties to the state's newspapers, and those connections doubtless served Mitchell well, as at about this same time he began contributing freelance pieces—so-called "Sunday features"—to a handful of the better ones: Raleigh's *News & Observer,* the *Charlotte Observer,* the Durham *Herald-Sun,* the Asheville *Citizen,* the Greensboro *Daily News.* A visit to the Wilmington newspaper, where an older colleague who had already graduated was working as a reporter, further whetted Mitchell's interest. Later, as his confidence grew and he expanded his range, he also published in *The Baltimore Sun.*

In terms of his development, more important than *what* he was writing was the mere fact that Mitchell *was* writing, seriously writing, both nonfiction and fiction—and that he was being published. Writing for him was not the dilettantish exercise it was for many of his campus counterparts, and he knew it. As it sank in that his future was not to be found back on the Mitchell homestead, "I knew I had to get some other way of making a living."

By the spring of 1928, Mitchell short stories were appearing regularly in *The Carolina Magazine.* If the work was literarily wanting in places ("I stumbled up the stairs and went into the coffee shop, and ordered a sardine sandwich because I always order a sardine sandwich when I get drunk and go into a coffee shop" or "Yuh can trust a good horse, but yuh can't trust women and mules"), in others it was surprisingly deft and insightful. A promising example was a piece entitled "Three Field Sketches." They are just that, sketches, in which little actually happens to the protagonists, all black field hands: A tenant farmer experiences a drought-quenching rain; a woman watches from the field with longing as a train pulls away and into the distance, leaving her to her life of unrelieved toil; and two black cotton hands are called in from the fields at day's end. But each sketch is lovingly observed, the writer clearly someone who has spent a lot of time in corn and tobacco and cotton fields himself and was paying close attention. And though the writer maybe has just turned twenty years old, the writing already has a muscular maturity. In this passage, the long-awaited cloudburst has finally arrived and the tenant farmer experiences it on a visceral level:

> He holds out his hand and the rain covers it, washes it. He cannot be certain just where his hand ends and the rain begins. He feels that he is part of the rain; part of the fluttering, streaming wet leaves of the poplar trees growing beside the shallow ditches, which carry the water from the fields to the swamp streams. One may see an experienced rider astride a swiftly loping, spirited horse, and think, The rider seems a part of the horse. Just so the negro thought himself one with the rain and one with the new life the rain is giving freely to the fields and the trees.

At this point Mitchell seemed as committed to his fiction writing as to his freelance news features, and he was able to publish sketches in several minor literary reviews. Then came his first major publication: the inclusion of the story "Cool Swamp and Field Woman" in the 1929 *New American Caravan,* an anthology of literature edited by, among others, his future *New Yorker* colleague Lewis Mumford. It was a substantial publication; the volume also contained the first published

short stories of a fellow Southerner, Erskine Caldwell, as well as poetry by Stanley Kunitz and E. E. Cummings. As a piece of writing,
however, the story is less satisfactory than "Three Field Sketches." It is
an arid tale of the gradual union of a man and a woman, again set
against the backdrop of Mitchell's familiar swamp and crop terrain.
Indeed, the unnamed protagonists are portrayed, in overwrought
prose, more as elemental extensions of the earth itself than as flesh-
and-blood people, and the language self-consciously tries too hard for
a literary detachment in the then-emerging modernist style. Parts of it
sound like a dubious mimicry of Hemingway, then coming into vogue
("They sat on the porch quietly and the night was the warmest of all
the nights. Sand was warm and rooms were warm"). Such forays didn't
really suit the young Mitchell, but he was a writing apprentice still
searching for his own style and voice. The same was true of a piece also
perhaps conceived while Mitchell was at Chapel Hill and published in
the 1931 *American Caravan IV*. This eerie story, called "The Brewers,"
feels almost like magical surrealism. Its brief tale of a desperate farmer
and mystical swamp woman collaborating to distill moonshine whiskey is written in an even more experimental vein, and it comes across
like a fever dream. This is the effect the author intended, but it again
feels forced. Just a few years later, Mitchell would be contributing
short stories to *The New Yorker*, likewise set in his home terrain but
rendered in a more unforced and droll voice, well on its way to the
kind of lyrical naturalism that would become Mitchell's writing signature. But, as with its predecessor, the true significance of the publication of "The Brewers" was the company Mitchell was keeping; fellow
authors in the 1931 anthology include Robert Penn Warren, William
Carlos Williams, Robert M. Coates, and William Faulkner.

In other words, Joseph Mitchell didn't have to wonder anymore
what he was going to do with his life. He was a writer.

On the journalism side, Mitchell in the summer of 1929 submitted
a feature article called "Tobacco Market" to the *New York Herald Tribune*. The lengthy piece, while factual, is full of observation and more
impressionistic in its approach than a conventional newspaper article.

In it, Mitchell reconstructs the vivid sights, sounds, and smells of Fairmont's Bulldog Alley tobacco market, which were second nature to him.

> In the street a horse trader is singing a song about mules. "Last call for the big horse and mule sale right around on Bulldog Alley, fine Tennessee and Kentucky mules sold for the highest dollar." A boy leads three stud-muscled mules; the trader, a young fellow with a hard blue face and a cigar in his mouth, turns to him and mutters, "Damn these people! They ain't got no money!"

The *Herald Tribune* accepted the submission and published it, on its op-ed page, on Sunday, October 13. Mitchell was elated. He had his first byline in one of the best papers in New York, the most important writer's market in the world.

Chapel Hill had given Joseph Mitchell an outstanding liberal arts education as well as direction, expertise, and professional connections. Now, emboldened by his freelance success, he made a decision. Done with college—he would leave the university several courses short of what it would have taken him to graduate, had he been able to—he would go to New York; he would be a newspaperman. He didn't really have any prospects per se, but he had something more important, his confidence—and one New York City byline.

Why was he so intent on leaving North Carolina? No one was ever completely certain, least of all Mitchell himself, who would spend much of the rest of his life trying to answer that question. But it was inevitable, really, and that much he *did* know. For years Mitchell had tried to suppress the gnawing, enveloping sensation that he had been born out of place, but Chapel Hill had proved it was true. How else to explain the fact that, as an adult, he routinely spoke not of "leaving" the culturally arid Fairmont but of "fleeing" it? As much as he loved home, the perceptive and creative twenty-one-year-old already understood that, in the end, it would mire him like an animal in the swamp. So he would escape—to what, he wasn't sure. But that naked confidence didn't surprise anyone who knew him well. "He was *so* determined," said a nephew, Jack Mitchell. "I call it deadly determination. He's like a hawk going after a small animal. A hawk will dive into a bush at ninety miles an hour to get his prey. That's deadly determination."

When at last Joseph mustered the courage to tell A.N. his intentions to go to New York and pursue a newspaper career, his father looked at him, the disappointment and a hint of disdain plain on his face. "Son," he said, "is that the best you can do, sticking your nose into other people's business?"

For all his misgivings—and they were many and grave—A.N. days later found himself driving Joseph the forty miles north to Fayetteville, where his eldest child would catch a northbound train to New York City and the uncertain future that awaited him there. It was a melancholy scene, both fully aware that the train was carrying off not just a son but the longtime expectations the father had of him. There was not a lot of conversation. As the train approached the small depot, A.N. finally said, "Well, son, do the best you can, and write to us."

CHAPTER 4

DISTRICT MAN

UNTIL I CAME TO NEW YORK CITY I had never lived in a town with a population of more than 2,699, and I was alternately delighted and frightened out of my wits by what I saw at night in Harlem. I would go off duty at 3 A.M., and then I would walk around the streets and look, discovering what the depression and the prurience of white men were doing to a people who are "last to be hired; first to be fired." When I got tired of looking, usually around daybreak, I would get on the subway and go to my $9 a week furnished room in Greenwich Village. When I got out of the subway at Sheridan Square I would get a *Herald Tribune* to see what the rewrite man had done with the stories I had telephoned in hours earlier. I had a police card in my pocket and I was twenty-one years old and everything was new to me. By the time the Harlem trick was over I was so fascinated by the melodrama of the metropolis at night that I forgot my ambition to become a political reporter.

—From My Ears Are Bent, *1938*

. .

In THE WAKE OF WORLD WAR I, THE GRAVITATIONAL PULL THAT NEW York City exerted on ambitious and literate young people from the American hinterland is impossible to underestimate. For those well read enough to imagine the life available out beyond the unbroken horizon, Manhattan meant sophistication, it meant liberation, it meant opportunity. It represented excitement and validation of talent. It was Sodom; it was Oz. "New York in the thirties, this city was so fantastic I can't get over it," said Mitchell's longtime friend and colleague Philip Hamburger. "It was really marvelous. It was the only place where Joe could have gone." The creative migration to New York in the twenties and thirties would catalyze the nation's cultural and intellectual development for the rest of the century. The pull of the city on Joseph Mitchell was almost precisely the same as it had been just a few years prior on a high school dropout turned newspaper roustabout from Utah, Harold Ross, who went to New York to prove himself and, once there, got it into his head that he could create a magazine setting a new standard for sophisticated reportage, light fiction, and humor. Early in 1925—just as Mitchell was looking forward to his high school graduation down in Fairmont—Ross launched *The New Yorker*. As it happened, Ross's spectacular success with *The New Yorker* would add immeasurably to New York's pull on all those other talented strivers out in the sticks, especially the ones who fancied themselves writers. As Mitchell himself acknowledged, "A great many New Yorkers knew when they were little children, when they were living in little towns all throughout the country, that they were going to come to New York."

In Mitchell's case, his imagination had been further sparked by some recent reading and thinking he'd been doing about his future. In the summer of 1929, just after he'd left Chapel Hill, Mitchell had his appendix removed. While recovering from the operation, he read the popular book *The American Commonwealth*, a political history written by Britain's former ambassador to the United States, James Bryce. It made such an impression that it reinforced a notion he'd already been considering, that of becoming a political reporter—yet another reason to set his compass for New York. So when the *Herald Tribune* purchased his submission about tobacco markets, it surely seemed an omen. It was time to make the leap.

Aspiration is one thing; timing is another. That train Mitchell boarded in Fayetteville in October of 1929 deposited him in New York just in time for the stock-market crash that marked the beginning of the Great Depression. After an overnight trip, Mitchell arrived at teeming Pennsylvania Station smack in the middle of the morning rush. He stowed his suitcase in a rental locker, got a bite of breakfast, and headed straight to the *Herald Tribune*. There Mitchell first met with the op-ed editor who had purchased his tobacco story, who in turn introduced him to Stanley Walker, the paper's city editor. After only a few short years in the role, Walker was something of a legend among New York's tribe of newspapermen. A fellow Southerner (from Texas), Walker liked his young visitor right off. He sensed in him the same enthusiasm and wide-eyed wonder about the city that Walker himself had brought to New York. As the *Herald Tribune*'s city editor, Walker championed a freer, more writerly approach to news reporting that, not coincidentally, resulted in a kind of talent pipeline to *The New Yorker*—Alva Johnston, St. Clair McKelway, John Lardner, Joel Sayre, and others would migrate from the paper to the magazine. Walker's passion was infectious; he so loved the thrill of the chase that he was known to tag along on police raids just for fun. At the same time he implored his reporters to be unafraid in the stories they pursued. "A paper which doesn't take chances is a dead paper," he would say a few years later, in 1934, when he literally wrote the book on how to be a city editor. It was for all these reasons that Walker was revered by so many of New York's newspaper reporters—the ones who worked for him, and the ones who wanted to.

But at the moment Walker had no jobs open. Besides, he was somewhat alarmed that Mitchell would make such a trip entirely on impulse, with no appointments and with no real prospects waiting for him. The editor advised him that the first thing he should do under the circumstances was to grab any job he could scare up—even in a soda shop, if need be; as he told the farm boy, "Half the soda jerks in the city are from the South." Walker, however, could see that Mitchell did not lack determination, and the budding reporter somehow came away from their lengthy discussion considerably encouraged. "He did not actually say so," Mitchell recalled years later, "but [he] gave me the impression that he would give me a job as a reporter as soon as I learned how to get around in the city." He retrieved his suitcase from Penn Station and got a cheap furnished room in Greenwich Village, near Sheridan Square, at a building that catered to newspapermen. There Mitchell quickly met a copy editor at the *New York World*, who said he would introduce Mitchell around. It appears Walker may have also made some calls on Mitchell's behalf. In short order Mitchell accomplished his aim: He'd secured a newspaper job, at the *World*—and a lavish salary of fifteen dollars a week. Of course, fifteen dollars could carry a frugal young man a long way, even in New York, when a loaf of bread was a dime, cigarettes were fifteen cents, and movies were a quarter—for a double feature.

As a copy boy, Mitchell ferried freshly written stories from reporters to editors and from editors to the composing room and performed the dozens of other dull tasks that kept a big-city newsroom humming. But it also was the kind of job that revealed a novice's drive to the paper's editors, and Mitchell made the most of his chance. Before long, the city room was assigning him to cover police blotters in the outlying boroughs, and on the side he began to contribute Sunday feature stories. Not long after that, just four months after that first impromptu job interview, Walker summoned Mitchell. He was going to work for the mighty *Herald Tribune*—at double his copy boy's salary, to boot.

Though he would work there less than two full years, Mitchell always considered his stay at the *Herald Tribune* "one of the most exciting periods of my life." For decades after he'd made his mark as one of the nation's most accomplished writers, and even after the paper's demise, he stayed in regular touch with many of his former *Trib* colleagues. But he was not alone in that; "*Tribune* men" had a unique *esprit* in the crowded New York newspaper universe. This was due in no small part to Stanley Walker's genius for identifying talent, which allowed him to build one of the most capable reporting staffs New York City had ever seen. The *Herald Tribune* of that era was widely considered the liveliest and best-written newspaper in the city; if *The New York Times* was the "paper of record," the *Tribune* crowd considered it dull going and inferior to what they produced day in and day out. Certainly Mitchell felt there was no better place in the world to apprentice his trade—and no better city editor to have as his mentor.

Mitchell started in February 1930, and Walker set him to work as a "district man." Newspaper district men were assigned to cover specific sections or neighborhoods of the city—the Village, the West Side, parts of Brooklyn or Harlem, say—and they typically worked into the wee hours if they were on morning papers like the *Herald Tribune*. They paid particular attention to the police activity in their district; in fact, their tatty little offices, or "shacks," often were literally appended to police headquarters. As Mitchell would recall in the introductory chapter of his 1938 collection of newspaper writing, *My Ears Are Bent*, with so many colorful reporters, cops, snitches, politicians, mobsters, and petty criminals parading in and out through the course of an evening, it was often hard to tell the good guys from the bad—such was the bracing complexity and moral ambiguity of Depression-era New York. When there was a police or fire call, the district man was expected to get to the scene, find out what happened as quickly as he could, and phone in the facts to the paper's rewrite desk.

Mitchell would work various districts during his initial time at the *Herald Tribune*, but he started out in Harlem. The experience proved to be revelatory. Yet Mitchell managed to make something of an impression on Harlem, too, or at least on the hard-bitten colleagues who covered it; they regarded the new man as an overeager puppy. The reporters' shack was on the ground floor of the Hotel Theresa, a Harlem landmark and cultural hub. "We used to sit in the doorway in swivel chairs and look out at the people passing to and fro on Seventh Avenue, Harlem's main street," he wrote. "There were four reporters in Harlem at night, three from the morning papers and one from the City News Association. My colleagues were veterans. The thing they disliked most in a reporter was enthusiasm, and I was always excited. When I got on the telephone to give my office a story . . . they would stand outside and point at their foreheads and make circles in the air, indicating that I did not have any sense."

In Harlem, as in his hometown, Mitchell experienced a jumble of races and classes. But the flamboyant characters he encountered there, and the jazzy, desperate extremes at which life was lived, were like nothing he'd ever seen in North Carolina. When things at the district shack were slow, Mitchell made the rounds of clubs, diners, storefront churches, and speakeasies, looking for stories. He quickly found his way to many of Harlem's more established eccentrics, every one of whom he filed away—and many of whom he revisited a few years later when he was writing features for the *New York World.* These included the gambler Gill Holton, who earlier in his career ran the Broken Leg and Busted Bar & Grill; the famous preacher and entrepreneur Father Divine; and the proprietor of the most patronized voodoo emporium in Harlem. Other times his police contacts got him into places that were as harrowing as they were exotic, such as the neighborhood's out-of-the-way marijuana dens. One night a black detective Mitchell knew offered to take him on his rounds along Lenox Avenue, to check in on some of the evening's "rent parties" (which tenants threw when they couldn't make their rent, beseeching the guests to chip in). After several raucous stops, Mitchell followed the detective into a sixth-floor tenement flat. In the dark, smoky space they found several well-dressed whites in the company of blacks, all smoking unfamiliar (to Mitchell) brown cigarettes. Then, from out of the haze, a shot rang out.

> Everyone was watching the tall detective. Suddenly he turned on his heel and grabbed a small, forlorn Negro. Then I saw that the fellow had a .45 in his hand. They caught at each other, and the detective kept a muscular grip on the small man's gun hand. They wheeled about the room, grappling, until the detective got one hand gripped about the gunman's neck. He began to choke him, steadily. They fell against the piano, and then the gun went off. It broke a key on the piano, and there was an explosion, and a tiny, futile tinkle came from the piano. All the people began to laugh. The detective choked the gunman to the floor, picked the pistol from his hand, and motioned me to open the door.
>
> He pulled his sparring partner to his feet, and the three of us stumbled out of the room. As I closed the door I saw the very pale man light another dark cigarette. We walked down Lenox Avenue, and people from the night clubs began to question us,

but we did not notice them. The detective was escorting the gunman to the precinct station.

"What kind of place was that?" I asked.

"That was a very nice place," the tall detective said, smiling.

At the time, Mitchell probably lived not far from the site of that rumble; one of the many places he occupied during his first few years in New York was in a largely Puerto Rican neighborhood on West 96th Street. As he relocated with his different district assignments, Mitchell lived in a series of "furnished-room houses and side-street hotels" in the early days of the Depression—among them various places on the Upper West Side, in Tudor City, in Greenwich Village, and in Times Square. In doing so, he was scrupulously following some of the advice Stanley Walker had given him in their first meeting. To really learn a city quickly, Walker had said, a reporter should live close to the areas he's covering. And he should walk, constantly. It was all right to take a trolley or streetcars, where you can see out, Walker told him, but it's vital to walk and take in as much as you can. "I started walking, all day, solitary walks, with a map in my pocket and a sandwich," Mitchell recalled years later in his journal. "Before long, he gave me a job but walking in the city had become addictive. When I left the [*Herald Tribune*] and went to the [*World*] I continued to walk on my days off. When I left the [*World-Telegram;* the two papers merged in 1931] for [*The New Yorker*], I continued, and I still do."

Walker gave his young charge one more piece of professional advice that stuck. Once Mitchell became a reporter, Walker instructed him to go to Brooks Brothers and buy himself a decent suit. He did, and for the rest of his life, the always smartly dressed Mitchell purchased every piece of his wardrobe, from socks to hats, from Brooks Brothers.

The education Mitchell was afforded during his *Herald Tribune* apprenticeship, in the totality of the experience, cannot be overestimated. More important than just learning the city, he was learning its rhythms, how it worked. He was figuring out whom to ask when you needed to get to the "right" people. He was encountering the city's

Having taken Stanley Walker's sartorial advice,
Mitchell—hat cocked just so—poses as a proud apprentice
member of New York's Fourth Estate.

myriad characters and sussing out who was worth a story from who was simply crazy. And he was learning how to get out of their way and listen.

Most important, the raw kid from Fairmont was gaining a big-city confidence. He recalled in his journal that once he went to New York and became a reporter, he began to detect a welcome transformation in himself. "Lost my shyness—would approach anyone from the mayor on. . . . 'This is Mitchell of the *World-Telegram* or the *NY Herald Tribune.*'"

That rising confidence didn't escape Walker's notice. In the fall of 1930, the city editor recalled Mitchell from the district shacks and put him to work as a bona fide reporter on the city desk.

SOMETIME IN 1930, WHILE on assignment at Madison Square Garden, Mitchell met a fellow reporter whom he found considerably more interesting than the story he was supposed to be covering.

Therese Jacobsen was working the same Garden event for the Mount Vernon *Daily Argus*. At the time it was unusual for a female reporter to be doing anything other than writing stories for the "women's pages." Even more unusual was the fact that Therese's older sister, Maude, was also a reporter and, like Therese, would go on to graduate from Columbia's prestigious journalism program. Therese was gregarious and had a talent for the work—in what would be an abbreviated print career, she wrote for such publications as the *New York World, Brooklyn Eagle, Irish Times,* and the *Argus,* the last located in suburban Westchester County, New York, where she shared an apartment with Maude at the time she met Mitchell. Therese was only twenty years old, a year and a half younger than Mitchell, and she was hard to miss, even in a crowd at the Garden: very attractive, with beautiful hazel eyes and an easy, engaging smile that conveyed an effervescent personality. Her confident demeanor showed she was thoroughly a city girl, and the farm boy was smitten immediately. Soon after meeting, the two were dating; sometimes they even arranged to cover stories together. But at first Therese's protective family didn't quite know what to make of this laconic, dark-haired Southerner. Not long after meeting him, Therese's father asked Mitchell if he owned anything. He thought for a moment, then said, "Well, I own a horse."

Born in New York, Therese (she sounded the "th" like "thimble,"

A bright and vivacious city girl, Therese Jacobsen charmed country boy Joseph Mitchell from their first meeting.

and her full name was pronounced the-RESSE) was the daughter of Scandinavian immigrants. Her father was a respected civil engineer, who was educated in his native Norway and then immigrated to New York, where he worked on the city's subway system and helped build the Lincoln and Queens–Midtown tunnels. Perhaps his proudest accomplishment, however, was being invited to design and construct the grand drive for Theodore Roosevelt's Sagamore Hill home in Oyster Bay, which yielded him several prized letters from the former president. Therese's mother was a native of Denmark; she met her husband-to-be on the boat they shared when he was first immigrating to America and she was returning from a visit home.

The Jacobsens settled in Brooklyn's Prospect Park neighborhood. Theirs was a close family, and the household was one of much warmth and humor, which helped shape Therese's outgoing nature and highly developed sense of fun. She was an excellent cook and an athlete who as a teenager swam and fenced competitively. Therese was, in sum, a bright and vivacious young woman who was sure of herself. "She . . . had a benign view of the world and could be very funny," recalled her daughter Nora. "She had a great sense of irony and of the absurd and did not take herself too seriously." An example Nora cites: Therese was brought up as a Lutheran, and all her life, when the Baptist-raised Joseph would take Communion, she delighted in calling him a "cannibal." This combination of qualities—beautiful, cheeky, as curious about other people as he was—made the young lady reporter enormously appealing to Mitchell.

On February 27, 1931, after having dated for the better part of a year, Joseph and Therese made the short train trip up to Greenwich, Connecticut, where they were married by a justice of the peace. If they were excited about eloping, they didn't seem especially anxious; they passed the time on the ride up by scoping out the first issue of the newly merged *New York World-Telegram,* which they couldn't know was soon to figure prominently in their lives. It's not clear why Joseph and Therese chose elopement or, more interestingly, why even after the fact they decided not to tell their parents what they had done. (Nora later speculated that it may have been a product of the Depression mentality—to safeguard their respective jobs when some editors at that time felt it wasn't fair for two positions to reside in a single household, with plenty of "good men" looking for work.) Maude was in on things, however, because she let the newlyweds take over the apartment she'd been sharing with Therese. But this ruse actually proved to be the undoing of their secret. When the telephone rang early one morning, Mitchell reflexively answered it; it was Therese's father on the other end of the line. When he sternly inquired what

Mitchell was doing at his daughter's apartment at that inappropriate hour, Mitchell had to confess to the elopement. Hurt and angry at having been misled, and mindful of appearances for their daughter, the Jacobsens arranged for an elaborate Norwegian "church wedding" in Brooklyn, to be held on the first anniversary of their elopement, after which Joseph and Therese's marriage was publicly announced. As for the Mitchells, when Joseph informed them, by telegram, of his marriage to a New Yorker of Scandinavian descent whom they had never met, A.N. is said to have replied, "You made your bed and now you better lie in it."

NOT LONG AFTER THE "real" wedding—the one in the church—Therese gave up her reporting career. She never told her family exactly why, and it's altogether possible it did have something to do with the hard-times "job rationing" then occurring in the industry. But years later her sister allowed that Therese considered it "inevitable" that her talented husband would outshine her as a writer; she decided that, instead of competing with him, she would pursue an alternate creative outlet. She did this with her usual enthusiasm. She loved photography, and now she took formal lessons to learn how to shoot professionally and develop her own photographs. Before long she had learned how to convert an apartment bathroom into a makeshift darkroom, and for the next fifteen years or so (until two young daughters made too many demands on her time), Therese Mitchell and her Rolleiflex were fixtures on the intimate streets of Greenwich Village, where the couple eventually settled.

Therese's forte, and her passion, was photographing candid scenes of the city's inhabitants. She didn't chase celebrities, and she wasn't interested in capturing scandal and crime for the tabloids. She took photographs of regular people—sometimes in extraordinary situations but as often as not just being themselves, not even aware of the photographer's presence. She paid particular attention to the working class, union members, and the working poor. When the couple would go to Fairmont for summer vacations, Joseph's "foreign wife" (as some in Fairmont initially referred to her) was no less engaged, taking photographs of the farms and warehouses and humble dwellings of the tenant farmers—as well as of the farmers themselves. Whether taken in the city or the countryside, her black-and-white images are natural and very affecting; she achieved an empathetic documentary quality akin to that of Dorothea Lange and other better-known photographers of the Depression years. Her photographs could have been taken only in those places and only at that time in American history. One other thing is evident in Therese's photography: She fully shared her husband's fascination with people whom others found odd or outcast. That palpable appreciation of a fundamental dignity in the less advantaged proved to be one of the most important and enduring aspects of their relationship.

At the *Herald Tribune,* Mitchell was quickly validating Walker's confidence in him. He seemed able to do anything, from working police sources to conducting quickie celebrity interviews to covering mobster funerals. And then, about the time of his elopement, early in 1931, he stumbled onto a story so sensational that it alone could have made his reportorial reputation in New York. According to Richard Kluger's account in his book *The Paper: The Life and Death of the New York Herald Tribune*—which he derived largely from Mitchell himself (and about which Mitchell left some corroborating journal notes)— the young reporter was covering the murder of a prostitute in Midtown Manhattan and went to the victim's apartment with a detective. There he saw the police investigators come upon her diary. The book turned out to contain the names of her well-known clientele—whom, it seemed, she had been blackmailing. The detectives also found drafts of a letter she was composing to the Seabury Commission, the state panel then investigating police corruption, offering to testify against vice-squad officers she alleged were framing her. Mitchell excitedly called Walker, who urged him to get as much information as he could before the police bounced him from the crime scene. He did, then returned to the city room to start writing his spectacular exclusive. The paper's managing editor, however, "decided the story was too hot to be entrusted to one of Walker's cubs," and he ordered Mitchell to turn

*Visiting Fairmont with her new husband, Therese often went
into the countryside to capture the Depression-era existence
of Tobacco Road sharecroppers.*

over his notes to a senior reporter who was friends with Ogden Reid, the *Herald Tribune*'s owner and editor-in-chief. The glory moment passed. As Kluger recounts, "Deprived of his scoop, back pounding the pavements of the Bronx on routine police stories, Mitchell burned. He did not know exactly who was responsible for what had happened, but his anger focused on Ogden Reid."

Mitchell nursed his grudge for months. Then one day, through a convoluted set of circumstances, he found himself effectively babysitting another of Walker's reporting protégés, Richard O. Boyer, who was trying to write an important story for the paper but who also had a strong proclivity for drink. Mitchell's assignment: Keep Boyer sober and on task. This Mitchell did. But when the story *was* finished, the two celebrated by getting thoroughly drunk, then went off to the paper to turn in Boyer's piece. Deep into his cups and still bitter at having had his big story snatched from him, Mitchell decided "he would tell Ogden Reid exactly what he thought of him." He may even have meant to resign his position—something he never would have done in a more sober condition. The two inebriated reporters stumbled around the premises; Boyer, in search of a bathroom, instead relieved himself in the coatroom. Mitchell made it to Reid's office, but the editor was momentarily away. His secretary said she would try to find him but tactfully suggested Mitchell might leave a note instead. As she headed off, however, Mitchell barged in to Reid's office. "Suddenly possessed by fury," he impulsively grabbed a decorative inkwell from the editor's desk and hurled it at the wall. "I still remember the beautiful crescent pattern," Mitchell would recall.

The next day Walker called a hungover Mitchell to say that Reid was fairly understanding about the drunken tantrum—but the managing editor, alas, "insisted that the cutups be made examples of." Walker, reluctantly, had to let Mitchell go.

In no time, the great Mitchell–Boyer inkwell caper—the sort of incendiary, insubordinate gesture every working journalist has contemplated but seldom carried out—would take on legendary status in newspaper circles, one that only built over the years. This came to be something of an embarrassment to Mitchell, a man of control who had allowed himself to get out of control. For the rest of his life, he would be asked about the episode and invariably had to set the questioners straight as to the facts of it, as opposed to the apocrypha that had built up around it. (The fastidious Mitchell took special pains to make clear he had not been the urinator.)

For now, Mitchell had a much larger problem on his hands than a sullied reputation. He was a newly married man in the worst economic climate in the nation's history, a long way from home, and he was suddenly unemployed. While he hoped Walker would be able to use his vast network to help him land somewhere, that might take a little time, and in any case the predicament was of his own making. For the

Mitchell, front center, surrounded by dozens of new friends in Leningrad, a relationship that a decade later he was made to regret.

moment he was back to one priority—get a job, any job. So that summer he undertook what would be one of the great adventures of his life: He signed on as a deckhand on a freighter ship, the SS *City of Fairbury,* destined for the Soviet Union.

Years later, from the vantage point of an established and well-known newspaperman, Mitchell would put a considerably lighter gloss on the circumstances of his maritime moonlighting, writing that "I got tired of hoofing after dime-a-dozen murders" and telling his seafaring colleagues that he feared he was getting a little "soft" and wanted some manual labor to toughen up. Elsewhere he would refer to the trip as a "summer vacation." None of these characterizations made any sense, of course, for a young newlywed in the teeth of the Depression. Like many of the less-experienced men on the *Fairbury,* Mitchell was there because it was honest work and it paid. But one thing he *did* make clear to his mates: This was definitely to be a one-time affair for him. And they understood. "This was no career for anyone who was educated," recalled Jack Sargent Harris, a noted anthropologist and United Nations official who, before he pursued his graduate education, sailed that summer on the *Fairbury* with Mitchell.

The *Fairbury* was one of the large, lumbering cargo vessels that were hastily turned out during the First World War at the Hog Island shipyard outside Philadelphia. Its itinerary for this voyage was a routine one: transport heavy machinery to Leningrad (as the Soviets had lately rechristened the imperial city of St. Petersburg) and return to the States with Russian timber. Along the way it would make stops in Copenhagen, Danzig, Stockholm, and a few smaller ports.

Mitchell's service began on July 8, 1931. Harris, who had done one prior transatlantic sail and would continue to work the Hog Island freighters for several years, said that Mitchell had signed on with a *Herald Tribune* colleague, Ben Robertson. They were all deckhands, and Mitchell did what everyone on the crew did during their daylong shifts: washed down decks, chipped away rust, painted—whatever needed to be done for the ship's upkeep. There were about fifteen men on the deck crew. Harris said Mitchell and Robertson devoted much of their downtime to reading and talking—though Robertson did most of the latter. Harris remembered the young Mitchell as taciturn. "There were very few words in Joe," he said. But Mitchell made an exception for Harris, whose native intelligence the writer sensed. He repeatedly encouraged Harris to continue his education at some point. "Joe liked to talk to me because I listened. I was interested. I think he saw me as someone with a mind that was just awakening," Harris said.

When the American freighters hit the Soviet ports, Harris recalled, the sailors seldom left the ships, because there weren't any prostitutes around, as there were in the more-libertine ports to the west. However, when the *Fairbury* arrived in Leningrad, it put in for the better part of two weeks, and many on the antsy crew took the opportunity to sightsee in the magnificent and historic city, still in the exhilarating first blush of the Communist revolution. The Russians, Harris said, "were very friendly to the Americans, they liked to see us. We were welcomed everywhere. It was quite warm—even though there were no whores."

When the *Fairbury* sailors went ashore, they were escorted by young Russian women—always women, given the evisceration of the male population in the war; "even the winch-drivers [on the docks] were girls," Mitchell said. The young ladies were more-charming fore-runners of the official "minders" who would shadow Western visitors to the Soviet Union during the Cold War. Mitchell wrote in some detail about his Leningrad stay in a feature story not long after his return and then several years later in his introduction to *My Ears Are Bent*. He and his *Fairbury* colleagues took their new Russian friends to a Charlie Chaplin movie, discussed their mutual affection for the work of Alexander Pushkin, and made a short train ride to the former summer residence of the Russian royal family, now converted into a rest home for Soviet workers.

It is south of Leningrad and the flat, swampy country reminded me of eastern North Carolina. Somewhere on the tremendous estate the two girls picked some wild strawberries, and that night they made some cakes, a wild Russian strawberry on the top of each cake. We ate them and got sick. I remember how proud they were when they put the cakes on the table, smiling at us, and how ashamed we were, an hour or so later, when we got sick. We figured out it was the change in the water, but we couldn't explain that to them because we knew no Russian. In Leningrad we swam naked each day in the Neva, under the gentle Russian sun. One afternoon we got together, the seamen from all the American ships in the harbor, and marched with the Russians in a demonstration against imperialist war, an annual event. One night a girl invited me to her house and I had dinner with her family, thick cabbage soup and black bread which smelled of wet grain. After dinner the family sang. The girl knew some English and she asked me to sing an American song. I favored them with the only one I could think of, "Body and Soul," which was popular in New York City when I left. It seemed to puzzle them.

Lighthearted and bucolic as that all sounded, Mitchell was quietly observing Leningrad's bustling populace, the ever-present propaganda, and "the smell of sacrifice in the streets," and he concluded the

Russians were distinctly unsettled as to how things were going to turn out for them under this experiment of Communism. He called Leningrad an "index city" for the rest of the country, and he was not sanguine. "The uneasy feeling of unrest there is perhaps not universal. However, except for the hospitality of the people . . . this minor desperation is the most lasting impression an American seaman has of the city." In this way Mitchell was a good bit less naïve than his fellow sailors and many other early Western visitors to the putative workers' paradise. Still, the layover in Leningrad would prove to have serious consequences for him, years later, when Mitchell was trying to get official clearance to work as a writer for the U.S. government during World War II.

The *Fairbury*, laden with Russian pulp timber, returned to the States at the end of August 1931, dropping off Mitchell in Albany, New York. He hopped a bus for New York, ready to return to his wife and, he hoped, his newspaper life.

Four decades later, making notes for a planned memoir, Mitchell typed these phrases on a sheet of paper: "Looking back on it, I think I got scared during the Depression and never got unscared" and "always lived with a feeling of anxiety" and "never been sure anything would last very long, particularly a job." It's not clear if he was referring specifically to the frightening turn of events with his employment in 1931, but it would scarcely be surprising if he was.

Mitchell's guardian angel, Walker, again came to the rescue: He arranged for Mitchell to get a reporting position at the *World-Telegram*. By early October, tanned and no longer "soft," and with his worldview heightened considerably, Mitchell was back on the news beat. Still freshly married, Mitchell was grateful to have a paycheck again. It would be a few years yet before he could appreciate just what a springboard Walker's intervention really was.

CHAPTER 5

ASSIGNMENT: NEW YORK

I HAVE BEEN UP IN SCORES of buildings of a wide variety of types
while they were being demolished (I have a passion for climbing up
on scaffolding), and I have been up in dozens of skyscrapers while
they were under construction, and I have been out on half a dozen
bridges while they were under construction, and I have been down
in three tunnels while they were under construction—the Queens
Midtown Tunnel, the Lincoln Tunnel, and the Brooklyn-Battery
Tunnel—and watched the sandhogs forcing their way inch by inch
through the riverbed. I am also strongly drawn to certain kinds of
subterranean places. . . . I have been down in the vaults under
Trinity Church and I have been down in the vaults under the Federal
Reserve Bank and I have been down in the dungeony old disused
warehouse vaults in the red-brick arches under the Manhattan end
of the Brooklyn Bridge, which still smell mustily but pleasantly of
some of the products that used to be stored in them—wine in casks,
hides and skins from the wholesale-leather district known as the
Swamp and now demolished that once lay adjacent to the bridge,
and surplus fish held in cold storage for higher prices by fishmongers from Fulton Market, which is nearby. . . .

—From Joseph Mitchell's unfinished memoir

. .

N 1931, AS MITCHELL WAS STILL LEARNING THE CITY IN HIS
Herald Tribune apprenticeship, he stumbled across one of its more
fascinating microcosms on Manhattan's Lower East Side. The Fulton
Fish Market was exactly the kind of sprawling, bustling, feast-for-all-

five-senses environment that Mitchell relished, with color and characters in any direction he turned. Each day before dawn, crates of freshly
caught fish and seafood of every variety arrived by boat and truck,
where they went into huge bins and hatches. Some of the fish would
be sold whole, and others were filleted by aproned workers wielding
their long blades like surgeons. The fish market, located in the shadow
of the Brooklyn Bridge, originally was operated by transplanted New
Englanders who sold the fish that their seafaring families brought to
the city. But with the polyglot evolution of New York, the market became a collection of ethnic populations—first the Irish, then Italians,
then Jews.

When Mitchell was introduced to the Fulton Fish Market, he
knew nothing of the fish business particularly, but he understood the
workings of a commodities market from growing up with his father's
cotton and tobacco businesses. The fish market would be one of the
first, and most enduring, emotional bridges between Mitchell's former
life and his new one. He found it a stimulating yet comfortable space,
and it was one he would return to, in different ways and in different
capacities, for the rest of his life.

Mitchell's "tour guide" to this new world was one of the market's
best-known figures—Joe Cantalupo, whom Mitchell would come to
consider "my oldest friend in New York." When Mitchell first met
him, Cantalupo was running his father's "carting" business, which was
responsible for hauling away all the trash from the fish market. The
two Joes bonded immediately; Cantalupo was a great talker and, because of his business, he seemed to know everyone in the market. He
was also a very large man, with an appetite to match; Mitchell likened
him to another Falstaffian figure, one he worked with at the *World-
Telegram* and who would also become a lifelong friend, the writer and
gourmand A. J. Liebling. ("He ate too much just like Joe Liebling,"
Mitchell said of Cantalupo years later, "but most of the people I ad-
mire seem to eat themselves to death.")

Maybe what Mitchell most appreciated about Cantalupo was
the commitment he had made to truly understand his people and
surroundings. Though not a fisherman or a fishmonger himself,

Cantalupo "was so involved in the fish market. He knew fish. . . . He knew where the shrimp came from. He had been on the shrimp boats. And on draggers in Boston and saw everything he knew. And so he got to be the most respected man in the market." Courtesy of Cantalupo, Mitchell would become friendly with the most established and influential members of what was then the Fulton Market Fish Mongers Association, some of whom would figure prominently in his later writing. He began to spend much of his spare time around the market, and in his own words he became a "fish market buff."

At the fish market Mitchell also was learning something that would prove immensely useful to a young reporter—what New York sounded like. In and around the stalls he was encountering Portuguese, Greek, Italian, Old Yankee, and other tongues heretofore alien to him; as he put it later, "I got a feeling for New York speech down there." In a sense he was training his ear.

Joe Cantalupo was just one of the unique people who made New York New York—one of hundreds of genuine characters that Mitchell had already met in a kind of big, messy, living novel. Of course, he had encountered many of the *most* memorable characters on the other end of Manhattan, in Harlem—the street preachers, speakeasy operators, prostitutes, detectives, beat cops, drug dealers, and drug users. To a still-transitioning Southern boy—and one who at this point in his career continued to feel he was as likely to pursue fiction as fact-based writing—they left an immense and lasting impression. He found especially compelling the black ministers, who had mastered the oratorical arts and who had such a cultural and moral pull in their communities. In fact, around this time Mitchell began to formulate the rough idea of a novel, one taking a distinctly Joycean approach to his garrulous new home. The book would record a day in the life of a newspaper reporter, and it would pivot on his meeting up with a black preacher in Harlem. The themes would be the large ones—life, death, redemption, and resurrection.

While nothing came of that idea, at least at the time, it's hard to imagine any person in any other occupation who was exposed to as much of thirties New York as Joseph Mitchell of the *New York World-*

Telegram. By mid-November of 1931, Mitchell was regularly turning out bylined stories for his new paper, and of increasing significance. For the next several years his work consisted mostly of "features"— color pieces, profiles, human-interest stories, hard-luck stories, and everything in between. He went to many trials, which he enjoyed somewhat, and even more gangster funerals, which he enjoyed a great deal. ("There would be a whole lot of wreaths, which would clash with the fact that the man was lying there, embalmed," he recalled. "The five-o'clock shadow: they were always kind of blue around the jaw. . . . 'Goodbye Old Pal' on the wreath.") And right from Mitchell's hiring, his editors liked his way with a newspaper staple: the celebrity profile. Bing Crosby, Ida Tarbell, Noël Coward, Emma Goldman, Aimee Semple McPherson—Mitchell visited with them all as they traipsed through the nation's cultural capital. Over three days he produced a droll, rolling profile of George Bernard Shaw, then eighty years old and irascible as ever, as he sparred with the local press. (Asked what he hoped to do in New York City, Shaw replied, "Get out of it.") Mitchell wrote about an offbeat young humorist and cartoonist named James Thurber, who in time would become Mitchell's friend and colleague at *The New Yorker.* Occasionally Mitchell indulged what would become one of his signatures—taking a story in a far different direction than its readers might expect. A good example was a lion-in-winter profile of Billy Sunday, which ran in January 1934, not long before the fiery evangelist died. Sunday is visiting New York with his wife, getting ready for a revival and wearing itchy woolen long underwear to ward off the chill. Instead of dealing head-on with Sunday's evangelism, Mitchell gets at the subject by having the old man talk about the people who have come by to reminisce about his long-ago first career, that of a professional baseball player:

> "[A]nother visitor was Mickey Welch, who used to pitch for the old New York Giants years and years ago. As a matter of plain fact, he quit playing ball in 1892. I played against him many a time.

"He brought up the story about the time I was scheduled to run a race with Arlie Latham—fastest man on the St. Louis team. I was the fastest man on the Chicago team, of course. Well, in the meantime I got converted at the Pacific Garden Mission, in Chicago.

"So I was very put out, as a practicing Christian, when I heard they were going to hold this race on a Sunday afternoon. I went around to my manager and I said, 'I've been converted and I can't run in this race on a Sunday.'

"And he said, 'The hell you can't. I got all my money on that race, and if you don't win it I'll have to eat snowballs for breakfast all winter.' So I said, 'The Lord wouldn't like for me to run on a Sunday.' Well, the manager looked at me and said, 'You go ahead and run that race and fix it up with the Lord later.'"

The New York World-Telegram *assigned the intrepid Mitchell to all manner of stories, as he seemed interested in everything.*

Besides celebrity profiles, Mitchell made a specialty of in-depth series. These typically appeared over four to six days, with all the pieces exploring a single subject in exhaustive detail. They covered a remarkably idiosyncratic range: the history of vaudeville, real estate auctions, the New York waterfront, Prohibition, and the 1933 Chicago World's Fair (which Mitchell was sent to cover). Sometimes the topics came from deskbound editors; others were Mitchell's own suggestions. Their significance in terms of a developing young writer far transcended the diverse subject matter, however. They show that Mitchell was turning out an astounding amount of copy in this first phase of his career. Each story in one of these series, for instance, typically ran to several thousand words, and the sheer amount of time invested in the interviewing and basic research was considerable. And it's not as though Mitchell would disappear from the paper for months before one of these series was published; he was pulling them together in the "spare" time between the daily features and profiles he was writing as a matter of course. Then again, in these salad days Mitchell wrote quickly, and his acute mind allowed him to shape vast amounts of information into coherent narratives prior to sitting down at the typewriter.

These early stories also reveal that from the outset Mitchell was a great and gifted listener, with a particularly refined ear for dialogue. Shy by nature, Mitchell quickly learned the reporter's bag of tricks for getting interview subjects to open up. He realized that most people are uncomfortable with silence and will talk to fill the void, so he was not above simply shutting up to see what the interviewee volunteered. But more typically Mitchell coaxed his subjects with a great and animated enthusiasm, as if the secret to happiness or the meaning of life could be found in their sometimes-dreary monologues. Often, in fact, Mitchell *was* transfixed—but certainly not always. He was unimpressed with the bulk of the celebrities or politicians he was assigned to interview, and he considered most successful industrialists and financiers self-important windbags. "After painfully interviewing one of those gentlemen," he would write, "you go down in the elevator and walk into the street and see the pretty girls, the pretty working girls, with their jolly breasts bouncing about under their dresses and you are relieved; you feel as if you had escaped from a tomb in which the worms were just beginning their work. . . ." He far preferred the authenticity of everyday people, who were not working off some unseen script. "The best talk is artless," he said, "the talk of people trying to reassure or comfort themselves, women in the sun, grouped around baby carriages, talking about their weeks in the hospital or the way meat has gone up, or men in saloons, talking to combat the loneliness everyone feels."

LIKE ALL YOUNG REPORTERS, Mitchell was intoxicated by the romance of newspapering in New York. He loved the fact that every day brought a new, unexpected assignment. He thrilled when the newspaper's huge presses rumbled to life, shaking the building and tingling the nerves. He loved the camaraderie of the newsroom and of the smoky newspaper bars to which Mitchell and his colleagues reflexively retired after work, the greenhorns hanging on to the practiced stories of the veterans. It was a sign of the respect Mitchell was earning that, still in his twenties, he was elected chair of the *World-Telegram* local of the Newspaper Guild, the national union of professional reporters and editors. But also like many young reporters, Mitchell envisioned himself branching out into broader pieces for magazines, for the exposure and to augment his modest income. He kept an eye on various publications for prospects for his kind of work. One magazine he was reading especially closely was a relatively new title but one that was already developing a solid reputation in the New York journalistic community. The respect came in large part because the magazine was recruiting top local talent to its reporting and editing staffs. It was called *The New Yorker*, and its editors gave nonfiction writers rare license both in terms of subject matter and writing approach. Mitchell was well acquainted with one of the magazine's most recent acquisitions, a fellow North Carolinian named Don Wharton, who had come to the *Herald Tribune* around the same time Mitchell did and who left in 1932 to become an editor at *The New Yorker*. It's likely Wharton played a role in opening the magazine's door to Mitchell.

It appears Mitchell had at least a hand in a short Talk of the Town piece that appeared in *The New Yorker* in June of 1933. Talk pieces were short and typically droll dispatches from around the city, and the subject of this item was one of the nation's few remaining manufacturers of silk top hats. Max Fluegelman had fashioned inaugural hats for both Theodore and Franklin Roosevelt, as well as for every U.S. president in between. For most of *The New Yorker's* history, Talk contributions were not signed, although the magazine's archive indicates that Mitchell was one of several contributors to this piece. It was common then for newspaper reporters to provide Talk ideas or even first drafts, which were then "run through the typewriter," or polished, by sundry *New Yorker* editors (including founder Harold Ross) to achieve the Talk of the Town department's desired tone of bemused detachment.

Mitchell's first substantive and undisputed contribution to *The New Yorker* appeared soon after, in November. This was a Reporter at Large article about Elkton, Maryland, a town just south of the Pennsylvania border, which had become somewhat notorious for providing quickie marriages for men and women desperately in need of them—a group that encompassed all types and classes of people, Mitchell wryly notes ("Persons whose names are in the *Social Registers* of two cities have waited patiently on the worn sofa in a marriage parlor while the minister finished mumbling the dreary service for a couple from a carnival"). Mitchell's dispatch, while straightforward enough, is elevated by a sardonic perspective evident from the report's opening paragraphs. Central to his story are the two elderly rival ministers who operate the town's marriage parlors, the Rev. R. W. Moon and the Rev. Edward Minor. Observes Mitchell:

> The driver brings the couple to the parlor and calls for the minister. If it is the Rev. Moon, he comes shambling in, a gaunt, shining-eyed man. While he examines the permit, he talks to the groom. His voice is servile. "What part of the country are you from, brother?" he asks. If the bride, nervous, usually weeping, lights a cigarette, he regards her severely. "Sister," he says, "I don't like to see the ladies smoke. It withers their memories and

makes their offspring puny." If the bride, forlorn in the drab room, sobs when the ceremony is completed, he pats her on the shoulder and says, "Now, now, marriage is the most beautiful thing in a woman's life."

Mitchell followed up this contribution quickly, producing a Profile of the popular singer Kate Smith, which appeared in March of 1934. At first glance this piece, entitled "Home Girl," would appear to be just another celebrity portrait, not unlike the ones Mitchell was turning out for the *World-Telegram*. But Mitchell affects a tone that is different, and darker, than that. For one thing, he telegraphs to the reader that he is not especially a fan of the singer's sentimental oeuvre, which itself gets your attention and makes you wonder what kind of treatment the Profile subject is in for. But more remarkable is the story's main theme, broached right at the outset, which is one of resentment—an emotion that has built up in the young woman after listening to countless vaudeville and radio comics make sport of her corpulence (in 1934, Kate Smith was just twenty-four years old and already two hundred twenty-six pounds). Mitchell devotes much of his allotted space to these slights, to the pain and anger they arouse in her, and to the image they have created of her in the public mind, one almost of a performing freak. Against this image he then juxtaposes the considerable (and largely unpublicized) efforts Smith devotes in her private life to helping the less fortunate. In this sense, the portrait can be seen as a forerunner of the more famous Profiles Mitchell soon would be writing of non-celebrity down-and-outers, which would explore so poignantly, and in much more depth, the theme of "otherness." Mitchell closed the Profile by discussing how pleased Smith was to be invited by the Philadelphia Orchestra to be a soloist for a fundraiser.

She decided to sing "My Heart at Thy Sweet Voice," and, when she arrived at the concert hall, frightened Leopold Stokowski by going over to him and saying sharply, "When you come to this note, hold it! See?" Each day she grows prouder of her infinitely sentimental contralto, and once she told an interviewer, "I'm big and I'm fat and I'm not a prize beauty, but I have a voice, and when I sing, boy, I sing all over."

Here was another indication that Mitchell was no daily hack but a thoughtful writer who was bringing irony, intentionality, even contrariness, to his narratives. As Mitchell knew long before the rest of the public did, even celebrities bruise.

More significant than the content of these early contributions, however, was that they put Mitchell firmly on the radar of *The New Yorker*'s editors. The magazine was keen to get even more Joseph Mitchell into its pages. But the editors of the *World-Telegram* knew they had something special in Mitchell, too. And they were working him, hard. He was writing literally every day, sometimes several stories per day. Even for a New York–based general-assignment reporter, the range of his interests and assignments was astonishing.

In June of 1934, for instance, Mitchell witnessed serial executions at Sing Sing penitentiary, as New York put to death three men convicted of methodically poisoning a drunken derelict whose life they had first insured, with themselves as beneficiaries. Every aspect of their tale— the perpetrators, the victim, the plot—was tawdry. But Mitchell's account of their execution is anything but, the scene's horror only reinforced by the understatement of his observations. "The relatives were waiting to claim the bodies of the three men who helped kill a barfly for $1,290. It took them a long time to kill Malloy. It took the State only sixteen minutes to kill them."

Then in July, during a particularly oppressive heat wave that had the city in its grip, Mitchell produced a string of almost impressionist pieces about it. Weather stories are the bane of every newspaper reporter, as it's challenging to find new or inventive ways to say, "It's hot (or cold, or rainy, or icy) out there." Mitchell solved the problem by taking a novelistic approach to the assignment, turning the journalistic trope on its head and making the heat palpable to his readers. "It takes ten beers to quench one's thirst," he writes. "The damp, insistent heat has placed blue lines beneath the eyes of subway passengers. The flags on the skyscrapers are slack; there is no breeze." A little later he lets the proprietor of a Romanian restaurant on the Lower East Side recount a "revealing" story, in his distinct patois.

> "It is hot and humidity all day down here, yes, but at night you sleep on the roof," [says Haimowitz]. "Nothing better at all. We lay blankets down in the dark and go to sleep, everybody, all the families. The other night something terrible happened on a roof in Hester Street. There is a fat guy, so big as me almost, a butcher. He has too much to drink. He goes home and takes off his clothes. He knows his wife is up on the roof. He goes stumbling up there and he lifts up a blanket. It is the wrong blanket, but he does not know it. It is some other lady, not his wife. He goes right to sleep and snores very big. The lady wakes up and takes a look at him. She screams and she yells. She flees away in a hurry and almost falls off the roof. Then his right wife she gets out from under her blanket and sees him. She gives a scream. She gives him a kick, but it is no good. He snores. They call a cop, and they pull him away to his own blanket. He does not wake up. He just dreams and snores. The whole neighborhood wakes up, but not him. It is good to sleep on roof. So cool. Better yet than any shore."

Mitchell's work during this stretch showed him to be a kind of journalistic prodigy; in essence still a post-apprentice, he could scarcely have been expected to be capable of such emotional nuance and writerly craft. Yet he was shrewd enough, too, to be aware that he and a number of other young practitioners were gradually elevating what New York daily journalism was capable of. Newspapering in this *Front Page* era was as clamorous and frenetic as New York itself, a kind of contact sport. In 1920 there were fourteen daily papers operating in the city; the competition was so fierce that the strong were on the verge of swallowing the weak in a wave of mergers or buyouts. Radio was fast emerging as yet another threat. For publishers keen to unload their two- and three-cent papers on as many readers as possible, speed often trumped accuracy, and titillation was more alluring than public-affairs news. With the exception of the staid *Times,* the more venturesome *Herald Tribune,* and a handful of other "serious" papers, this was a tabloid age. Partisan politics suffused much of what passed for news content, and scant attention was paid to genuine social ills. In the Depression environment, editors figured readers wanted distractions from their troubles. So columnists purveyed gossip and rumor and their own colorful nocturnal activities. The average reporter, who learned on the job, had little incentive to attempt true storytelling or focus on real people. Mitchell and a younger generation of newspaper journalists wanted to change this unsatisfying state of affairs. Later in life, Mitchell talked about that desire and the hubris it engendered in them. "There was a peculiar journalistic world—Lucius Beebe and [Walter] Winchell—but we were above that," he would say self-effacingly. "We were superior to other reporters and the *Daily News,* but we weren't arrogant. We were observers, kind of Olympian—when really we were ignorant young people trying to act like we knew everything."

Proud as he was of what he had accomplished in a few short years in New York, Mitchell nonetheless clung to his North Carolina tether. Back home, the Mitchell family not only was weathering the Depression, but A.N. actually profited by acquiring a number of farms that his neighbors couldn't keep up with. The enterprise was becoming more challenging to manage by himself, though. Joseph and Therese returned to Fairmont at least once a year, usually in summer, and if anything the growing family business only increased the continuing, if largely unspoken, pressure on the eldest son to come back home for good once he got the New York adventure out of his system. In reality, the visits were persuading Mitchell that he was becoming a kind of "exile," a man emotionally torn between two worlds. This was a theme he would explore for the rest of his life, as he grappled with the guilt of leaving home and spurning his father's wishes. Yet each trip to Fairmont underscored for Mitchell how much he had come to love New York, how much he missed its action and sensory bombardment when he was away. Invariably, the minute he arrived in North Carolina he started longing again for New York. It was a dichotomy Mitchell never really reconciled.

AFTER MORE THAN THREE YEARS of nonstop features, major series, and oddball miscellany, Mitchell got a "reprieve" of sorts at the beginning of 1935, when the *World-Telegram* included him on the team it dispatched to cover the "trial of the century."

At a courthouse in Flemington, New Jersey, about fifty miles west of New York, a German émigré named Bruno Hauptmann was to be tried for extortion and murder in the kidnapping and death of the infant son of Charles Lindbergh, who eight years earlier had flown solo across the Atlantic to become America's hero and an international sensation. The child was taken from the Lindbergh home in Hopewell, New Jersey, in March of 1932; a ransom was demanded and paid, but Charles Jr.'s remains were discovered that May. The nation breath-

Mitchell at the out-of-the-way New Jersey inn that became a second home during Bruno Hauptmann's "trial of the century."

lessly followed the tragic story. It would be another two years before Hauptmann was arrested and charged with the crime.

In September and October of 1934, after Hauptmann's arrest, Mitchell was one of the legions of reporters on the case, writing the occasional news update—for instance, when Lindbergh showed up to testify at the grand jury for Hauptmann, or when Hauptmann was transferred to Flemington to await trial. But with the trial's start on January 2, 1935, the New York media swept into Flemington like a military invasion. The *World-Telegram* mounted a team of ten journalists on the scene to cover the trial, and Mitchell would say that "compared with our competitors we were understaffed."

He filed for the paper almost every day. Some of these contributions were more feature-oriented, describing the atmosphere around the courthouse for readers back in the city. Some were straightforward accounts of the day's testimony; other times he simply gathered odds and ends from the trial. Mitchell produced about two-dozen pieces in all. But even writing the "straight news," Mitchell brought a more acute sense of observation than the average reporter on the scene, conveying a subtler humanity instead of the easy pathos others went in for. Here, for instance, was how he began his news story about Anne Morrow Lindbergh's testimony early in the trial:

FLEMINGTON, Jan. 3—The questioning of Mrs. Anne Morrow Lindbergh by Attorney General David T. Wilentz resembled a tense private conversation. The voice of the mother of the murdered child was so low as she said that Charles Augustus Lindbergh, Jr., was normal, healthy and blue-eyed that the Attorney General impulsively moved several steps forward and stood almost directly in front of her.

The two were so near that the questions and answers could not be heard, and Judge Trenchard, leaning forward, said, "If the jurors do not hear the testimony, let them speak up and we will see to it that they do hear it." Mrs. Lindbergh looked startled. She sat even more erect in the chair. Her eyes blinked and she clinched her jaws. Thereafter her voice was louder.

To shield its staff from the hothouse media environment and the camp followers in Flemington proper, the *World-Telegram* housed its reporters and editors miles away, at a small, family-run hotel in Stockton, New Jersey. It took over the hotel completely, installing a news wire and turning one of its larger spaces into a makeshift newsroom. Over the nearly two months of the trial, the team got into a kind of routine. While the trial was playing out during the day, Mitchell and the other reporters constantly phoned in updates on the testimony. Then at night, after a hearty, home-cooked communal dinner, they retired to the newsroom to start writing their "overnights"—the stories the paper would run in its early editions, until the trial had resumed and the paper could be freshened with the latest news for its home-delivery editions. "By ten P.M. the room would be full of cursing reporters whacking out nonsense on portable typewriters," Mitchell later wrote. The men lived for the weekends, when Therese and the other wives were permitted to join their exhausted husbands in Stockton.

Outside was the depressing northeastern winter, with its short days and cold nights. The Stockton hotel was situated one block from the Delaware River, and for Mitchell the setting afforded a chance to escape the trial's relentless deadlines. "We used to go down there at night and with slabs of ice as big as box-cars piling up against the bridge pillars," he wrote. "Late at night we could stand on the porch of the hotel and hear the crunch of the ice in the river." Sometimes they would sled on the nearby frozen canals. Family lore has it that one day Mitchell teamed up with *Herald Tribune* columnist Lucius Beebe to climb up the side of the building adjacent to the jailhouse, a vantage point from which they supposedly could see Hauptmann pacing in his cell.

Writing about the trial several years after the fact, Mitchell was almost blithe in recalling how the experience provided him a welcome interruption from the grind of the city beat. Still, he fully appreciated the serious business playing out in that New Jersey courtroom. After Hauptmann's conviction and two more years of appeals, he would be put to death. Mitchell by now had been a witness to several state executions; they had shaken him, and he said it would take him a long time to get over what he had seen. He captured that gravity in summarizing his Flemington experience:

> In the morning all the ashtrays would be full of butts and the wastebaskets would hold piles of crumpled copy paper and empty applejack bottles. Whenever I see a bottle of applejack I think of the Hauptmann trial. It was a mess. I have seen six men electrocuted, and once a young woman who had been stabbed in the neck died while I was trying to make her lie still, and one night I saw a white-haired Irish cop with a kindly face give a Negro thief the third degree, slowly tearing fresh bandages off wounds in the Negro's back, but for unnecessary inhumanity I do not believe I ever saw anything which surpassed the Hauptmann trial—Mrs. Lindbergh on the witness stand, for example, identifying her murdered child's sleeping suit, or Mrs. Hauptmann the night the jury came in, the night she heard that her husband was to be electrocuted. The older I get the less I care to see such things.

Professionally, however, the most important thing that happened to Joseph Mitchell in Flemington had nothing to do with the Lindberghs, the Hauptmanns, the media frenzy, or the trial itself. Barely a week into the proceedings, he got a note from St. Clair McKelway, a reporter and editor at *The New Yorker*—and who soon would be named the magazine's first managing editor in charge of nonfiction stories, or what everyone there called "Fact" pieces.

Three years older than Mitchell, McKelway, too, was a native of North Carolina, though he spent his boyhood in Washington, D.C. He began his newspaper career there, but he made his reputation at the *New York Herald Tribune*. An outstanding reporter with a jeweler's eye for detail, McKelway as a writer had a lovely, carefree touch that reflected his own personality and perfectly suited the crime stories that became his specialty at *The New Yorker*. He would also produce one of the most celebrated Profiles in the magazine's history, a six-part evisceration of Walter Winchell, when the gossip columnist was at the height of his influence. Handsome and unhurried, as dapper as he was droll, McKelway once sat down to do a performance review with a then-new reporter at the magazine, John Bainbridge, and offered this lone piece of advice: "Be more debonair." He would marry five times, and he suffered spectacular bouts of manic depression that could send him skittering from reality. (As an Air Force information officer during World War II, for instance, McKelway sent a telegram to the War Department, accusing Admiral Chester Nimitz of treason; influential higher-ups quashed it before McKelway could get into serious trouble.) But during these early years of *The New Yorker*, McKelway was among a handful of people who helped Harold Ross establish its breezily sophisticated tone and its journalistic standards. He also specialized in recruiting some of the best reporting talent in New York.

Which was why he had reached out to Mitchell. Specifically, McKelway wished to discuss some potential Reporter at Large story

The dashing St. Clair McKelway, Mitchell's first editor at The New Yorker, *would marry five times. His fourth marriage was to Martha Kemp Mature, soon after her divorce from Hollywood leading man Victor Mature.*

ideas—but, more broadly, he wanted to talk about Mitchell's future. "When the Lindbergh trial is over (or is it ever going to be over?) I'd like very much to have a talk with you about how you are getting along in your work for this periodical," McKelway wrote.

McKelway was ardent. That March, with the trial's close, he was pitching Mitchell on a Profile of a well-known yachtsman and "caviar king." A few months later he suggested a Reporter at Large piece on nude beaches. By that fall Mitchell's old mentor, Stanley Walker, had joined Ross's editing staff, and he, too, was trying out story ideas on his protégé. Mitchell was flattered by the attention, but, revitalized somewhat by the forced time away from the city, he was already back on the daily treadmill. Not long after the trial, he was putting the finishing touches on a mammoth six-part series on the nation's best-known liberal journals, including *The Nation*, the *Daily Worker*, *Commonweal*, and *The New Republic*. (Said the headline on the opening piece: LIBERAL JOURNALS ARE INFLUENTIAL BECAUSE THEIR SUBSCRIBERS ARE ENLIGHTENED CITIZENS.) Other series during this "second stage" of Mitchell's *World-Telegram* tenure involved profiling New York's busiest social caseworkers, sagest magistrates, and bravest firefighters, the last stories liberally illustrated with their heroic exploits. He continued to crank out the celebrity profiles like a mimeograph machine: Eleanor Roosevelt, Kitty Carlisle, Jimmy Durante, George M. Cohan, Tallulah Bankhead, and Gene Krupa, to name just a few. Nor did he neglect the city's curiosities: New Yorkers who wanted to pull down all the city's statues, lady parachutists, and the inventor of the combination toothbrush/hairbrush/shoe brush.

Odd or mainstream, long or short, almost every story Mitchell now wrote appeared on the *World-Telegram*'s front page or main feature page. His stories were popular with readers, who connected with their humor and humanity. The paper in turn fueled that popularity by making Mitchell one of the reporters it featured on the side-panel billboards of the *World-Telegram* delivery trucks that raced around the city. Meantime, Mitchell continued to refine the unconventional, understated, and elegant style that was a precursor to his later *New Yorker* work. Other than a little sentiment now and again, his work at this point was largely absent of authorial emotion. But he let that façade crack in a powerful story that appeared in late 1935.

Mitchell visited a hospital that housed wounded veterans from the World War, men who had sustained the gravest kinds of physical and psychological injury. He gained access to one of the back wards, where the most profoundly damaged men stayed. Mitchell described how some of them seemed unable to move; others wore frozen, emotionless expressions. The more socialized of the patients were sitting at a table, trying to make baskets from reeds. "Outside the leaves on the maples in the eighteen acres of hospital grounds were yellow and red," Mitchell wrote, "and on Kingsbridge Road kids were throwing a football about and yelling, and on the blue Hudson two young men were rowing a boat, and inside, huddled around the radiators, five middle-aged men whose nerves had been blasted out of coordination by screaming shells were struggling with reed baskets. It takes them hours to do the work a child can do in no time. It made one furious watching them struggle with the lengths of reed, trembling and fumbling."

The *World-Telegram* was also sending Mitchell to where important news was occurring—and one such instance nearly cost him his life. In the late winter and early spring of 1936, the Ohio River was flooded for its entire length, and Mitchell traveled to see the situation for himself. He was scheduled to fly out of an airport in Cleveland in a small airplane, to survey the upper reaches of the Ohio over two days and document the extent of the damage. The first day's trip went off without incident. But day two—March 20, 1936—proved more eventful.

Mitchell was in the single-engine craft with the pilot and two other newspaper reporters. Approaching takeoff, the plane clipped a snowdrift along the runway and flipped, coming to rest upside down. Mitchell and the others, strapped securely into their seats, were pulled out by horrified onlookers. They were shaken but unharmed. In short order, in fact, the group had secured another plane and took off as planned to finish the assignment. "It all happened too fast for us to get scared," Mitchell told the *World-Telegram*, which also ran a small photograph of the mishap. Then the paper printed his report on the flooding, which was typically thorough and made no mention of the accident.

———

IN THE THIRTIES, as was the case in preceding and succeeding decades, the gears of the New York media world were lubricated at certain favorite bars. Newspaper reporters and editors, magazine contributors, theater publicists and producers, agents, and assorted friends of the court came together there to gossip and drink. On occasion they were even known to gamble. Among the most welcoming of these establishments was Bleeck's (pronounced "Blake's"), a onetime speakeasy that went legitimate with the repeal of Prohibition.

This night, as most nights, there is a "match game" under way in the cramped back room. A bemused Joseph Mitchell—still in one piece after his flirtation with mortality in Cleveland—takes it all in from a small peanut gallery that's formed up just behind the long table of a dozen or so players. Among these are Walker and Beebe and past and present staffers from the *Herald Tribune,* as well as a sizable cohort from *The New Yorker*—McKelway, Thurber, Alva Johnston, Wolcott Gibbs, John O'Hara, and John Lardner. Then there is the lone woman at the table, a petite, fetching blonde named Ann Honeycutt. As night wears on, the barbs sharpen and carom around the room. Mitchell observes the lady and nods in approval as she gives it to the boys as good as she gets.

Bleeck's was located on West 40th Street between Seventh and Eighth Avenues. Conveniently enough, it was right out the back door of the old *Herald Tribune* building, on 41st Street, which meant that Bleeck's for years effectively doubled as an auxiliary newsroom for the paper's staff. And it remained a popular hangout even for those, like Mitchell and McKelway and Johnston, who had moved on to other places. Some editors wouldn't have wanted temptation residing quite so close to their reporters, but Walker didn't mind. "It was a hell of a lot better to know that your good men were probably there," he explained, "than in assorted bedrooms from Staten Island to Speonk."

By the mid-thirties, the match game at Bleeck's was almost as much a New York institution as the bar itself. In the game, each player got three matchsticks. With both hands behind their backs, players decided if they would hold three, two, one, or no matches. They then presented a closed fist on the table, and, in clockwise order, each player guessed how many total matches were being held by the entire group. The person guessing the correct number was excused, and this continued until there remained only the loser, who was obligated to buy drinks for the lot. The match game was useful because it could accommodate any number of people and could be played in various stages of sobriety. It also provided a good excuse to drink into the wee hours (Bleeck's stayed open until 4:00 A.M.), and with the attendant side wagering and blue commentary, it was just as much fun to watch as to play.

At Bleeck's, as at McSorley's, women had been kept out for many years, but that barrier finally fell in the early thirties. And Ann Honeycutt—"Honey," as she was known to all—had helped bring it down. It was a role she was used to playing.

Born in tiny Plain Dealing, Louisiana, Honeycutt made her way to New York in 1923 and immediately set about reinventing herself. She became friends with fellow Confederate expat Walker, and with his entrée she was soon a regular at the bars frequented by the city's newspapermen. At speakeasies like Tony's, she also fell in with the circle of the talented (and then mostly single) young men who were helping Harold Ross build his new magazine. Though she had been in New York only a little longer than many of them, she came across very much as a "woman about town," in Mitchell's recollection. She reveled in the liberation New York afforded, and that uninhibited enjoyment was part of her strong appeal to men. Honeycutt herself spoke about the thrill of being young in the city, in that golden time between the wars. "My memories of that period are all speakeasy memories. . . . [Y]ou got out of the home, you walked out the door and you were *free.*"

With her vivacious personality and quick wit—Mitchell would later say that some of the lines credited to Dorothy Parker were actually Honeycutt's—she was catnip to the *New Yorker* men. She occasionally dated Gibbs. Thurber fell head over heels in love with her and wooed her for years, though unsuccessfully. (He was doubly wounded when she instead wed the charming McKelway, whom Thurber admired in every other way; the marriage, however, was short-lived.) In the thirties and early forties, Honeycutt spent so much time in the company of *New Yorker* staffers that Ross sometimes forgot that she didn't work for him, too, to the point that he assigned her stories to write. Charles ("Chip") McGrath, who many years later was deputy editor of *The New Yorker* under William Shawn, called Honeycutt "a Molly Bloom figure to a whole generation of writers and artists and editors."

They loved her because she was beautiful and she was funny. But mostly they loved her because, unlike most women of their acquaintance, she seemed one of them. Whether it was drinking with them or fighting with them, Honeycutt held her own. She got plenty of practice, too, particularly in her long and complicated relationship with Thurber.

Already having lost most of his sight because of a boyhood accident, Thurber grew bitter when he drank, and he drank a lot. It was not uncommon for him to sail into rages, like the one Honeycutt recalled for Thurber's biographer, Burton Bernstein. They were at "21," and Thurber "slapped me from across the table," she said. "So I threw a glass of Scotch right back at him. We were thrown out, but we finished the fight on the sidewalk. It was like that in those days."

Professionally, too, Honeycutt made her way in what was largely a man's world. Having gotten her foot in the door at CBS as a singer, she worked her way up to become a radio-program producer. She was an accomplished writer, as well, and in 1939 she would turn out a delightful book about how to raise dogs in the city, a work whose popularity was enhanced considerably by its illustrations—Thurber's inimitable canines.

Walker introduced Honeycutt to Mitchell, and she liked the lean, laconic Carolinian from the start, in part for the same reason so many women gravitated to Mitchell: He listened to them. He was genuinely interested in their careers, their opinions, their lives. But for Honeycutt, who had grown up with a peripatetic father and who seemed ineluctably drawn to unreliable men, Mitchell was dependability itself.

If he said he would do something for her, he did, and this was the foundation for what became a close friendship. Though Honeycutt was seven years older than Mitchell, he was fascinated by how her backstory seemed to mirror his own—two displaced Southerners, kindred spirits trying to break away from their pasts and prove their mettle on the toughest stage there was. As he got older, in fact, Mitchell grew obsessed with the synchronicity of their lives, a connection he wanted to somehow document and devoted much of the rest of his life to futilely chasing.

With Mitchell spending ever more time with the *New Yorker* crowd, the temptation grew to make a professional change. He craved more time to work on good stories than his paper—*any* paper, really—could afford. He longed to write more substantive, and narrative, articles. And he wanted to surround himself with people who took the calling as seriously as he did. The more his own craft improved, the more dim his view became of the reporters who were joining the *World-Telegram* from other "Scripps-Howard towns" and who, in his eyes, weren't willing to put in the time or effort New York truly required of a reporter—the kind of investment Walker had asked of him when *he* first arrived. "The reporters on the [*World-Telegram*] were geniuses from Akron and Cleveland and Toledo and places like that," Mitchell wrote years later in his journal. "Instead of getting to know the city, as soon as they got here they moved to Rye or Orange or some other suburban place, and they knew hardly anything about the city. Most of the time, it was a hollow newspaper, exposing sheriffs, and the like of that. I really never gave a damn. [The corporate motto] Give Light and the People Will Find Their Way of the Scripps-Howard papers . . . the sanctimoniousness."

After an absence of two and a half years, Mitchell finally managed to produce another *New Yorker* piece, "Bar and Grill," which appeared in November of 1936. Little more than an extended sketch, if an amusing one, it described a neighborhood dive and the Runyonesque characters (including, again, many newspaper reporters) who frequented it. At Dick's Bar and Grill, it seems the clientele went in for a lot of drinking, dicing, fighting, and occasionally shooting. But the customers were no more colorful than the proprietor, Dick, who was known to all as simply "The House." The House, Mitchell wrote, is "a sad-eyed and broad-beamed Italian who often shakes his fat, hairy fists at the fly-specked ceiling and screams, 'I am being crucified.'" The *New Yorker*'s editors loved this peek into one of the city's grimier precincts; they were also delighted that a nonfiction slice of life could be as cheeky as a good short story.

Other publications beckoned Mitchell, as well. For instance, in early 1937, *McCall's* invited him to write about Edward VIII's recent abdication of the British throne for Wallis Simpson. As an established national publication with a circulation in the millions, *McCall's* could offer Mitchell considerably more money than the still-young and penurious *New Yorker*. But Mitchell thought the magazine's content so unserious that he couldn't bring himself to write for it.

His next freelance piece for *The New Yorker*, another Reporter at Large, appeared in July of 1937. Entitled "Mr. Grover A. Whalen and the Midway," it was a portrait of a young woman named Florence Cubitt, "Queen of the Nudists at the California Pacific International Exposition," whose ambition was to succeed Sally Rand as the nation's most ogled fan dancer. Her specific aspiration was to be a star attraction of the 1939 New York World's Fair—notwithstanding the vow of the fair's president, Grover A. Whalen, that such lewd acts would be entirely unwelcome. Mitchell had written about nudists, fan dancers, strippers, and the like for the *World-Telegram*, and this piece essentially reworked one he'd produced a year earlier after a memorable interview with the shapely Miss Cubitt. In fact, when she came through the door to meet him, Mitchell wrote, "She was naked. It was the first time a woman I had been sent to interview ever came into the room naked, and I was shocked. I say she was naked. Actually, she had a blue G-string on, but I have never seen anything look so naked in my life as she did when she walked into that room." Again, *The New Yorker* was pleased to publish a droll Fact piece, especially one that pitted a beautiful fan dancer's dreams against a stuffy bureaucrat's determination to extinguish them.

Still, the transition from newspaper to magazine writing was not an easy one, even for someone with Mitchell's skills. His early work did need some editing, if much less than most non-staff contributions did. But Mitchell had a more basic challenge than learning magazine style: He wasn't sure in what direction to take his writing career. *New Yorker* correspondence from this pivotal period in Mitchell's development reveals that the magazine's cultivation of the writer was serious but also frustrating—in essence because *The New Yorker* knew what it wanted, and Mitchell didn't seem to.

In November of 1936, for instance, Mitchell told McKelway that he was working on "a story about an inquisitive out-of-town boy in New York City, something on the order of a composite profile" (a concept that would resurface, in a far different context, later in his career). The piece obviously would have autobiographical overtones. But after reading it, McKelway turned it down. "Frankly, we are a little puzzled by it and, after the 'Bar and Grill' piece, disappointed," he wrote. "This Mr. Griffin doesn't seem to come up through this piece as a character at all. One time he seems to be one guy and another time another. I am afraid it is one of those pieces where fact and fiction have got sort of mixed up together with an unfortunate effect. When you first spoke to me about the subject I got the idea that this was to be a piece about the first few years of an out-of-towner in New York—more of a factual piece telling the strange life that such a man leads and the things that he thinks and does which are unfamiliar to most New Yorkers. This turns out to be almost entirely a fictional sketch and I am afraid it doesn't satisfy us either as fact or as fiction. He just seems to be a pretty ordinary fellow, not very interesting and rather common, if I may use that questionable word." McKelway went on to say that "I hope to God" the young writer didn't find his cool reception too deflating. But he pleaded with Mitchell to try something "more tangible."

A proposed Reporter at Large about an amateur local detective was rejected as insufficiently interesting. Then, in the fall of 1937, Mitchell made yet another stab at some autobiographical fact-fiction mélange. But McKelway again demurred, his vexation more palpable. "The essential trouble with these stories is that they're not really *stories*, but sort of fragments of experiences, which don't fit into the factual side of the magazine, or the fictional either," he wrote Mitchell. He goes on, however, to quote his boss, Ross, as saying Mitchell is a *"damn* good" writer, and Ross wondered if Mitchell should be encouraged to try his hand at more fiction, a prospect that continued to intrigue Mitchell. McKelway, in the meantime, reiterated his concern that the rejections not discourage Mitchell.

If Mitchell wasn't discouraged, exactly, he certainly shared McKelway's frustration—although it's less clear whether his frustration was with *The New Yorker,* for its reluctance to explore even more-experimental creative frontiers, or with himself.

ABOUT THIS SAME TIME, Mitchell received a telephone call that caught him entirely unawares yet thoroughly delighted him. On the other end of the line was Mitchell's undereducated shipmate on the *City of Fairbury,* Jack Sargent Harris. It seems he had indeed gone on to make something of himself, just as Mitchell had urged him to do on their transatlantic sail six years earlier. When Harris finally gave up as a merchant seaman, he was accepted into Northwestern University, where he studied anthropology. Now, in an even more remarkable turn, he was working on his PhD at Columbia University and was a graduate assistant for Franz Boas. Even a layman like Mitchell recognized Boas as the most influential anthropologist in the world. Seventy-eight years old and recently retired, Boas had trained a veritable army of anthropologists who were radically redefining race and civilization and reshaping how the West understood cultures once considered simply "primitive." It was Boas's earlier work that had largely disproved notions of "superior race"—which now, in a terrible irony, had reemerged so virulently in the scientist's native Germany. Indeed, Boas lived long enough to see Nazis burning his books in a square outside his alma mater, the University of Kiel, which over the years had bestowed on him its highest honors for his contributions to understanding the family of man.

Harris arranged for Mitchell to meet his mentor, who in turn agreed to be interviewed for a series in the *World-Telegram.* Mitchell's conversations with Boas and many of his protégés resulted in six long pieces that ran in early November 1937. These included an overview of the state and importance of anthropological studies; a profile of Boas himself; and stories specifically focused on the Ojibwa and Pawnee tribes, the Dobu natives of New Guinea, and the collection and recording of aboriginal music. The stories make for good reading, if rather highbrow for *World-Telegram* readers. But for Mitchell, the experience represented something much more profound; it was a kind of graduate-level seminar in anthropology that caused him to rethink, as a reporter, why people are who they are and do what they do. It would be a career-altering revelation.

Mitchell went into the interviews with Boas with the typical mindset of a reporter approaching an expert, which is to say he hoped he could find a way to put across his subject's work to a non-scientific audience in an interesting, coherent fashion. Yet it was Boas himself who upended the usual journalistic transaction, Mitchell would recall years later. As the two men settled into conversation, the reporter began to realize that Boas was paying more attention to him than to his questions, essentially an anthropologist observing a curious specimen—the New York newspaperman. Boas was becoming increasingly engaged—"not in me," Mitchell explained, "but in my ignorance." As Boas tried to explain his research principles, he suddenly told Mitchell, "Read this," and handed him a copy of his book *Anthropology and Modern Life*, which Mitchell would in fact read, and he "began telling me how to look at the world. He said, 'Don't take anything for granted, don't take yourself for granted, or your father.'" Mitchell was exhilarated by it all. He would remember coming away from the experience "feeling born again."

The insights from preparing the anthropology series caused Mitchell to reflect on his own life's work to date, a review that left him feeling somewhat unsettled. "I began to see that I had written a lot of things that were highly dubious," he recalled, in particular the stereotypical drinking stories so popular at that time (such as "Bar and Grill" from the previous year's *New Yorker*), which tended to wink at heavy imbibing as relatively innocent or even amusing behavior, when in fact

Mitchell was beginning to think the truer question was, "What's so great about all this goddamned sloshing?" He also realized that such stories were, in a sense, too easy to execute; he was better than that. This self-awareness was one of the main reasons that, in time, Mitchell's subject matter would move in far more substantive directions. In relating the stories of Mohawk steelworkers, gypsies, sideshow acts, and fishermen, Mitchell brought to them a new depth and context—a clear anthropological approach to understanding his subjects as members of distinct communities, with their own values, histories, and prejudices. For instance, when years later he would profile the venerable George Hunter, Mitchell took pains to set the story against the decline of Hunter's Sandy Ground hometown, lending the tale considerably more richness and meaning. Like a good novelist, Mitchell was moving ever closer to discovering his characters' fundamental motivation.

Even as he was pulling together the anthropology stories, Mitchell was putting the finishing touches on another project that, in its own

Therese took this photograph of her husband passed out on their couch, with New York's newspapers strewn about. Mitchell included this image in his first book, My Ears Are Bent.

way, would take his writing career to a new level. By now a bona fide newspaper "name," Mitchell had been approached by a small New York publisher, Sheridan House, about putting out a collection of the best of his journalistic work as a book. Initially, Mitchell was not inclined to do it; he believed that journalists should keep themselves largely out of the picture so that their stories, and their subjects, get the readers' full attention. But Sheridan's editors were persistent, and Mitchell began culling almost a decade's worth of material. He recast some of the pieces and added interesting, and sometimes racier, details that his newspaper editors had cut out of the originals.

The book was entitled *My Ears Are Bent,* a coy play on Mitchell's almost masochistic ability to listen at length to all types of New Yorkers, dozens of whom march through his first book like a gaudy parade down Broadway. In the opening chapter, a kind of foreword, Mitchell discusses the art of conversation—how he goes about it and why he loves it. "Now and then . . . someone says something so unexpected it is magnificent," he writes. He cites a time early in his career when he was working on a story about voodoo and black magic in Harlem and was present when an assistant district attorney questioned a prostitute. The prosecutor was pressing her because he was convinced the woman had been used as an altar in a black mass. As their interview dragged on, however, she wasn't especially helpful on this point, and at length the exasperated interrogator asked why she had become a prostitute in the first place. "I just wanted to be accommodating," she replied. Mitchell was enchanted.

Even eight decades after the material was produced—most of it under unforgiving deadline—a reader is struck by several things about the stories contained in *My Ears Are Bent.* Foremost is how fresh Mitchell's voice was and how consistent that voice remained from story to story throughout a remarkable range of subjects. Then there is the fact that he was able to establish such a distinct voice at all in a medium so hidebound by its rules and prejudices that it almost by definition suppressed a writer's individuality. The material has a distinct maturity in outlook and a wry humor throughout. There is a tinge of world-weariness here and there, perhaps surprising from a writer so young but not surprising at all to anyone who knew Mitchell, an "old soul" from his boyhood days. And there is the Mitchell trademark—empathy for his fellow man, even when that man is certifiably crazy.

When it was published, *My Ears Are Bent* garnered considerable reviews and press attention in New York, virtually all positive. Not surprisingly, one of the friendliest, but also the most prescient, was written by Stanley Walker for the *Herald Tribune*. "Perhaps no other city in the world offers such a lush field for a man with Mr. Mitchell's talents as New York. This lovely and confusing and uproarious city is made to order for the knowing observer of human curiosities," Walker wrote. New York's fine newspapers do their best to reflect this "color and glory," he continued, "but somehow they never quite do the job, for the elusive quality of the city is the despair alike of poets and short story writers and historians. If Mr. Mitchell sticks to his knitting he should be able to turn out something of infinitely greater value than this present little volume, charming though it is."

The book generated flattering newspaper stories about Mitchell back in North Carolina, as well. One reminded readers that North Carolina had previously exported O. Henry to New York. Elsewhere the publisher, Sheridan House, speculated that, in time, Joseph Mitchell might match the success of another Southern writer—Margaret Mitchell. The author was uneasy about this kind of premature flattery, of course; he understood his talent, but he also knew he was just getting started. That hint of dismay can be detected in a publisher's photograph accompanying these stories. They show a handsome young man staring intently into the camera, unsmiling and suppressing all his usual amiability, as if being photographed against his will. His eyes are inquisitive, his dark hair combed neatly and beginning to recede ever so slightly from his forehead.

That summer, Mitchell sent a copy of *My Ears Are Bent* to his parents. Inside the front, he inscribed, "For Mamma and Daddy, with my love and with the promise that my next book will be much better. J.Q.M."

CHAPTER 6

A REPORTER AT LARGE

JANE BARNELL OCCASIONALLY CONSIDERS herself an outcast and feels that there is something vaguely shameful about the way she makes a living. When she is in this mood, she takes no pride in the fact that she has had a longer career as a sideshow performer than any other American woman and wishes she had never left the drudgery of her grandmother's cotton farm in North Carolina. Miss Barnell is a bearded lady. Her thick, curly beard measures thirteen and a half inches, which is the longest it has ever been. When she was young and more entranced by life under canvas, she wore it differently every year; in those days there was a variety of styles in beards—she remembers the Icicle, the Indian Fighter, the Whisk Broom, and the Billy Goat—and at the beginning of a season she would ask the circus barber to trim hers in the style most popular at the moment. Since it became gray, she has worn it in the untrimmed, House of David fashion.

—From "Lady Olga," 1939

. .

B Y 1938, DEPRESSION-WEARY AMERICANS WERE ALREADY LOOKING back on the twenties with nostalgia. That decade, as intoxicating as its successor had been desperate, had represented not only an age of personal liberation but one of cultural liberation. American literature moved in a bolder, more provocative, more naturalistic direction. The emerging motion-picture industry rooted itself in the latter-day paradise of Hollywood. Radio as a commercial medium spread coast to coast with astonishing speed. And print media evolved, as well, perhaps most notably in the rise of bold new magazines. To be sure, many of the venerable titles in American publishing were still around to usher in the Jazz Age—*Collier's, Liberty,* and *The Saturday Evening Post,* for instance, not to mention a shelf full of the still-popular "women's" magazines. Yet such periodicals were hardly *of* the Jazz Age; for the postwar generation, they came across as staid and out of touch. Young entrepreneurs recognized an opening for magazines with a more contemporary focus. They sought to make cultural statements, to take political stands, to take a fresh look at news—and just maybe, in that great American tradition, to get rich. Among the most important magazine launches in the wake of World War I were H. L. Mencken and George Jean Nathan's *The American Mercury* (founded in 1924); DeWitt Wallace's *Reader's Digest* (1922); and Henry Luce and Briton Hadden's groundbreaking *Time* (1923)—to be followed in short order by such other Luce titles as *Fortune* (1930) and the picture magazine *LIFE* (1936).

Then there was *The New Yorker,* founded in 1925. By now, with the thirties slogging to a close, Harold Ross's shiny weekly was regarded by people who made their living with words as something special, and distinct from the rest. "We were reading *The New Yorker* all the time and I saw what the possibilities were," Joseph Mitchell recalled in his 1989 interview with Norman Sims. "That's the magazine that changed everything."

The New Yorker was Ross's brainchild, and a more unlikely marriage of man and idea can scarcely be imagined. A roughneck and a high school dropout, Ross was born in Aspen, Colorado, and raised in Salt Lake City, Utah, when both were little more than frontier settlements, as wide open and woolly as Ross himself. He spent a number of years roaming the United States (and into Panama for a while, during the canal's construction) as a "tramp" reporter for dozens of newspapers before enlisting in the Army with America's entry into World War I. In France he became managing editor of the newly established *Stars and Stripes* service newspaper, and after the war he settled in New York City, intent on starting a magazine.

Ross toyed with several ideas, but his main one envisioned a new kind of publication that would reflect the glamour and excitement of twenties Manhattan. To his numerous friends in the media, theater, and arts (he was a charter member of the Algonquin Round Table crowd), the notion of a rube like Ross as an arbiter of urbanity was preposterous. He looked like a blacksmith and he swore like one. He brushed his coarse black hair straight up into a kind of three-inch hedge. His clothes were rumpled and ill-fitting, and he wore high-button shoes long after they ceased to be fashionable. His laugh, while infectious, was explosive and snorted, and it exposed a cavernous gap between his two front teeth. Chic he was not. Nevertheless, Ross was as stubborn as he was confident, and he persuaded the heir to a New York commercial-baking fortune, Raoul Fleischmann, to bankroll the enterprise.

The New Yorker launched in February of 1925, and its early issues were so editorially infirm that the whole venture nearly died in the crib. Its few curious readers didn't know what to make of it. Before it landed upon its famously aloof and amused tone, *The New Yorker* came across as clumsy and shrill and trying too hard. Editorial content was wildly uneven and error-ridden; aiming to be *au courant*, it simply was tripping over itself. About the only thing Ross got right from the out-set was the artwork and cartoons—but that wasn't enough to keep readership from atrophying throughout the spring and summer fol-lowing its launch. Fortunately for Ross, Fleischmann was an inveter-ate gambler, and against his better judgment he kept infusing the start-up with cash.

Finally, in the fall of 1925, with the arrival of a new cultural season and Ross securing stronger material, *The New Yorker* started to catch on. Through sheer force of will, Ross was conjuring the mix of wit, voice, and storytelling (both fact and fiction) that would prove to be a winning formula for readers of a certain means and discernment—and, even more important, for the advertisers who wanted to reach them.

It's true Ross was not a sophisticated person, but he had highly sophisticated editorial instincts, including an uncanny nose for talent. Indeed, his recruiting ability turned out to be the primary driver for

When he hit New York in the early twenties, Harold Ross still looked like the Utah rube he was. By the time he hired Joseph Mitchell at The New Yorker, *in 1938, Ross had cleaned up considerably.*

The New Yorker's success. He relentlessly sought out creative people, be they editing lieutenants (Ralph Ingersoll, Katharine S. White, Stanley Walker, William Shawn); cartoonists and artists (Peter Arno, Helen Hokinson, Whitney Darrow, Jr., Rea Irvin); humorists (James Thurber, Robert Benchley, S. J. Perelman); critics (Wolcott Gibbs, Lewis Mumford, Clifton Fadiman); essayists (E. B. White); fiction writers (Clarence Day, John O'Hara, Sally Benson, John Cheever); or the journalists who made up the magazine's so-called Fact staff (St. Clair McKelway,

Janet Flanner, Meyer Berger, Alva Johnston). By the late thirties, *The New Yorker* was secure enough, and staffed-up enough, that Ross could have relaxed his recruiting efforts and let talent simply come to him. Instead, he accelerated his search, looking in particular to build up his reportorial staff to help the transformation of his onetime "comic paper" (as he always called, and fancied, his creation) into a kind of global journal. In time, Ross would assemble a stable of nonfiction talent that became synonymous with American literary journalism—A. J. Liebling, Philip Hamburger, E. J. Kahn, Jr., Lillian Ross, Brendan Gill, Geoffrey Hellman, Emily Hahn . . . and the man who was perhaps the most enduring of all: Joseph Mitchell.

No surprise given his itinerant reporting history, Ross was a newspaper addict. He read the boisterous New York City newspapers the way a major-league scout watches high school baseball games, looking for prodigies. As such, in the early thirties he took note of a newcomer at the *World-Telegram* who was regularly producing the most compellingly told stories in the paper. This Joseph Mitchell could turn a phrase, had an eye for detail, and saw stories where few others did. More important, the young man seemed to share Ross's appreciation for the comic possibilities of the human carnival. So it was that their courtship began.

This is where things stood five years later when Mitchell, in the spring and summer of 1938, submitted two final freelance contributions to *The New Yorker*. The first, "The Kind Old Blonde," was a slight fiction sketch that appeared in June, and a bit of a backslide toward the kind of boozy tale he ostensibly now eschewed. In it, a woman—a "big, sound, well-dressed blonde" with a fondness for Old-Fashioneds—and her companion are in a bar, where she is trying to dissuade him from suddenly giving up drinking, which a bad medical report inclines him to do. (When the waiter brings her order of little-neck clams, she sounds rather like Mitchell himself talking: "If you don't mind, these clams are mighty small. I'd like to have the cherrystones. If you don't mind.") His second, considerably more substantial submission, that July, was a Reporter at Large entitled "Hit on the Head with a Cow" (the curious title derives from a mishap during

Mitchell's childhood, told in the story's opening, in which he was knocked unconscious while helping hoist a cow for butchering). It's actually the story of Captain Charley's Private Museum for Intelligent People, an astoundingly indiscriminate collection of Egyptian mummies, stuffed animals, Chinese coins, snakeskins, the parasol of an infamous New Orleans madam, and so much more, all housed in the basement of a brownstone tenement near Columbus Circle. The lone criterion for something to be added to the collection was whether the proprietor, Charley Cassell, considered it interesting. Mitchell's account of visiting Captain Charley's museum helped cement what was quickly becoming the writer's specialty for *The New Yorker*—finding characters of such bold hues, they were nearly off the color wheel. In a note accepting the story for publication, McKelway told Mitchell that Ross had gone out of his way to compliment the piece, something "very unusual" for the editor to do. The piece appeared in the magazine in August, and the same month Ross and McKelway summoned Mitchell to a luncheon meeting.

Mitchell had a strong inkling Ross was going to offer him a full-time job at *The New Yorker,* and he went in a state of high anticipation. Yet as they sat at their table at the Blue Ribbon, a staff haunt near the magazine's offices, it seemed that all Ross wanted to do was talk shop about the *World-Telegram* and the city's other newspapers. Ross was animated in the discussion, Mitchell remembered, which didn't especially surprise him, given that the newspaper industry had been such a formative influence on Ross, as it had been for Mitchell. Eventually Ross segued to another topic he and Mitchell shared—growing up in small towns. Mitchell was enjoying the conversation, but as the time passed, the meal finished, and they were departing the restaurant, he wondered if he had misread the purpose of the meeting. Then, as they made their way up the street and were about to part company, Ross abruptly stopped and turned to the writer. "Look, Mitchell," he said, "if you'd like to come up here, it's a hell of a place to work. Do you think you'd like it?" Mitchell, relieved, simply smiled for a moment. "Oh, yes," he said.

Ross made Mitchell's hiring official with a letter outlining the terms. The original contract was for twenty-six weeks, renewable for a second twenty-six weeks if both parties were agreeable; in other words, there was to be a kind of probationary period. (Ross had confidence in Mitchell but had found that, sometimes, even the most talented daily journalist never really got the hang of a magazine's pace and writing with a more subjective point of view.) He would be paid one hundred dollars a week, a small increase from what he was making at the *World-Telegram*. Once the particulars of the position were laid out, Ross concluded the letter on a more personal note, and with a prediction: "This formality being over, I would report that I am exceedingly glad to hear of your decision [to join the magazine staff] and think that good things will come of it."

ON SEPTEMBER 26, 1938, Joseph Mitchell, having only recently turned thirty years old, reported for his first day of work at *The New Yorker*. The one extraordinary aspect about his otherwise-straightforward employment was that Mitchell would be paid a conventional weekly salary. A man flummoxed by numbers wanted no part of the byzantine, much-reviled compensation system Ross had devised for other writers at his magazine—one that left many of them owing their soul to "the company store" like beaten-down miners.

At *The New Yorker*, even full-time staff writers were paid by the piece; but, unlike freelancers, staffers collected a weekly "draw" against future stories in lieu of a salary. The amount collected weekly often exceeded what writers were credited with for their work. It was a system the magazine had developed over time, an effort by Ross—an unreconstructed tinkerer, who put great store by "systems"—to motivate editorial production while also providing staffers a modicum of financial security. His pay system also took into account story length and overall productivity, but along the way it got so complicated that few writers actually understood it. "Half the people here were always in debt," Mitchell recalled years later. "I mean even Thurber and [Wolcott] Gibbs. McKelway was always in debt. That's why they made him managing editor—to give him a regular income."

McKelway recalled that offering Mitchell a straight salary as opposed to the usual drawing account proved to be key in dislodging him from the security of the *World-Telegram*. The idea of a draw "terrified" Mitchell, McKelway said. And it was not hard to see why, once you examined the underlying logic of the draw, which wanted to treat editorial output as if it were a smooth-running assembly line rather than the fit-and-start product of neurotic, temperamental, and often alcoholic human beings. Internal memos written five years after Mitchell came to *The New Yorker* provide some hints as to the complexity of the compensation there. In 1943, William Shawn, then heading up the Fact writers, proposed that Mitchell receive a ten-dollar weekly raise. While this would seem a simple enough proposition, *The New Yorker's* business executives were so notoriously tightfisted that such a thing required courtlike briefs. Shawn made his case:

Mitchell, who has been working for us since 1938, has always been on a salary rather than a drawing-account arrangement. However, books have been kept on him [as if he had been on a regular drawing account] and he shows a bookkeeping deficit of over $6,000. This figure is deceptive, I hold. We have paid him in salary a total of $16,630. Deducting $1,705 in credits for seven casuals (paid for at prevailing rates), we are left with $15,925 [sic] to be accounted for. Altogether, we have accepted nine Profiles and twelve Reporters [at Large] in the period in question. Mitchell's pieces, as we are probably agreed, cannot be evaluated in any ordinary way. The value of the individual piece is extremely high, and there is an additional value in the very fact that a man of his caliber is willing to devote all his time to writing for us (making a bare living) and in the complementary fact that we are wise enough to keep him around (at an apparent loss); serves as some kind of inspiration to the other writers and to the editors. All right, to get back from inspiration to dough, if we figure that each of his nine Profiles was worth $1,000 and each of his Reporters was worth $577.90, we balance the books.

Actually, in the late thirties and early forties—when the average American earned less than two thousand dollars a year and the newly established federal minimum wage was twenty-five cents an hour—one hundred dollars a week afforded a Manhattan resident a passable standard of living. A Broadway ticket or a meal at a decent restaurant could be had for a few dollars, one of Mitchell's sharp double-breasted suits for twenty-five. Even allowing for this reasonable quality of life and the stability of his guaranteed salary, Mitchell constantly fretted about money—as he would for the rest of his days. Part of this was an organic impulse in the writer, who was a chronic worrier, anyway; part of it was the memory of his summary dismissal from the *Herald Tribune;* and part of it was due to the parlous times he was living in. Whatever the root cause, Mitchell's anxiety over compensation would evolve into a smoldering bitterness over the years, as he saw *The New Yorker* enjoy lavish profitability, thanks largely to the high-quality content he and other longtime staffers had provided at bargain-basement rates.

Ironically, by insisting on being paid by the week instead of by the word, Mitchell may have shortchanged himself in his first several years at the magazine. That's because his initial output was nothing short of Olympian. Perhaps it was his background working for newspapers, where writing two or three substantive stories a day was routine. Perhaps it was the probationary language in his first two six-month contracts. But Mitchell got off to a roaring start at *The New Yorker.* Four of the pieces he would eventually include in his 1943 book-length collection of stories, *McSorley's Wonderful Saloon,* appeared in the magazine within the first three months of his arrival there. More astonishing, in 1939 *The New Yorker* would publish no fewer than thirteen Mitchell pieces, plus several smaller Talk of the Town contributions. (One of these stories prompted a droll "protest" from *New Yorker* contributor and Ross friend H. L. Mencken. In a Reporter at Large about a purveyor of diamondback terrapin, Mitchell asserted that Maryland-style terrapin stew contains cream. The Sage of Baltimore was aghast. "Tell Mr. Mitchell that someone has misled him into a gross libel," Mencken wrote to McKelway. "It is the inborn and ineradicable conviction of all

Marylanders above the level of Y.M.C.A. secretaries that to put cream in terrapin is exactly on all fours with peeing in the piano." Mitchell replied that while Mencken was entitled to his view, cooking authority Sheila Hibben's recipe for Maryland terrapin stew included cream. "All the terrapin experts I consulted listed cream as well as sherry in their recipes for terrapin stew Maryland," Mitchell told McKelway. "However, I don't want to get in an argument about this; thousands of men have lost their lives in arguments over tomatoes in clam chowder, cream in terrapin stew, etc." Mencken conceded the point. "Tell Mr. Mitchell that I forgive him, though I don't also forgive Mrs. Hibben. She should know better.")

More than prolific, Mitchell represented a refreshing departure in the magazine. He was introducing cultured *New Yorker* readers to places they would never visit in person (at least on purpose) and to people they would have no reason to know. These were places like Dick's Bar and Grill, or Captain Charley's Private Museum, or My Blue Heaven Italian restaurant in Hoboken—a ferry ride away but where the risotto and calamari are worth the trip, even as a disquieting little drama unfolds at the next table over. These early Mitchell pieces were thin slices of life—the weightless, shapeless, hard-to-categorize "casuals" Ross championed in *The New Yorker*'s first years and much terser than the accounts of skyscraper-raising Mohawks and eccentric street historians that would later establish Mitchell's reputation. If they lack the heft of his later work, the shorter pieces are no less keenly observed by the young writer with a gift for the telling detail.

Consider "I Couldn't Dope It Out," which appeared in December of 1938. Here the reader finds Charlie, his blue serge suit too tight, bullying other diners in My Blue Heaven and belittling his companion, a woman in her late forties, "small and red-haired and quite good-looking in a scrawny, slapdash way." Charlie's treatment of the woman—who responds with strained smiles, nervous laughter, and, finally, tears—drapes the dining room in tense silence. It's a most uncomfortable lunch. Then later, Mitchell writes, on the ride back to Manhattan:

Mitchell working intently at his typewriter. The act of writing did not come easily to him.

While the ferry was moving out of the slip the man and woman walked out on the deck, arm in arm. They walked up and put their elbows on the rail. The woman stood right beside me. They were talking. He said something to the woman that I didn't hear, and she laughed and said, "You wouldn't kid me, would you?" I didn't hear his answer. Then the woman, laughing happily, said, "I bet you tell that to all the girls." They were talking that way, laughing and talking, all the way across the river. I couldn't dope it out.

That kind of behavioral study had always appealed to Mitchell, and there was still a big part of him that aspired to be a writer of fiction. At this time it was still possible for a *New Yorker* writer to work both sides of the aisle—turning out Fact pieces one month and fictional ones the next. Indeed, fully half of Mitchell's pieces that first year were short stories. Many of these, such as "The Downfall of Fascism," his darkly comic account of the aborted Klan raid of his youth, were set in Black Ankle County, the fictional version of Mitchell's home.

HAVING DUAL OUTLETS ALLOWED Mitchell to give voice to the dual allegiances—old home versus new home—that weighed on his conscience. His short stories helped him stay connected to small-town North Carolina. But his reporting celebrated his new home, of which he was enamored. With his artful journalism, Mitchell threw a spotlight on the largely ignored and taken-for-granted underclass of the world's greatest city. He was starting to utilize the time and space and freedom offered writers at *The New Yorker* to serve up entertaining reports enlivened by detail, dialogue, and droll humor. A standout appeared in April of 1939. "All You Can Hold for Five Bucks" is Mitchell's evocation of the traditional New York steak dinner, or beefsteak: "a form of gluttony as stylized and regional as the riverbank fish fry, the hot-rock clambake, or the Texas barbecue," he wrote. It's a story so visceral that the reader can almost smell the roasting meat and hear the grease dripping onto the hot coals. In its sophistication and the mastery of the material—and in representing the kind of surprising story no *New Yorker* reader would have seen coming—it also amounted to an announcement that a major new voice had arrived on the scene.

The focus of these gatherings, hosted by men's clubs and political organizations, is beef and beer. Beefsteaks had been around for decades, part of the Tammany tradition. A typical beefsteak in those earlier times would feature perfectly aged steaks, all you can eat, complemented by platters of double-rib lamp chops and lamb kidneys—no utensils permitted. In his story, Mitchell visits with Sidney Wertheimer, the master butcher behind many of the city's best beefsteaks, as he prepares another feast. "In the old days they didn't even use tables and chairs," he says. "They sat on beer crates and ate off the tops of beer barrels. You'd be surprised how much fun that was. Somehow it made old men feel young again. And they'd drink beer out of cans, or growlers. Those beefsteaks were run in halls or the cellars or back

rooms of big saloons. There was always sawdust on the floor. Sometimes they had one in a bowling alley. They would cover the alleys with
tarpaulin and set the boxes and barrels in the aisles. The men ate with
their fingers. They never served potatoes in those days. Too filling.
They take up room that rightfully belongs to meat and beer."

The subsequent verging of Prohibition and women's suffrage
caused the beefsteaks to go co-ed, and as a result they became considerably more refined, at least outwardly. Tuxedos, shrimp-cocktail ap-
petizers, and actual silverware became *de rigueur;* the traditional
oompah bands gave way to dance orchestras. A lot of the old-timers
found these civilizing influences unfortunate—as, clearly, did Mitchell. A strain of wistfulness runs through the story like the marbling in
Sidney Wertheimer's steaks.

This nostalgic overtone would become a Mitchell signature. A
similar, if more overt, example can be found in "Obituary of a Gin
Mill," published in January of 1939. Mitchell revisits the once-loud
and rowdy speakeasy of "Bar and Grill," which has subsequently relocated six blocks away and, in the process, gone respectable. Mitchell
admits that walking by the old location makes him lonesome. And the
new iteration has made "The House"—the proprietor, Dick—
miserable. Now he finds himself running a "big, classy place with a
chromium and glass-brick front, a neon sign in four colors, a mahog-
any bar, a row of chromium bar stools with red-leather seats like those
in uptown cocktail lounges, a kitchen full of gleaming copper pots, a
moody chef who once worked in Moneta's, a printed menu with
French all over it, and seven new brands of Scotch," Mitchell writes.
The writer can bear the changes, sort of, until the day he notices that
Dick's renowned turtle livers are listed on the menu as Pâté de Foie de
Tortue Verte: "Until I saw those pretentious words I never fully realized how dead and gone were the days when Dick was the plain-
spoken proprietor of a dirty, lawless, back-street gin mill. I am aware
that it is childish, but sometimes, leaning against the spick-and-span
new bar, I am overcome by nostalgia for the gutter."

That nostalgia—to the extent a thirty-year-old *can* be genuinely nostalgic—was tied to Mitchell's near-obsession, cultivated over a decade pounding pavement for newspapers, with the city's "lowlife," as that class was known around the editorial offices of *The New Yorker.* The nostalgia also reflects a sense of romance about the drinking life that many young people have before they witness, or experience themselves, its darker consequences. This propensity was something Mitchell was already beginning to see in himself after his encounter with Franz Boas. Nonetheless, such material remained popular with readers and editors, and a high percentage of the stories Mitchell wrote in 1939 feature drunks. There is Peggy, a bitter, brandy-swilling beauty who terrorizes a little girl in "Goodbye, Shirley Temple." Or Mike, struggling with his six-week-old sobriety, whose tumble off the wagon Mitchell chronicles in heartbreaking detail in "Sunday Night Was a Dangerous Night." ("Eating his steak and potatoes, Mike felt at ease. The atmosphere of the barroom, the bickering of the men at the bar, the beer smell comforted him.")

Still, that summer of 1939 Mitchell escaped the bars long enough to take *New Yorker* readers for the first of what would be many guided excursions to the city's docks and waterways. In "A Mess of Clams," Mitchell rides the *Jennie Tucker,* "a battered, stripped-down, 38-foot sloop powered with a motor the Captain took out of an old Chrysler." The *Jennie Tucker* is a buy-boat of the clam-shipping firm Still & Clock, which purchases the day's work of clammers who extract the littleneck and cherrystone clams found in New York restaurants and the Fulton Fish Market from the black mud of Long Island bays. After introducing his readers to Captain Archie M. Clock, Mitchell tells us a pertinent bit about himself. He was starting to do this more often now in setting up certain stories; the effect was to come across as less a narrator than an amiable travel companion. "I sat down on the bucket and told [Captain Clock] that one Sunday afternoon in August, 1937, I placed third in a clam-eating tournament at a Block Island clambake, eating eighty-four cherries," he writes. "I told him that I regard this as one of the few worth-while achievements of my life." The two men later share forty-three cherrystone clams only minutes removed from the muck.

When the valves were pried apart, the rich clam liquor dribbled out. The flesh of the cherries was a delicate pink. On the cups of some of the shells were splotches of deep purple; Indians used to hack such splotches out of clamshells for wampum. Fresh from the coal black mud and uncontaminated by ketchup or sauce, they were the best clams I had ever eaten.

"A Mess of Clams" also represented Mitchell's first mention in *The New Yorker* of the Fulton Fish Market, and in fact the story sets the table for some of Mitchell's most memorable characters, including the "seafoodetarian" Hugh Flood, who would appear just a few years later.

BY EARLY 1940, MITCHELL had not only passed his probationary period but was developing into what Ross might well have considered an exemplar of a Fact writer—a lovely and clean stylist, and someone who brought plenty of fresh characters to the magazine. Having gained confidence with longer-form writing, and fully enjoying his reportorial freedom, Mitchell began to modulate his manic production, putting more time into his reporting and letting the stories get progressively lengthier and more layered. He also finally stopped his flirtation with short fiction. But at the same time, he was utilizing commonly employed fictional techniques in his factual Profiles and Reporter pieces. Rather than marching his stories forward in the prosaic fashion of conventional magazine journalism, which was then little more than glorified newspaper writing, Mitchell instead tended to unspool them novelistically, often ending up in places a reader could scarcely have predicted at the outset. More and more he was letting his subjects reveal their stories—and character—in long monologues. He eschewed black-and-white protagonists and embraced those who inhabited the grays. Endings were seldom tidy. And his sense of irony, always acute in real life, turns up more regularly on the page.

Indeed, in the half dozen Fact articles he published in 1940, Mitchell produced a string of some of the most memorable characters of his career: these included "Lady Olga," his Profile of a bearded lady in the circus sideshows; "Mazie," a Profile of the charitable owner of a Bowery movie theater; "Santa Claus Smith of Riga, Latvia, Europe," an edgy account of a charismatic, check-kiting hobo; and "The Old House at Home," his long love letter to McSorley's.

Careful followers of Mitchell's career might have recognized several of these, as they represented a revisiting from when he had written about them in the *World-Telegram*. "For quite a while, the people I wrote about here [at *The New Yorker*] were people I had [written about] on the newspaper, like Mazie and Commodore Dutch and [piano prodigy Philippa] Schuyler," Mitchell would explain. "A lot of the people I knew on the newspapers, I wanted to write more about and here was the opportunity."

Mazie is a good case in point. Mazie "ran a movie theater and I wrote about her for the *World-Telegram* and I would go by there," Mitchell recalled late in his life. "I got to know her more and more without her being aware I did. Stopping by there on occasion and talking to her—nothing special. When I came [to *The New Yorker*] I had a background I could draw on."

Mazie P. Gordon is the brassy, benevolent owner of the Venice Theatre, a seedy "dime house" at the edge of the Bowery that served as a sort of shelter for the down-and-out, providing refuge for drunks and the emotionally unstable for the length of "two features, a newsreel, a cartoon, a short, and a serial episode." Mazie, whom Mitchell once described as a latter-day "Wife of Bath" character, spends long days in the Venice's ticket booth and then at night roams the Bowery, passing out nickels and dimes and tending to the comfort and welfare of the bums who inhabit its shadowy alleys.

When Mitchell sketched Mazie in the newspaper (and reprinted it in *My Ears Are Bent*), the piece ran to a little over one thousand words. When she reappeared in *The New Yorker* just a few years later, the piece was seven thousand. She was the same person but not the same subject. "In *My Ears Are Bent* Mazie is indeed a curiosity: a bosomy blonde Jewish woman in her forties, rumored to have been a burlesque girl in her youth, now a tough-talking version of Mother Teresa," literary critic Noel Perrin would observe in 1983. But later, in *The New Yorker*, "she is a complete person. You get both a much fuller—and a wildly funny—account of the way she operates the movie theater, and the story of her life. A brilliant sketch has turned into a portrait full of light and shadow."

For instance, Mazie's policy toward disruptive drunks in her theater warrants just a few lines in the newspaper account:

> Sometimes a bum goes in at 10 o'clock in the morning, and at midnight he is still there, sleeping in his seat, snoring as if he owned the joint. Mazie does not mind, but if one begins to yell derisively at the actors on the screen, giving them good advice, she goes in and pulls him out by the slack of his worn pants.

The magazine article offers a much more vivid—and amusing—rendering:

> Now and then, in the Venice, a stiff throws his head back and begins to snore so blatantly that he can be heard all over the place, especially during tense moments in the picture. When this happens, or when one of the drunks gets into a bellowing mood, the women and children in the reserved section stamp on the floor and chant, "Mazie! Mazie! We want Mazie!" The instant this chant goes up, the matron hastens out to the lobby and raps on the side window of Mazie's cage. Mazie locks the cash drawer, grabs a bludgeon she keeps around, made of a couple of copies of *True Romances* rolled up tightly and held together by rubber bands, and strides into the theatre. As she goes down the aisle, peering this way and that, women and children jump to their feet, point fingers in the direction of the offender, and cry, "There he is, Mazie! There he is!" Mazie gives the man a resounding whack on the head with her bludgeon and keeps on whacking him until he seems willing to behave. Between blows, she threatens him with worse punishment. Her threats are fierce and not altogether coherent. "Outa here on a stretcher!"

she yells. "Knock your eyeballs out! Big baboon! Every tooth in your head! Bone in your body!" The women and children enjoy this, particularly if Mazie gets the wrong man, as she sometimes does.

Mazie sat in the ticket booth, a dog in her lap, every day from mid-morning until 11:00 P.M.—conducting business, chatting with visitors, passing out change to shaky bums—and Mitchell, it seems, was there to witness all of it. Then every night after work, Mitchell writes, "she makes a Samaritan tour of the Bowery." And, again, Mitchell is there.

He was a witness who saw what he saw, not always what he wanted to see and certainly not what he expected to see. But he never patronized, never judged. No matter how downtrodden his characters might be, no matter how laid low by misfortune, Mitchell lent them a fundamental decency and humanity. They might be different from you or me, he seems to say, but they have their dignity.

Readers loved characters like Mazie. So, too, did Ross, although it took him longer, perhaps, to warm up to the odder of Mitchell's odd-balls—or, more important, to figure out precisely how they "fit" into his carefully tailored magazine of sophistication. Ross "had a view of those people," Mitchell told Norman Sims. His term for them was "lowlifes," and in general Ross paid rather less for such Profiles than for so-called "highlifes," those being entertainers or other swells. Then again, he did recognize that Mitchell was cultivating new terrain—essentially inventing what Ross finally and inimitably came to classify as the "highlife-lowlife" piece.

Another memorably rendered highlife-lowlife was Mitchell's 1940 portrait of Jane Barnell, the bearded lady known professionally as Lady Olga. Barnell has spent almost the entirety of her sixty-nine years barnstorming the country with one circus or another. But the main point of the story—and what gives it its resonant poignancy—is the effort she makes to try to achieve something like a normal domesticity. Her greatest desire, in fact, is to one day work as a stenographer. Yet she knows this isn't really possible; as Mitchell says, she "long ago . . . learned there is no place in the world outside of a sideshow for a bearded lady." Mitchell tells her tale, as he did Mazie's, in prose that is straightforward, detailed, unflinching—and without a hint of pity, which Barnell doesn't want in any case. She takes a defiant pride in her work and even in the labels others insist on applying to her and her sideshow friends. The Profile ends in one of the most famous lines of Mitchell's career. "If the truth was known," Barnell tells him, "we're all freaks together."

Lady Olga represents one of the earliest manifestations of a Mitchell staple character—the "other." No doubt the attraction had something to do with Mitchell's own sense of being an outsider, the farm boy abroad in the big city. And even though he himself grew up with some trappings of privilege—or maybe it was *because* of that privilege—Mitchell had a lifelong innate connection to the disaffected and downtrodden, and especially the underdog. Whatever the reason, Mitchell "looked at freaks with love and affection and understanding," said his colleague Philip Hamburger.

Twenty years after the Lady Olga Profile, a then-emerging photographer named Diane Arbus would call Mitchell one day to talk about the piece, and the two developed a substantive but telephone-only friendship. Arbus later photographed some of the same people Mitchell profiled. In her biography of Arbus, Patricia Bosworth quoted Mitchell as saying, "I urged Diane not to romanticize freaks. I told her that freaks can be boring and ordinary as so-called normal people. I told her what I found interesting about Olga, the bearded lady, was that she yearned to be a stenographer and kept geraniums on her windowsill. . . ." Arbus may have shared Mitchell's fascination with freaks, but Mitchell accorded them a singular dignity, said Hamburger—something he, at least, didn't believe Arbus did. As he put it, "The difference between Joe Mitchell's portrait of a freak and Diane Arbus's photograph of a freak is the difference between a humanitarian and a nosy-body without a heart."

WHILE MITCHELL WAS WRITING about Bowery angels and gluttonous beefsteaks, another former newspaper reporter was developing a comparable reputation profiling boxers and showmen and charlatan street preachers. Like Mitchell, A. J. (for Abbott Joseph) Liebling was known to friends as Joe, and before long "the two Joes" were in their way doing for *The New Yorker* what Babe Ruth and Lou Gehrig had done for the Yankees. But Mitchell and Liebling were more than colleagues; they were best of friends and kindred literary spirits.

They met while working at the *World-Telegram.* "Liebling had read a story I'd written," Mitchell would recall. "Liebling was a pretty unfriendly guy. Not unfriendly, really, but self-sufficient. A few days after I got on the paper, we were going down the elevator and he said something about the story I'd written, and introduced himself. I'd seen his work before. Anyway, we went up to the corner to the coffee place there and we got to talking. It was amazing how many writers he and I admired." It turned out that one particular (if now somewhat obscure) influence they shared was a nineteenth-century British writer, George Borrow, much of whose work focused on Europe's Romany, or gypsy, population. Borrow was "a forerunner of Joe's and my interest in what they called lowlife at *The New Yorker*," Mitchell would say. "We found a mutual bond in other authors concerned with lowlife—Villon, Rabelais, Sterne, Dostoevsky."

Four years older than Mitchell, Liebling joined *The New Yorker* in 1935. Like the other Joe, he was a prodigious talent, but he had a much harder time making the transition from newspaper to long-form writing than Mitchell would a few years later. Once he did, he turned out some of the most vivid reportage *The New Yorker* would publish over the next several decades—including gleefully tart press criticism.

Outwardly, they made for an odd couple. Liebling was as rotund as Mitchell was trim; he was as unkempt as Mitchell was fastidious. Liebling was the native New Yorker to Mitchell's drawling émigré. When they walked the streets together, Liebling matched Mitchell's smart fedora with a bowler hat too small for his head. Liebling wrote quickly; Mitchell was deliberate. Mitchell working on a story was a study in quietude and concentration; Liebling would pound on his typewriter and snort with delight, rereading his own handiwork. Then again, he usually had good reason. Few have ever put words to page with as much relish as A. J. Liebling. For instance, in an evisceration of the powerful publisher of the *Chicago Tribune,* Liebling wrote that Colonel Robert R. McCormick "daily assures Chicagoans that personal violence, national bankruptcy and extinction by guided missiles are the normal expectation of man in Chicagoland.... In compensation for the grim fate in store for them, the Colonel offers Chicagolanders a guarantee that life everywhere else is much worse." And this wry note on another of his favorite subjects, food: "In the light of what Proust wrote with so mild a stimulus, it is the world's loss that he did not have a heartier appetite."

Whatever their apparent differences, Liebling and Mitchell shared many values and passions. And as writers they influenced each other profoundly. This influence was not really about the other's prose or style. Nor did they run drafts of their stories by each other; on the contrary, as much as they talked about favorite writers, they seldom spoke of what they happened to be working on. But both were drawn to subjects not unlike themselves—Mitchell in a more psychological sense, Liebling in that he preferred his characters larger than life. And because both were focusing on untraditional subject matter and utilizing more-literary approaches than was possible at daily newspapers, they spurred one another on. As Mitchell would later explain, it "liberated me to talk to Joe about writing, and he gave me a great feeling...." They understood that they were looking at New York in essentially the same way.

As close as they became, the two writers were also to some extent rivals, remembered Roger Angell, longtime fiction editor at *The New Yorker.* And he said the thing that most bothered Liebling about Mitchell was that he seemed to know everything, no matter how arcane the fact. One day in the forties, Angell said, Liebling was walking along Sixth Avenue when he spotted a taxidermy shop and, on impulse, ducked in. On a shelf he noticed a peculiar assemblage of small bones. The proprietor explained that those were the bones of a small male opossum, taking pains to point out to Liebling the peculiarly shaped penile bone. For a few dollars Liebling purchased the bones, which he carefully wrapped in his handkerchief. Back at *The New*

Yorker he found Mitchell at his desk, typing. Liebling wordlessly unwrapped the bones, arraying them on the desk before Mitchell. Mitchell studied them for a moment, then said, "Pecker bone of a young male possum. What do you want to know about that, Joe?"

Beyond story subjects, there was one other crucial area where their interests converged. Mitchell and Liebling were among the great eaters in the history of New York City, and frequent dining companions. According to Liebling biographer Raymond Sokolov, Mitchell "understood the complicated importance of gutbucket gluttony in Liebling's life. The two Joes had been stopping at crummy basement Italian restaurants together since the Depression, eating sheep's heads, down to the eyes." Liebling, a man of enthusiastic, outsize appetites to begin with, shared Mitchell's love of seafood especially. The two enjoyed nothing more than gorging on oysters, clams, squid, octopus, or what-

A. J. Liebling met his New Yorker *running mate Mitchell years earlier at the* New York World-Telegram.

ever other denizen of the deep had found its way onto the daily special, washed down with a drinkable wine. After Mitchell's death, longtime colleague Brendan Gill captured the pair's gustatory passion. "The Joes often went to the Red Devil, an Italian restaurant in the neighborhood," Gill recalled. Around Christmastime one year, the owner came out after Mitchell and Liebling had polished off a huge meal; he was carrying two glasses and a bottle of brandy, and to their great surprise he told them to drink their fill. Just as they were starting in on this remarkable offer, however, a grease fire broke out in the kitchen. Flames crackled in the back and smoke began pouring into the dining room. "The situation posed a dilemma for Joe and Joe," Gill continued. "It was the first time they had ever been so generously treated by the proprietor, and they certainly intended to take full advantage of the gesture. At the same time they wished to save their lives." Walking away with the bottle would seem ungrateful, even unfeeling. So they hit on a compromise—they stepped out into the street with the brandy, just beyond the smoky chaos, and "toasted the spirit of Christmas there."

Therese Mitchell was also a close friend of the first of Liebling's three wives, Ann McGinn, a schizophrenic who was later institutionalized. The Lieblings were frequent dinner guests at the Mitchell apartment. The two couples often went to Rockaway Beach together, Sokolov writes. "Therese Mitchell took photographs of them on the sand, a strange but happy-looking couple, Ann ravishing, Joe all pudge, she weirdly vacant, he with an amused glint in his eye."

Until World War II, Liebling, like Mitchell, had worked almost exclusively in New York. Then, in the fall of 1939, *The New Yorker* dispatched him to Paris to fill in for its longtime European correspondent, Janet Flanner, who was returning stateside for what was supposed to be a temporary leave. When Germany commenced its blitzkrieg across northern Europe, Flanner couldn't get back to Paris. Liebling would spend the rest of the war producing some of the most powerful and enduring journalism to emerge from the European theater, including a particularly moving first-person account of the Normandy invasion. Mitchell, for his part, would try every way he could think of to become involved in the war effort, from attempts at enlistment to endeavoring to work for the Writers' War Board—only to be thwarted at each turn by a combination of bad luck and bad health.

Indeed, sometime in the spring or summer of 1941 Mitchell began feeling unwell, and this vague malady persisted for months. He and Therese decided to go ahead with their usual summer trip to North Carolina, where Mitchell hoped the respite would fix whatever was wrong. Instead, his health worsened. He was compelled to check in to a hospital in Fayetteville, where he was diagnosed with an ulcer. In a letter to McKelway in late September, he reported being put on a milk diet and being held for three weeks; upon his release, he was under doctor's orders to stay in Fairmont for several additional months of rest, where, according to Mitchell, all he did was read Dickens and take walks in the woods. It wasn't until the following January that Mitchell was cleared to return to work in New York.

HIS POSITION AT *The New Yorker* firmly secured, Mitchell was determined to put even more depth into his pieces, which were appearing less frequently as they expanded considerably. He found himself spending more time simply wandering the city's five boroughs, taking in . . . well, everything. He described the process in his unfinished memoir:

> What I really like to do is wander aimlessly in the city. I like to walk the streets by day and by night. It is more than a liking, a simple liking, it is an aberration. Every so often, for example, around nine in the morning, I climb out of the subway and head toward the office building in midtown Manhattan in which I work, but on the way a change takes place in me—in effect, I lose my sense of responsibility—and when I reach the entrance to the building I walk right on past it, as if I had never seen it before. I keep on walking, sometimes only for a couple of hours but sometimes until deep in the afternoon, and I often wind up a considerable distance away from midtown Manhattan—up in

the Bronx Terminal Market maybe, or over on some tumble-down old sugar dock on the Brooklyn riverfront, or out in the weediest part of some weedy old cemetery in Queens. It is never very hard for me to think up an excuse that justifies me in be-having this way (I have a great deal of experience in justifying myself to myself)—a headache that won't let up is a good enough excuse, and an unusually bleak and overcast day is as good an excuse as an unusually balmy and springlike day.

When he wasn't on foot, Mitchell was crisscrossing the city by subway or, for a better view, by bus.

There is no better vantage point from which to look at the com-mon, ordinary city—not the lofty, noble silvery vertical city but the vast, spread-out, sooty-gray and sooty-brown and sooty-red and sooty-pink horizontal city, the snarled-up and smoldering city, the old, polluted, betrayed, and sure-to-be-torn-down-any-time-now city. I frequently spend an entire day riding on the New York City buses, getting off at junction points and changing from one line to another as the notion strikes me and gradually crisscrossing whatever part of the city I happen to be in. I might ride in a dozen or fifteen or twenty different buses during the day.

Mitchell was investing more in his reporting because his work was widening to capture entire cultures, not just a single person like Mazie or a single place like Dick's Bar and Grill. This evolution is plain in "King of the Gypsies," published in August of 1942. The piece starts out as a portrait of Johnny Nikanov, a self-appointed gypsy king of indeterminate age. (He estimates that he's between "forty-five and seventy-five, somewhere in there," he tells Mitchell. "My hair's been white for years and years, and I got seventeen grandchildren, and I bet I'm an old, old man.") King Cockeye Johnny, as he is sometimes called, is a thief and, again, a drunk. His drink of choice is equal parts gin and Pepsi-Cola, a concoction he calls "old popskull."

But while Johnny is the protagonist, he isn't the only actor in the piece. It is populated with such secondary characters as Detective John J. Sheehan, a member of the New York Police Department's pickpocket squad, who has "worked exclusively on gypsy crime for the last nine years," and Johnny's fortune-teller wife, Looba. And the piece reflects reporting done over a long period—early in the article Mitchell notes that he first became acquainted with Sheehan six years earlier, while a newspaper reporter. That was the same time he met Johnny Nikanov, and they had stayed in touch. "Once he invited a few of the Criminal Courts loafers, including myself, to his home on Sheriff Street for a *patchiv*, or gypsy spree," Mitchell writes. "We ate a barbecued pig, drank a punch composed of red wine, seltzer, and sliced Elberta peaches, watched the women dance, and had an exceedingly pleasant time. Since then I have often visited Johnny. Whenever I am in the Sheriff Street neighborhood I call on him."

The deeper and more textured reporting—the desire to write the story behind the story, if you will—may well have been a by-product of Mitchell's exposure to anthropologist Franz Boas. But it also speaks to Mitchell's prowling curiosity and his propensity to immerse himself in a subject, not merely to dabble in it. For instance, in pursuing his Profile of King Cockeye Johnny and later writing about other aspects of the gypsy culture, Mitchell sought out tutorials with police experts and even became a member of the Gypsy Lore Society, remaining a regular reader of its journal for years. Such an immersion allowed Mitchell to write with authority about not just *a gypsy* but *all gypsies*. With broad, bold strokes, Mitchell writes:

> Johnny does not know how many gypsies there are in the city, and neither does anyone else. Estimates range between seven and twelve thousand. Their forefathers came from every country in Europe, but the majority call themselves Russians, Serbians, or Rumanians. They are split into scores of vaguely hostile cliques, but they intermarry freely, speak practically the same dialect of Romany, the universal gypsy language, and are essentially alike. They are predominantly of the type that anthro-

pologists call nomad gypsies; that is, unlike the Hungarian fiddler gypsies, for example, they never willingly become sedentary. They are contemptuous of the Hungarians, calling them house gypsies. In the past the nomads straggled from Maine to Mexico, spending only the winters in the city, but since the depression fewer and fewer have gone out on the road. Johnny has not been farther away than Atlantic City since 1934. At least two-thirds receive charity or relief of one sort or another. The gypsy kings are authorities on relief regulations; they know how to get their families on relief and keep them there. In the city, gypsies prefer to scatter out, but there are colonies of them on the lower East Side, on the Bowery, on the eastern fringe of Spanish Harlem, and on Varet Street in the Williamsburg neighborhood of Brooklyn. They rent the cheapest flats in the shabbiest tenements on the worst blocks. Three or four families often share one flat. They move on the spur of the moment; in the last two years one family has given seventeen addresses to the Department of Welfare. In the summer, like all slum people, they bring chairs to the sidewalks in front of their houses and sit in the sun. They nurse their babies in public. They have nothing at all to do with *gajo* neighbors. Even the kids are aloof; they play stick- and stoopball, but only with each other. The children are dirty, flea-ridden, intelligent and beautiful; one rarely sees a homely gypsy child. They are not particularly healthy, but they have the splendid gutter hardihood of English sparrows.

"King of the Gypsies" represented Mitchell's first true effort at profiling an entire culture, and, like the works to follow, it's an often-wistful profile of a culture in decline, a culture undermined by the changing city. A whole people—not just one bar, not just one tradition like the beefsteak—are victims of "progress." And though still a young man, Mitchell already was concerned enough about the impact of New York's breakneck changes that he was starting to channel that distress through his stories. In "Gypsies," he let Cockeye Johnny do the lamenting of days gone by, writing: "Johnny sighed and slopped some more gin into his glass. 'Things have been getting worse and worse for gypsies ever since the automobile was put on the market,' he said. 'When I was a little knee-high boy the U.S. was gypsy heaven. Everybody was real ignorant and believed in fortune-telling.'"

WHILE HER HUSBAND WAS chronicling New York's disparate communities with his typewriter, Therese was doing much the same with her camera. Though she photographed all over the city, her favorite subject was her home neighborhood, the Village. With Washington Square Park at its center and (roughly) bounded by Broadway to the east, the Hudson River to the west, Houston Street to the south, and 14th Street to the north, Greenwich Village was by this time well established as an enclave of bohemian culture, home to writers, radicals, artists, poets, avant-garde theater, art galleries, and more than a few flat-out loons. Many found its exotic atmosphere alarming; for the Mitchells, it was entertaining and comforting all at once, a kind of carnival that never closed up or left town. And one of the best shows in the Village was an irrepressible character who would provide the most memorable subject of Joseph Mitchell's career to date.

Joe Gould "wasn't just a bum, he was a bum of a certain genius," writes Ross Wetzsteon in his history of Greenwich Village in the first half of the twentieth century. He was "the leading beneficiary of the Villagers' enduring fantasy of a link between the social misfit and the cultural rebel—after all, who better understood society's hypocrisies than society's outcasts?"

Gould, a Harvard graduate and, for a brief time, a newspaper police reporter, was generally homeless and hungover. He made his way by hustling for meals, drinks, and spare change. Poet E. E. Cummings was among Gould's benefactors, giving him money and cast-off clothing. Gould told people he had several pet seagulls when he was a child and knew their cawing "language" well enough to communicate with them; as if to prove it, at parties he would remove his shoes and socks and take off in "awkward, headlong skips about the room, flapping his arms and letting out a piercing caw with every skip." The bizarre performances earned Gould the nickname "Professor Sea Gull." But what set Gould apart from the other hard cases roaming the city were his garrulous personality, his need to be the center of attention, his obvious intelligence—and his astonishing claim to be writing the *Oral History of Our Time,* an exhaustive, handwritten work chronicling life in New York. The history was said to fill hundreds of notebooks. A 1934 story in the *Herald Tribune* reported that the oral history was then more than seven million words, and a follow-up four years later said it had grown to almost nine million words, although no one had seen the entire omnibus in one place.

Mitchell would recall first encountering Gould at a Greek diner in the Village during the hard winter of 1932. The young reporter was drinking coffee while on a break from covering stories at a nearby courthouse, and the ragged bohemian was cadging a free meal. Mitchell would come to know Professor Sea Gull much better later on, after he moved to the Village, and he kept notes on Gould and his quixotic oral history for several years before pitching *The New Yorker* on a Profile, in mid-1942. "I remember telling [my] editor that I thought Gould was a perfect example of a type of eccentric widespread in New York City, the solitary nocturnal wanderer, and that that was the aspect of him that interested me most, that and his oral history," Mitchell would say later. Mitchell passed word around the Village that he wanted to talk to Gould. Before long, Gould phoned him at *The New Yorker,* and they met the next morning at a diner. Gould drew himself up on his counter stool and said, "I understand you want to write something about me, and I greet you at the beginning of a great endeavor."

It was an endeavor that would require hours upon hours of interviews with a man who was, essentially, mad. Mitchell often bought Gould breakfast during the course of their interviews, meals Gould extended by dumping copious amounts of ketchup onto his plate and eating it with a spoon. Mitchell trailed his subject on his evening perambulations, in which he sometimes crashed parties of well-known figures from the theater and arts communities, some of whom, like Cummings, had adopted Gould as a kind of amusing mascot. More typically, however, Gould "prowls around the saloons and dives on the west side of the Village, on the lookout for curiosity-seeking tourists from whom he can cadge beers, sandwiches, and small sums of money," Mitchell wrote. "If he is unable to find anyone approachable in the tumultuous saloons around Sheridan Square, he goes over to Sixth Avenue and works north, hitting the Jericho Tavern, the Village Square Bar & Grill, the Belmar, Goody's, and the Rochambeau." This went on for months.

Mitchell's patience paid off in an unusually rich Profile piece: "Professor Sea Gull" was published in December of 1942, and it was a reader sensation. It was also just the second piece Mitchell had in *The New Yorker* all year. While this paucity was attributable in part to his ulcer and recuperation, it also suggests how all-consuming his commitment had been to the Gould Profile and to getting it just right. Mitchell's utter fixation with Gould is not especially difficult to appreciate. In Gould, Mitchell found a near-doppelgänger—if one who slept in doorways, seldom bathed, wore filthy rags, and had long ago lost his teeth. Gould tells Mitchell he is writing "the informal history of the shirt-sleeved multitude"—not a bad description of Mitchell's own portfolio to date. Like Mitchell, Gould had left behind his home and a disappointed father. Like Mitchell, Gould was a practiced listener. Indeed, where others saw in Gould—eccentric even by Village standards—a panhandling if occasionally charming drunk, Mitchell saw an oddly disciplined reporter:

> Although Gould strives to give the impression that he is a philosophical loafer, he has done an immense amount of work during his career as a bohemian. Every day, even when he has a bad hangover or even when he is weak and listless from hunger, he spends at least a couple of hours working on a formless, rather mysterious book that he calls *An Oral History of Our Time*. He began this book twenty-six years ago, and it is nowhere near finished.

Mitchell reports that Gould would fill composition books with a barely legible scribble "in parks, in doorways, in flophouse lobbies, in

Joe Gould—a.k.a. Professor Sea Gull—takes flight during a party in the early forties. Mitchell made the Greenwich Village vagabond famous.

cafeterias, on benches on elevated-railroad platforms, in subway trains, and in public libraries." He wrote in furious bursts—one all-night session recounted by Mitchell resulted in eleven thousand words. But of the ostensible millions of words so far committed to the history, Mitchell said, "hundreds of thousands . . . are legible only to him."

Mitchell went on to describe the oral history as "a great hodge-podge and kitchen midden of hearsay, a repository of jabber, an omnium-gatherum of bushwa, gab, palaver, hogwash, flapdoodle, and malarkey, the fruit, according to Gould's estimate, of more than twenty thousand conversations." Mitchell reached that conclusion having had the opportunity to read only a fraction of Gould's ostensibly sprawling opus, and he hadn't found anyone else who'd seen much more of it. What little of the oral history Mitchell *did* read was limited to "rambling essays on such subjects as the flophouse flea, spaghetti, the zipper as a sign of the decay of civilization, false teeth, insanity, the jury system, remorse, cafeteria cooking, and the emasculating effect of the typewriter on literature." He continued:

> Only a few of the hundreds of people who know Gould have read any of the Oral History, and most of them take it for granted that it is gibberish. Those who make the attempt usually bog down after a couple of chapters and give up. Gould says he can count on one hand or one foot those who have read enough of it to be qualified to form an opinion. One is Horace Gregory, the poet and critic. "I look upon Gould as a sort of Samuel Pepys of the Bowery," Gregory says. "I once waded through twenty-odd composition books, and most of what I saw had the quality of a competent high-school theme, but some of it was written with the clear and wonderful veracity of a child, and here and there were flashes of hard-bitten Yankee wit. If someone took the trouble to go through it and separate the good from the rubbish, as editors did with Thomas Wolfe's millions of words, it might be discovered that Gould actually has written a masterpiece."

The literary merit of the oral history notwithstanding, Mitchell's Profile made Gould a celebrity well beyond the Village and cemented the relationship between the two men—this last not exactly the outcome Mitchell would have wished for. Enchanted or sympathetic readers began to send money to the "Joe Gould Fund" in care of Mitchell at *The New Yorker*, which Gould encouraged by giving people the magazine's address as his own. Gould began routinely dropping by the *New Yorker* offices and monopolizing Mitchell's time. When Mitchell finally got up the nerve to object to the constant interruptions, Gould would have none of it. "Look," he said. "You're the one who started all this. I didn't seek you out. You sought me out. You wanted to write about me, and you did, and you'll have to take the consequences."

CHAPTER 7

THERE ARE NO LITTLE PEOPLE

WHEN [COMMODORE] DUTCH IS introduced to someone, he usually makes fun of his own face. He shakes hands and says, "Pleased to meet you, pal." Then, opening his mouth as wide as possible and exhibiting his solitary tooth, he giggles and says, "Look, pal! I'm an Elk!" He seems most pleased with himself when people are making jokes at his expense and laughing at him. It makes no perceptible difference to him whether their laughter is scornful or good-natured. "When a fella is laughing at me, I'm sizing him up," he once told an intimate. "I'm giving him the old psychology."

—From "A Sporting Man," 1941

· ·

I N 1942, HAVING SPENT HIS FIRST DECADE IN NEW YORK LIVING SOME-thing of a gypsy existence himself, pinging from boardinghouse to boardinghouse and flat to flat, Mitchell finally put down roots, moving with Therese into the Greenwich Village apartment that would be home for the rest of their lives. And they were now not just a couple but a family; in July of 1940 they had welcomed their first child, Nora—not coincidentally, the name of James Joyce's wife.

The Mitchell apartment was on the sixth floor of a ten-story building at 44 West 10th Street, between Fifth and Sixth Avenues. Their small unit was at the back of the building, on the southeast corner. There were two bedrooms; Joseph and Therese occupied one and Nora the other. (When in 1948 the family added another daughter, Elizabeth, she got her parents' bedroom; from that point on Joseph and Therese slept on a foldout sofa bed in the living room.) The kitchen was so tiny that with four people sitting at the breakfast table there wasn't enough room to stand and open the refrigerator. If something was needed, someone sitting at the table had to open the refrigerator door and reach in for it.

The intimate space didn't keep the Mitchells from entertaining. Quite the contrary, they maintained an active social schedule and had people in often for drinks or dinner. Liebling, Hamburger, and many other *New Yorker* colleagues were frequent guests. "They lived in this cramped little apartment which was about as cozy as any place I have ever been," Hamburger remembered. And while the kitchen was small, Therese, a highly accomplished cook, coaxed feasts from it. Friends made a point of saying that of Therese's many fine qualities, that was one her food-loving spouse found particularly endearing. "Dinner would always start out with an enormous Swedish-Norwegian smorgasbord followed, usually, by a big roast of lamb," Hamburger said. "They ate well."

The Mitchells were a playful and affectionate couple. They loved to sing around the apartment, almost as much as they enjoyed needling each other, as she would do about his esoteric collecting and he

A photo-booth image from early in the Mitchells' relationship reflects the easy affection they would share throughout their long marriage.

would do about her unwavering positivity. As a young wife, Therese began a private ritual that continued until late into their lives—presenting her husband with original love poems for Valentine's Day. The verses might be silly or serious; often they managed to be both. ("Is me and has been all these years/The one who helps to dry your tears/And sends you out each day anew/to fight another battle through/Then home to labskaus, fish or steak/And risengrod and chestnut cake.") Their happiness radiates from a tiny image of the couple taken at a photo booth early in their marriage. Mitchell is smartly turned out in a coat, silk tie, and topcoat, but his hat is pushed back incongruously on his head. Eyes narrowed in a laugh, he has the moony, cartoonish expression of a man in love. Therese is leaning into her husband, her chin resting on his shoulder, bright eyes gazing up at him with a laughing smile. The mugging pair in the photograph, two very attractive people in their twenties, are clearly in the first blush of a romance, and family and friends attest that they were comfortably affectionate in this way their entire marriage.

Mitchell was an attentive father. As soon as Nora was walking, they began to explore the Village's parks and lanes hand in hand, much as his parents had introduced him to the mysteries of the farm as a toddler. There was a precocity about Nora; when she was not quite four and on her first visit to a museum, the Whitney, she took in a number of paintings before stopping in front of a nude. She commented to her father, "Look at the bosom."

At night, Therese's kitchen often doubled as her darkroom. As she had all through the thirties, Therese was photographing the city. She captured everyday people on the streets, on the job, selling their wares, parading on holidays. The striking black-and-white images evoke the great city trying to wrest itself from the Depression's grip and coping with the early years of World War II: People crowded beneath the Williamsburg Bridge. A parish priest keeping an eye on things from the rectory doorway. A Greenwich Village mother and her young daughter hunched over a stroller, framed by an archway. Workers at a wig shop, all sporting their own handiwork as they march down the street asserting their right to organize. Men sitting atop a Brooklyn

*Joseph and Therese
at the beach
in the forties.*

*Mitchell was as intent
on revealing the
wonders of New York to
daughter Nora as his
parents had been in
showing him the North
Carolina countryside.*

esplanade, legs dangling. A cop on horseback. Drunks and prostitutes, peddlers and preachers. Similarly, the photographs she took in and around Fairmont document, in unemotional, head-on fashion, the unrelieved want of the rural South. Houses are as swaybacked as old mules, their clapboards peeling away or missing altogether. There are open square cutouts in the walls where proper windows should be. Women and small children are captured as they impassively grade tobacco leaves, barefoot and wearing clothes that are little more than rags.

Because Therese photographed solely for her own satisfaction, only close friends and family got to appreciate the results. Watching her mother convert negatives into powerful images is among Nora's most poignant childhood memories. "She used to . . . work into the night, hanging contact sheets and prints on the shower curtain rod over the bathtub," Nora wrote in the program for an exhibition of her mother's work in 2000, sponsored by the Municipal Art Society of New York and the Greenwich Village Society for Historic Preservation. "I would often sit with her during these times and I remember them as magical—the darkness, the closeness, the images swimming up out of the chemical baths. . . ."

JOSEPH MITCHELL WAS THIRTY-THREE YEARS OLD when Japan attacked Pearl Harbor, pushing a theretofore reluctant United States into World War II. By this point, perhaps surprising even himself a little, Mitchell had become the picture of domesticity, at least by Greenwich Village standards. He was established as a respected staff writer at *The New Yorker*. He was adjusting to the family's new home. And he was a husband and new father. Nonetheless, after Pearl Harbor, Mitchell, like so many comparably settled American men, was determined to get into the war.

In the summer of 1942—a bleak period in the early hostilities, with America's lone consequential victory coming over the Japanese fleet at the Battle of Midway—Mitchell, the onetime freighter deckhand who was still interviewing a crazy man who talked to sea gulls, applied for a commission with the United States Naval Reserve. To his great disappointment, his application was rejected; a letter that August from the Office of Naval Officer Procurement cited his "inability to meet physical requirements." The rejection stemmed from the gastric ulcer that laid him low the previous year in North Carolina but subsequently had given him no problems. Later in the war, when summoned to appear by his local draft board, Mitchell was actually classified as 4-F because of the ulcer history. It was terribly frustrating to be thwarted by his medical past, all the more so because Mitchell now considered himself to be in robust health.

Precluded from active duty, Mitchell sought to serve through his communication abilities. In April of 1943, he applied for a position as a senior script editor with the newly formed Office of War Information—an agency that, ironically, *The New Yorker* had a direct hand in creating. Early in 1942, Mitchell's colleague at the magazine E. B. White had written a Notes and Comment piece suggesting that the numerous and confusing "information bureaus" cropping up in wartime Washington should be consolidated into a single entity. White even nominated the person to run it: prominent news commentator Elmer Davis. And in a matter of months Davis in fact was named to run the newly formed Office of War Information.

The OWI coordinated communication efforts on the home front, including the release of war news, printing of patriotic posters, and production of radio broadcasts that were essentially infomercials for the war effort. An overseas branch produced propaganda campaigns intended for enemy audiences. A number of Mitchell's friends and professional acquaintances wound up working there, including Philip Hamburger, who had left *The New Yorker* in 1941 to write for the U.S. Office of Facts and Figures and then moved over to the newly constituted OWI. Despite these various connections, Mitchell's hopes would be dashed again—this time by that distant and impetuous sea voyage to Leningrad, an innocent trip now being viewed by Washington clearance officers through the paranoia of wartime politics. Indeed, it could be argued that it was a single sentence from the introduction to *My Ears Are Bent,* the anthology of Mitchell's newspa-

Two typical New York street scenes from Therese. Her black-and-white photos were documentary in nature yet radiated great empathy.

per columns released five years previously, that kept him from working for the government.

In December of 1943, fully eight months after he applied for the OWI position, Mitchell was summoned to a meeting with an investigator for the U.S. Civil Service Commission office in New York, who was assigned to Mitchell's case. It's not known whether Mitchell considered the meeting in any way unusual or merely part of a protracted bureaucratic vetting. Regardless, the point of the session became quickly apparent. According to a short "Report of Interview and Special Hearing" transcript, the investigator, Henry Beckwith, ominously informed Mitchell that "the purpose of this interview is to allow you an opportunity to answer questions concerning information which has been received by the Civil Service Commission about alleged activities on your part."

After establishing the perfunctory facts of Mitchell's life, Beckwith asked the writer why the employment history in his application didn't include his summer excursion to Leningrad twelve years earlier on the *City of Fairbury*. "I didn't remember the dates," Mitchell replied—disingenuously, as he knew full well it wouldn't help his cause to disclose even a brief trip to Communist Russia. Besides, for more than a decade his employment had been as a professional journalist, which spoke directly to the expertise he brought to the position in question. He explained that he "did not want to complicate this thing with faulty information, and I did not consider it to be important enough to mention. It was in the summer vacation of 1931. The trip lasted three months altogether."

Mitchell's inquisitor bore in. "In your book, *My Ears Are Bent*, you state: 'One afternoon we got together, the seamen from all the American ships in the [Leningrad] harbor, and marched with the Russians in a demonstration against imperialist war,'" Beckwith said. The implication was that Mitchell had been something of a ringleader in the "demonstration," and Beckwith wanted an explanation. But Mitchell dismissed the idea. "I liked the Russians," he said, "and in a spirit of adventure, I marched with them and with the sailors from these ships in a demonstration against imperialistic war that, as I understand it, is an annual celebration over there, and whatever kind of parade it had been, I would have marched in it."

Mitchell was pressed on several other matters. One had to do with a short story he published in 1939 in the Communist magazine *New Masses.* "I wrote a series of articles on Black Ankle County, in North Carolina, where I was born, and *The New Yorker* took three of them," Mitchell explained, but a fourth piece—"The Ruination of Judge MacDuff," the tale of a cornpone local magistrate whose penchant for practical jokes backfired on him—was rejected. He tried selling it to several other magazines, but when none would buy it he offered it to *New Masses.* Beckwith then asked Mitchell about his signing of a nominating petition for American Communist leader and fringe presidential candidate Earl Browder in 1940. Mitchell was unapologetic. "I believe that Browder has the right to run if he desires," he said.

Joseph and Therese Mitchell counted a number of friends who were, or had been, registered Communists. But in a closing statement, Mitchell asserted, "I am not and never have been a Communist Party member, however I have sympathized with some of their activities from time to time. In other cases I have opposed Communist activities. Actually, I consider myself a Democrat and have registered as a Democrat in various national, state and city elections. I have several times, however, voted for American Labor Party, Republican and Communist candidates." Mitchell in fact would demonstrate these left-leaning but eclectic political inclinations all his life. For instance, less than a year after the Civil Service Commission interview, in November of 1944, he was one of about a dozen high-profile magazine writers and editors who signed an advertisement endorsing Franklin Roosevelt's reelection. The signers represented many political views but said Roosevelt's leadership was too important to interrupt at that crucial point in the war. A former Newspaper Guild local representative, Mitchell was strongly pro-labor and he cared passionately about issues of social justice. He would be disgusted by the McCarthyism of the fifties, and he despised Richard Nixon on general principle; on the other hand, as he aged, his antipathy for *all* politicians grew, including Democrats. In his notes, Mitchell indicated he had little use for John

Kennedy, disliked George McGovern, and eventually soured on Bill Clinton.

The Civil Service Commission's mini-inquisition rattled Mitchell, and the heavy suspicion evident in the hearing must have carried over into the panel's deliberations of his suitability to serve in a sensitive wartime capacity. He would hear nothing further for another five months. After a while he made a new inquiry, this one with the Writers' War Board (then headed by the crime writer Rex Stout, creator of Nero Wolfe), submitting another summary of his professional experience. At last came a terse letter from the OWI, dated May 29, 1944, saying the agency could not hire him "due to our inability to get the necessary clearances for you." This was a hurtful blow; a latent ulcer was one thing, but to have one's patriotism questioned quite another. Even so, it appears Mitchell made one final effort to receive a government clearance—if for no other reason, perhaps, than to vindicate his name—and in March of 1945 he was at last adjudged by the Civil Service Commission to be "eligible on suitability for federal employment." It's not clear whether he had finally persuaded the bureaucrats of his trustworthiness or just worn them down. By then, however, Allied forces were closing in on Berlin, and Allied planes were bombing Tokyo. Mitchell's window to serve had effectively closed.

His inability to play a role in the war effort nagged at Mitchell for the rest of his life, a mixture of guilt and resentment that was only exacerbated by the reputation-making war correspondence his friend Liebling produced throughout the entire conflict—not to mention the work of so many other gallant New Yorker writers, among them Mollie Panter-Downes, E. J. Kahn Jr., St. Clair McKelway, Philip Hamburger, Janet Flanner, Daniel Lang, and brothers John and David Lardner. Indeed, The New Yorker turned out some of the most literate reportage of that or any war, from the front lines and beyond. It was a performance that lifted the magazine from its once narrow (if sophisticated) aspirations to become an international icon, one with a cultural influence that founder Harold Ross could scarcely have imagined two decades earlier.

Mitchell was left to channel his frustration into his work. After Pearl Harbor and for the next several years, *The New Yorker* yielded up to the war effort an almost crippling wave of male editing and writing talent, while an inflow of unknown faces arrived at its West 43rd Street offices to attempt to fill the breach. Staggered by the loss of so many of his stalwarts, Ross longed for stability, and Mitchell provided at least a measure of it. Even as the writer was trying everything he could think of to get into the war, Mitchell continued to turn out some of the magazine's most accomplished and admired writing, such as his 1942 Profiles of Joe Gould and Gypsy King Johnny Nikanov. He was also hip-deep into his reporting for a triptych of pieces based on the Fulton Fish Market, which would become the next sensation among his growing legion of readers. Then, in the summer of 1943, the publication of a second book of collected Mitchell stories helped assuage the sting of his wartime rejection. Entitled *McSorley's Wonderful Saloon,* after the subject of one of his best-loved *New Yorker* pieces, the book was a sort of "greatest hits"—his stories about Mazie, Lady Olga, the musical prodigy Philippa Schuyler, Captain Charley's Private Museum for Intelligent People, Cockeye Johnny Nikanov, Joe Gould, Santa Claus Smith (who "paid" for meals and services with beautifully rendered—and counterfeit—checks), Commodore Dutch, and many more.

McSorley's, issued by New York publisher Duell, Sloan and Pearce, reached the bestseller lists and was greeted by critical acclaim. Review after review remarked on the depth of detail Mitchell brought to his portraits. That said, most remained transfixed by the "oddball" nature of his subjects, with Mitchell often cast as a slightly mad scientist orchestrating them all. "For years he has been studying, with the prying patience of a botanist, the queer human weeds he finds growing in the dingier interstices of Manhattan's bum-littered Bowery," *Time* magazine proclaimed. Mitchell had grown weary of those who, intentionally or not, marginalized his characters as curiosities. In a foreword to the book, he struck an uncharacteristically sharp tone to answer them, in a few lines that became the best known of his career. "The people in a number of the stories are of the kind that many writers have recently got in the habit of referring to as 'the little people,'" he wrote. "I regard this phrase as patronizing and repulsive. There are no little people in this book. They are as big as you are, whoever you are." It was a noble affirmation of his subjects' innate dignity, of course. But at the same time it neatly preempted any diminishment of the author by diminishment of his subjects.

In a review in the *Herald Tribune*, Stanley Walker again gave his onetime protégé a helpful roll of the log, pointing out how truly difficult it is to produce nonfiction of this caliber. There is no alchemy involved. "He is a remarkably competent, careful workman, and the apparently casual and effortless result comes from days and nights of research and toil which would flabbergast the ordinary reporter," Walker wrote. "There could be no greater fallacy than to assume that the people of Mr. Mitchell's chosen world are easy to write about."

More important than regular reviews was that *McSorley's* got the attention of some literary critics, who took a deeper look at what Mitchell was accomplishing. A particularly influential assessment came from Malcolm Cowley, who suggested that, with *McSorley's*, a genuinely fresh American writer had emerged, one who possessed the skills of a top novelist but who was applying them to true-life material. Ten years older than Mitchell and a friendly acquaintance of his, Cowley had the intellectual standing to cause other opinion-makers to pay attention. "Mitchell's collection of portraits is the exact opposite of the books that choose an important subject, but are hastily written and have nothing much to say," Cowley wrote in *The New Republic*, where he was an editor. "These books, which form the bulk of current writing, always make you feel as if you had paid for looking into the wrong end of a telescope. Mitchell, on the other hand, likes to start with an unimportant hero, but he collects all the facts about him, arranges them to give the desired effects, and usually ends by describing the customs of the whole community." Cowley went on to liken Mazie and many of Mitchell's other curious characters to those found in Dickens, although he pointed out that the authors came to them from entirely different directions.

In Mitchell's factual writing, it is hard not to see an image of the factual lives we lead, under the dictatorship of numbers, statistical averages and mass movements. Yet perhaps this impression of Mitchell is merely superficial. Reading some of his portraits a second time, you catch an emotion beneath them that curiously resembles Dickens': a continual wonder at the sights and sounds of a big city, a continual devouring interest in all the strange people who live there, a continual impulse to burst into praise of kind hearts and good food and down with hypocrisy. Unlike Dickens, he represses this lyrical impulse, but it controls his selection of details. You might say that he tries—often successfully—to achieve the same effects with the grammar of hard facts that Dickens achieved with the rhetoric of imagination.

Cowley also applauded the literary sweep of Mitchell's work, even if it was somewhat disguised by his understated prose. As an example he cited the tale of Commodore Dutch, who was the sole beneficiary of his popular charity ball. Cowley wrote, "Mitchell doesn't try to present him as anything more than a barroom scrounger; but in telling the story of his career, he also gives a picture of New York sporting life since the days of Big Tim Sullivan." And his story about Cockeye Johnny "is even better," Cowley continued. "It sets out to describe Cockeye Johnny Nikanov, the spokesman or king of thirty-eight gypsy families, but it soon becomes a Gibbon's decline and fall of the American gypsies; and it ends with an apocalyptic vision that is not only comic but also, in its proper context, more imaginative than anything to be found in recent novels."

As it happened, Mitchell's next work *would* be a novel, of sorts—but one that only two people at the time knew was fiction.

CHAPTER 8

MR. MITCHELL AND MR. FLOOD

MR. FLOOD'S ATTITUDE TOWARD seafood is not altogether mystical. "Fish," he says, "is the only grub left that the scientists haven't been able to get their hands on and improve. The flounder you eat today hasn't got any more damned vitamins in it than the flounder your great-great-granddaddy ate, and it tastes the same. Everything else has been improved *and* improved *and* improved to such an extent that it ain't fit to eat. Consider the egg. When I was a boy on Staten Island, hens ate grit and grasshoppers and scraps from the table and whatever they could scratch out of the ground, and a platter of scrambled eggs was a delight. Then the scientists developed a special egg-laying mash made of old corncobs and sterilized buttermilk, and nowadays you order scrambled eggs and you get a platter of yellow glue."

—*From "Old Mr. Flood," 1944*

. .

HUGH G. FLOOD LIVED IN THE HARTFORD HOTEL, A NEW YORK waterfront establishment located on Pearl Street, near the Fulton Fish Market. Born on Staten Island before the Civil War, Mr. Flood (as he was invariably called by Mitchell) was long retired after having made a comfortable living as the owner of a house-wrecking company. He was a flinty man of firm habits and equally firm opinions. He liked his Scotch even as he lamented the toll he'd seen spirits exact on so many weaker souls than he. "His eyes are watchful and icy-blue, and his face is red, bony, and clean-shaven," Mitchell wrote of him. "He is old-fashioned in appearance. As a rule, he wears a high, stiff collar, a candy-striped shirt, a serge suit, and a derby. A silver watch-chain hangs across his vest. He keeps a flower in his lapel."

Mr. Flood was ninety-three years old in January of 1944, when Mitchell first related his story in *The New Yorker,* and his only remaining goal in life was to reach the age of one hundred fifteen. This was an almost absurd notion, of course. But once readers became better acquainted with "Old Mr. Flood," few doubted that he might just do it.

Again, not a lot "happens" in Mitchell's yarn. It essentially consists of a visit between the two men, which affords the writer a chance to render a carefully observed study of a character eccentric even by Mitchell's high bar. Mr. Flood, for instance, is a self-described "seafoodetarian," who for the better part of six decades has eaten little beyond fish—and fried cod tongues and clams and crab and octopus and lobster and eel and all other manner of things fishermen pull from the sea and sell at the Fulton Market. (About the only exceptions to his strict seafood regimen are a few items he considers proper accompaniments: bread and butter, onions, and baked potatoes.) He is convinced a seafood diet is the key to a long life. Every weekday morning he heads to the Fulton Market, where he is as much a part of the landscape as the vendors and the chefs, and he walks the stalls until a certain piece of fish catches his eye. This he purchases and takes to a trusted restaurant—usually Sloppy Louie's, also one of Mitchell's favorite haunts—and precisely instructs the annoyed cooks how to prepare it. Mr. Flood considers oysters an almost magical cure-all. When another elderly resident of the Hartford complains of feeling poorly and is headed for the doctor's office, Mr. Flood's retort is sharp and certain:

"Oh, shut up," he said. "Damn your doctor! I tell you what to do. You get right out of here and go over to Libby's oyster house and tell the man you want to eat some of his big oysters. Don't sit down. Stand up at that fine marble bar they got over there, where you can watch the man knife them open. And tell him you intend to drink the oyster liquor; he'll knife them on the cup shell, so the liquor won't spill. And be sure you get the big ones. Get them so big you'll have to rear back to swallow, the size that most restaurants use for fries and stews; God forgive them, they don't know any better. Ask for Robbins Islands, Mattitucks, Cape Cods, or Saddle Rocks. And don't put any of that red sauce on them, that cocktail sauce, that mess, that gurry. Ask the man for half a lemon, poke it a time or two to free the juice, and squeeze it over the oysters. And the first one he knifes, pick it up and smell it, the way you'd smell a rose, or a shot of brandy. That briny, seaweedy fragrance will clear your head; it'll make your blood run faster. And don't just eat six; take your time and eat a dozen, eat two dozen, eat three dozen, eat four dozen. And then leave the man a generous tip and go buy yourself a fifty-cent cigar and put your hat on the side of your head and take a walk down to Bowling Green. Look at the sky! Isn't it blue? And look at the girls a-tap-tap-tapping past on their pretty little feet! Aren't they just the finest girls you ever saw, the bounciest, the rumpiest, the laughingest? Aren't you ashamed of yourself for even thinking about spending good money on a damned doctor? And along about here, you better be careful. You're apt to feel so bucked-up you'll slap strangers on the back, or kick a window in, or fight a cop, or jump on the tailboard of a truck and steal a ride."

A FEW MONTHS LATER, in April, Mitchell published a tale that, in its own way, came across nearly as fantastical as the Mr. Flood Profile. The story was entitled "Thirty-Two Rats from Casablanca," though when it appeared years later in an anthology, Mitchell gave it its more straightforward and enduring title: "The Rats on the Waterfront." And that's exactly what it was—a detailed, fascinating, and not a little curious portrait of the fecund vermin that populated every seeming nook of the metropolitan harborside.

Mitchell's encyclopedic account plumbs rat biology and physiol-

ogy, the rat-friendliness of old New York buildings and the ratproof-
ing of modern ones, health authorities' various efforts to control rat
populations, and the ever-present concerns about a resurfacing of bubonic plague. He focuses his tale on the three rat varieties most common to New York: the black rat, indigenous to India ("It is an acrobatic
beast. . . . It can gnaw a hole in a ceiling while clinging to an electric
wire"); the Alexandrian rat, a native of Egypt and a cousin to the black;
and the brown rat, from Central Asia—the most abundant in the city,
not to mention "the dirtiest, the fiercest and the biggest." All three
strains spread into Europe in the Middle Ages with the explosion of
global trade, and in like fashion they found their way to America
aboard the merchant and slave ships of the colonial era. Once established, New York's rat population grew dramatically, as the animals
litter multiple times a year. While no one could be entirely sure, of
course, authorities in 1944 believed there were at least as many rodent
New Yorkers as there were the human variety.

The story likely arose from Mitchell's experience at the Fulton
Fish Market, where rats were an annoying fact of life—although, as he
pointed out, New York's resourceful rodents were to be found everywhere their voracious appetites took them, from the subway system to
five-star hotels. Besides, at that particular moment the city's rat population seemed to be spiking, as it always did during wartime, with the
increased seaport activities. Not coincidentally, the story of Gotham's
rats is also one Harold Ross would have cherished—for its colorful
arcana and for the slightly repellent chord the subject would surely
strike in his upper-crust readers, who had never before given a thought
to what was lurking inside their apartment walls. Mitchell did not
disappoint. Here, employing some dark anthropomorphism—rats
portrayed almost as gang members—he captures his subjects' unsettling essence:

> As a rule, New York rats are nocturnal. They rove in the streets
> in many neighborhoods, but only after the sun has set. They
> steal along as quietly as spooks in the shadows close to the
> building line, or in the gutters, peering this way and that, sniff-

ing, quivering, conscious every moment of all that is going on around them. They are least cautious in the two or three hours before dawn, and they are encountered most often by milkmen, night watchmen, scrubwomen, policemen and other people who are regularly abroad in those hours. The average person rarely sees one. When he does, it is a disquieting experience. Anyone who has been confronted by a rat in the bleakness of a Manhattan dawn and has seen it whirl and slink away, its claws rasping against the pavement, thereafter understands fully why this beast has been for centuries a symbol of the Judas and the stool pigeon, of soullessness in general. Veteran exterminators say that even they are unable to be calm around rats.

"Rats" is atypical Mitchell in several respects, not only because his protagonists are literally vermin but because it is fully two-thirds of the way through before he discloses what could be considered the true point of the piece. And, in a final departure, he does this by breaking actual news—and near-terrifying news, at that. Over the years New York had had several close calls with the bubonic plague, the flea-borne, rat-abetted pestilence responsible for the Black Death in medieval Europe. But in early 1943, in what shaken public-health officials called simply "the *Wyoming* matter," it experienced perhaps its narrowest escape ever, and Mitchell patiently reconstructs the previously hush-hush episode.

The drama began when a French freighter, the *Wyoming,* arrived in New York Harbor that January, having come from Casablanca in North Africa, where there had recently been a plague outbreak. Health officials had put an elaborate system in place to check all vessels for rat infestation as they arrived in New York, and the captain of the *Wyoming* produced a certificate that his ship had been fumigated in Casablanca. The ship docked at a pier in Brooklyn to off-load mail, then moved on to a Hudson River pier in Manhattan to deposit the rest of its cargo. There, longshoremen reported seeing rats aboard the freighter, and health authorities ordered it fumigated. They found dead rats and ran test cultures that, several days later, confirmed the presence of plague in the animals. "It was the Black Death, no doubt about it," Mitchell quotes one health official as saying. "We had found it in the harbor for the first time in forty-three years." By the time of this discovery, however, the *Wyoming* had moved on to a *third* New York port, in Staten Island, for repairs. Now nearly frantic that they had a plague ship traversing the city, health officials found the *Wyoming*, re-boarded it, ripped holes into all the enclosed holds, fumigated it again—and found yet more infected rats.

The great fear was that the *Wyoming*'s rats had gotten to shore, perhaps in three different boroughs, and were now commingling with the resident rat population, exchanging fleas and thereby spreading the plague bacteria. Authorities got up teams of rat-trappers and quietly dispatched them to catch hordes of the vermin near the various piers where the *Wyoming* had docked. Once a rat was trapped, it was tested for plague. Each test came back negative, but the trapping of the waterfront rats continued for several months, until health officials were certain the crisis had passed. The city had averted a calamity, though until Mitchell produced his riveting narrative, New Yorkers didn't even know they had been in danger.

THAT NOVEMBER, THEN, MITCHELL revisited Mr. Flood. In a second story that in later collections was entitled "The Black Clams," Mr. Flood has summoned Mitchell to share an exciting discovery. Upon arriving, Mitchell hears some of the other residents of the Hartford maintaining how Mr. Flood, now ninety-four, is finally slipping, how he's been more irritable than usual, how he's been talking delusionally about a mythical "black clam." But when Mitchell comes upon Mr. Flood, it turns out that the black clams *do* exist—and to prove it he has a bushel of them to share. The story is redolent of the multisensory detail characteristic of Mitchell. In a passage about how the black clams are retrieved, one can almost smell the ocean brine and hear the gulls overhead.

"The bed this basket of clams came out of is called Bed Number Two," said Mr. Flood. He is one of those who can talk and eat at once. "It's located two and an eighth miles east-southeast of the whistling buoy off Point Judith, Rhode Island. The water out there is eighty to a hundred and twenty feet deep. That's why it took so long to find the blackies. The bottom of Number Two is muddy, what the Coast and Geodetic charts call sticky, and it's just about solid with clams. They're as thick as germs. Bay clams come from much shallower water. To give you an idea, the water over most of the quahog beds in Great South Bay is only twelve feet deep. The Rhode Island clammers are working the ocean beds with the same kind of dredge boats that oystermen use, except the cables are longer. They lower a dredge on a steel cable and drag it over the bottom. The dredge plows up the mud and the clams are thrown into a big chain-metal bag that's hung on the tail of the dredge. They drag for fifteen minutes, and then they haul up and unload the bag on the deck. The ocean clammers are making a ton of money. They're getting a dollar to a dollar and a half a bushel."

As Mr. Flood sits in a nearby ship's chandlery with its proprietor and with Mitchell, devouring the delicious clams, his thoughts—and the story—pivot to the subject of mortality. A year closer to his goal of hitting one hundred fifteen, Mr. Flood had certainly enjoyed a full life, but even more delicious is the sensation of outliving *other* old people. "This is something I got no business telling a young man," Mr. Flood says, "but the pleasantest news to any human being over seventy-five is the news that some other human being around that age just died."

A third and final installment, "Mr. Flood's Party," appeared in August of 1945. More-discerning *New Yorker* readers may have recognized this as the title of an elegiac poem by Edwin Arlington Robinson, about "old Eben Flood"—and thus catch the first sly tip-off from Mitchell that, where *his* Mr. Flood was concerned, all was not as it seemed.

The occasion is Mr. Flood's ninety-fifth birthday party. Mitchell and a handful of Mr. Flood's friends are assembled in the old man's room at the Hartford, which he has tidied up for the party. The story begins as a paean to the life-giving elixir that is the oyster. Mr. Flood relates the unlikely tale of Sam, a twenty-two-year-old draft horse that pulled a delivery wagon for so long he no longer had the energy to flick his tail at the bothersome flies. But when a shucker slips some oysters into Sam's feedbag as a gag, the horse suddenly becomes so frisky that he later breaks his leg chasing after a mare on an icy street. Mr. Flood then discloses that a certain racehorse owned by an oysterman at the market is fed oysters or clams in preparation for a race. "He's not much of a horse—no looks, no style; he only cost eleven hundred dollars—but he wins every race they want him to win," Mr. Flood says. "They don't let him win every race he runs; that'd look peculiar."

From this point on, the piece plays out like a latter-day *Canterbury Tales,* with each character recounting a story in turn, each one a testament to the fickle and unknowable nature of life. Indeed, the next-to-last word in the story goes to an embalmer, Mr. Bethea ("If I had it to do all over again, I don't know as I'd choose embalming as my life's work. You don't get the respect that's due you").

Mitchell's stories turned Mr. Flood into a minor celebrity. But he was an elusive one. Newspaper reporters and *New Yorker* readers would come by the Hartford Hotel in hopes of visiting with him, to no avail. After "The Black Clams" appeared, publisher M. Lincoln Schuster was so inspired that he sent Mitchell a telegram with a proposal. "Tell the mayor of the fish market we are fascinated by his philosophy of life and death, his taste in Arctica islandica and the superb way you and he together have put it all into words," it read. "Don't you think his salty experiences, his flavorsome ideas and his mind 'a turmoil of regrets' would make a colorful and vivid autobiography especially if you could give a helping hand? Do you believe the mayor of Fulton Fish Market would let us send an editor down to investigate?"

In reply, Mitchell was polite but curt. "Thank you ever so much for your telegram about the story on Hugh G. Flood," he wrote. "I'm glad you liked it. I'm sorry, but I don't think Mr. Flood would be interested in doing an autobiography. As a matter of fact, I'm working on a biography of him. It will be published by Duell, Sloan and Pearce, probably late in 1945."

WHAT MITCHELL DECLINED TO say was that he couldn't introduce Schuster, or one of Schuster's editors, or anyone else for that matter, to Mr. Flood. The old man didn't exist. He was a composite, comprising elements of several long-established figures at the Fulton Fish Market—with a large dollop of Mitchell himself thrown in for good measure. But it would be several more years before readers knew the truth of the situation. When the three Mr. Flood pieces were published as a slender book in 1948, Mitchell added in an author's note: "These stories of fish-eating, whiskey, death, and rebirth first appeared in *The New Yorker*. Mr. Flood is not one man; combined in him are aspects of several old men who work or hang out in Fulton Fish Market, or who did in the past. I wanted these stories to be truthful rather than factual, but they are solidly based on facts."

Why a composite? Forty years later, Mitchell explained that the device was about the only way he could really put across the story he had been driven to tell from his first exposure to the Fulton Fish Market as a cub newspaperman. Mitchell had not entirely given up the idea of producing an epic tale of New York, his adopted home. Once he'd imagined that would be a sweeping novel, but by now he had come to think he might accomplish much the same thing in a story of the fish market and the characters who populated it. "I had been trying to write this thing about the Fulton Fish Market in a kind of Melvillean way," Mitchell told Norman Sims. "I feel funny to say such a thing. I read *Moby-Dick* in college and it had a great effect on me. I had often thought about a Melvillean background with the Fulton Fish Market."

In a decade of gathering material on the Fulton Market, Mitchell had developed a warm relationship with William A. Winant, a prominent purveyor in the market whose family had worked the trade for several generations. Because of Winant's advanced age, colorful personality, widespread connections, and deep roots in the market, Mitchell thought him a logical and attractive centerpiece for his tale. There was just one problem. "Well, Mr. Winant wouldn't cooperate," Mitchell explained. "He'd talk to me. We were great friends. He was quite old then. And Mr. Gus Lockwood, his partner, he wouldn't cooperate. There were several elderly men down there. Chesebro Brothers, Robbins and Graham. They were the same way."

Mitchell said that one day he was talking with *New Yorker* editor Harold Ross about the dilemma, when Ross offered a potential solution. "There had been a number of composite profiles [in the magazine]," Mitchell said, "a composite profile of a policeman, for example, that McKelway had written. So [Ross] said, 'Why don't you write a composite?'

"I did. I developed Old Mr. Flood."

According to Mitchell, Ross instructed the writer to make the tale as accurate in its contextual details as possible. So while the main character and most of the secondary characters in the Mr. Flood trilogy were fictional, some of the latter were real. Real, too, were some of the settings and the specifics of Mitchell's reportage, such as the laborious process of how clammers dredged up their precious cargo.

Looking back at the trilogy years later, Mitchell produced a memo that painstakingly sorted out the Mr. Flood fact from fancy. The memo is undated and it's not clear what its purpose was, though it was included among other reporting-related information in his journal materials. Mitchell may have written it simply to remind himself what was what:

The Hartford House was a real place, but it doesn't exist any longer. Since the book appeared, it went through three changes in ownership, and was torn down in 1958.

Maggiani's fishing-boat chandlery, in which the second story in the book is laid, is entirely fictional, as is Mr. Maggiani himself.

Several other places mentioned in passing, such as S.A. Brown's drugstore, Mrs. Palumbo's bakery, and the Purity Spice

Mill do or did exist. S.A. Brown's went out of business, and the building has been torn down.

Sloppy Louie's exists. . . .

The following characters are entirely fictional: Mr. Flood; his daughter Louise; Mrs. Birdy Treppel the fishwife; Mr. Ah Got Um; Mr. P.J. Mooney; Tom Maggiani; Old Dan the barber; Peter Stetson; Jack Murchison the waiter; Tom Bethea the embalmer; Matthew T. Cusack the watchman; Ben Fass; Sam the horse and Woodrow his driver; Gus Lowry; Charlie Titus; Captain Oscar Doxsee; Mr. Unger; Archie Ennis.

The only real people in the book (they appear only incidentally, and their names could and should be changed) are Mrs. James Donald, who was the owner of the Hartford House; James Donald, who was the bartender there; Gus Trein, who was the manager; Drew Radel, the oysterman (he died after the book came out); George Still (also dead); and Edmond Irwin.

While in retrospect this approach to a *New Yorker* story seems strange or even inexplicable, it was consistent with Ross's personality and his quirks as an editor. As Mitchell indicated, *The New Yorker* had published composite characters before, and it would again; the dubious technique would not really disappear from the print media's bag of tricks until the general elevation of journalistic standards several decades later. In its early years especially, *The New Yorker* routinely merged fact and fiction in the short, confectionary sketches it called "casuals," which it didn't bother to label for readers—who couldn't have cared, anyway, since the pieces were so ephemeral as to be harmless. It must also be remembered that for Ross, the primary purpose of *The New Yorker* was to mine humor from the city it covered; he always said he began the magazine as a "fifteen-cent comic paper," and he worked tirelessly to make sure it never took itself too seriously. And, of course, Joseph Mitchell was one of the magazine's few staffers who had substantive portfolios in both fact and fiction. Which is to say, Ross had confidence that as a writer Mitchell would be able to handle the composite adroitly—his main concern.

Then, finally, was this highly germane fact: Joseph Mitchell had done it before.

IN A 1961 LETTER to *The New Yorker*'s in-house attorney, Milton Greenstein, Mitchell explained that in "King of the Gypsies," his popular 1942 Profile, Cockeye Johnny Nikanov was likewise a composite. "Insofar as the principal character is concerned, the gypsy king himself, it is a work of the imagination," he wrote. "Cockeye Johnny Nikanov does not exist in real life, and never did." Mitchell was explaining the situation to Greenstein because at the time he was working with a producer to create a musical based on the Profile (and a kind of sequel he wrote in 1955), but another theatrical script—by a then up-and-coming producer and writer named Sidney Sheldon, later famous for his popular television series and novels—had surfaced. Mitchell had read it and felt the treatment appropriated too much of his gypsy stories. "No matter how true to life Cockeye Johnny happens to be, he is a fictional character, and I invented him, and he is not in 'the public domain,' he is mine," Mitchell insisted. In fact, his main purpose in disclosing all this to Greenstein was to inquire as to what legal recourse he had, if any, to block Sheldon's prospective production.

Mitchell explained that his interest in gypsies went back to his Southern boyhood, when he first encountered them, and grew when he was a newspaperman becoming acquainted with various New York families. He had read dozens of books on gypsies and was intimately familiar with their history and traditions. He secured Ross's approval to do a Profile about a gypsy king that would double as a vivid cultural portrait of the gypsy people for *New Yorker* readers. But that idea proved difficult in execution, as Mitchell revealed to Greenstein:

In 1942, after doing the reporting for the gypsy king Profile, I told Mr. Ross that because of wartime conditions not a single one of the gypsy kings in the city at that time was a really representative one and that a picture of gypsy life built around any one of them (which was what we were trying to do) would be a distortion. Consequently, with his knowledge and approval, I invented Cockeye Johnny Nikanov. Contained in him are aspects of a number of gypsy kings I had known in previous times in the South and in New York City and I think I can safely say that he is truer to life than I would've been able to make him had he been a real person—most of the gypsy kings I have known have had long records of arrests but no convictions, at least for felonies (it is the women who have criminal records), and such men can sue for libel or invasion of privacy, or threaten to, the same as men whose reputations are flawless.

The fact that Mitchell, with Ross's imprimatur, had already presented a composite character as a real person surely made their decision to create Old Mr. Flood much easier when Mitchell confronted an ostensibly comparable barrier to writing about the Fulton Fish Market. But unlike with Mr. Flood, Mitchell, for as long as he lived, never made any public acknowledgment about Cockeye Johnny's fictional pedigree. Then again he hadn't had to, as gypsies by nature were peripatetic and there had never been any public questioning of Nikanov's existence.

In a sense, the true misleading of readers came in how the magazine labeled the Mr. Flood stories, and Cockeye Johnny's before that. If a *New Yorker* story was identified as a Profile (as the first Mr. Flood story and "King of the Gypsies" were) or a Reporter at Large (as the two Flood sequels were), readers simply assumed them to be factual; it would never have occurred that the characters might be fictions or fabrications. But even in this departure, Ross—a lifelong lover of practical jokes—was tapping in to some of his deeper instincts. He would have been especially delighted to know he was "pulling one over" on sophisticates like M. Lincoln Schuster and other literary friends, and there is evidence he clearly relished this particular ruse. At the same time that Schuster had queried Mitchell, the publisher also wrote Ross about a possible Mr. Flood book. Ross passed along that correspondence to Mitchell with a note of his own, saying that "ten or twelve people have spoken of the last Flood piece with the usual enthusiasm and extravagance that always marks the appearance of one of your pieces. Don't picture Mr. Flood as more eccentric than he is in his diet. You know damned well he eats cole slaw, and a few other things in addition to potatoes and onions. He's not that cracked."

Ross also was an editor who liked to keep his readers alert. Indeed, a year after the third Mr. Flood installment, Ross stunned his audience when, with no tip-off whatsoever, he turned over a complete issue of *The New Yorker* to a single story, John Hersey's journalistically ground-breaking account of the dropping of the atomic bomb on Hiroshima.

Nevertheless, it is a genuine paradox that Ross, so finicky about accuracy that he established an entire department for fact-checking *New Yorker* stories, could be so cavalier about the most fundamental "fact" of all—the actual existence of a Profile subject. He somehow drew a distinction here, telling himself that he wasn't so much tricking readers as presenting them with a gift they couldn't have had otherwise—which was arguably true.

Despite Ross's support, Mitchell found the popular reaction to Mr. Flood's debut unsettling. "People, throngs of people, went down there to the hotel where he was supposed to live," Mitchell said. "I told them at the hotel to just tell them he's up at Norwalk at his daughter's. I never intended to . . . foster a hoax or anything. That was the farthest thing from my mind. The idea was to get the spirit of the fish market." After that initial Profile and its visceral public response, Mitchell even wondered whether they should continue with the follow-up pieces. "We began to feel strange about this," Mitchell said. "But Ross said, 'Oh, go ahead.' I don't think, except with his approval, that it would have been possible. We weren't trying to fool anybody, really."

Only those few editors at *The New Yorker* who needed to know the circumstances were let in on the truth. But Mitchell's colleague Philip Hamburger recalled years later that there were at least some suspicions at the time about the extravagantly crusty and sagacious Mr. Flood. "When I first read ['Old Mr. Flood'], I took it at face value," he said. "And then I began to think about it and said to myself: 'You shrewd little bastard. He's making this up.'"

Trickery aside, from a writing standpoint what is perhaps most significant about the Mr. Flood pieces is how they allowed Mitchell to channel, unfettered by facts, his own feelings about life and a world-view that was already lamenting a New York quickly passing away. Ever the old soul—"Joe has been working hard at being an old man since he was in short pants," observed a longtime friend, bar owner Tim Costello—Mitchell was fascinated by the elderly. As a reporter he loved the way they talked and how their unfiltered nature often exposed hard truths that less forthright (or "more polite") people would avoid. The themes he dealt with in the Mr. Flood pieces—the inexorable march of mortality, the serendipity of life, the fickle humor of our condition, the power of good food and drink, modern life's undermining much of the best of the past—represented Mitchell's own attitudes and preoccupations. Indeed, in many ways Mitchell *was* Mr. Flood, and he drops numerous hints to that effect. He gave the old man his own birthday (July 27). Mr. Flood shares a first name and middle initial with Hugh G. Mitchell, one of the writer's most prominent ancestors. Writer and subject have the same taste in literature: Mr. Flood's small room is cluttered with yellowed clippings of the columnist Heywood Broun and books that include the Bible, the collected works of Mark Twain, and a "beautifully written" government guidebook, *Fishes of the Gulf of Maine*, which few laymen but Mitchell would even know existed. Both are devotees of seafood in all its incarnations, and both deplore that much of New York's architectural heritage is being lost to the wrecking ball. Indeed, time after time Mr. Flood says things that one can easily hear coming out of Mitchell's own mouth, or that he would say or write in his journals years later. To cite just a few examples:

On his ambivalence about strong drink: *"Still and all, there've been times if it hadn't been for whiskey, I don't know what would've become of me. It was either get drunk or throw the rope over the rafter."*

On pretentiousness: *"I love a hearty eater, but I do despise a goormy."*

On "new and improved" foods: *I'm not against vitamins, whatever to hell they are, but God took care of that matter away back there in the hitherto—God and nature, and not some big scientist or other."*

On religion and the hereafter: *"[Mr. Flood] comes of a long line of Baptists and has a nagging fear of the hereafter, complicated by the fact that the descriptions of heaven in the Bible are as forbidding to him as those of hell. 'I don't really want to go to either one of those places,' he says."*

On life: *"Nobody knows why they do anything."*

In his interview with Sims, Mitchell acknowledged there is much of himself in Mr. Flood—including, at least to some extent, his diet. "All the things I said in there about eating fish, that's what I believe," Mitchell said. "Seafoodetarian." Observed Philip Hamburger, "Joe was a man who dwelt at great length with, and was always conscious of, mortality. And the magnificence of Old Mr. Flood actually to me was the way in which a young man projects himself into the body and mind of an old man and does it with such literary style. But Joe is thinking about his own death. There's no question."

Thus for Mitchell, the invention of Mr. Flood—and the invention of Cockeye Johnny Nikanov before him—represented not a prank but a pursuit for a larger truth. "Sometimes facts don't tell the truth, you know," Mitchell told Sims, pointing out that he'd read many feature stories over the years about the Fulton Market, but for him they never got at the underlying "truth" of what actually happens there, or why. He went on to say that virtually all "nonfiction" works represent a subjective shaping of the "facts" by the author or reporter that may or may not add up to the truth. "When I'm working on a story," he said, "before I'm through I have a huge collection of notes. Typewritten. And then I realize: All these are facts, and the truth lies within these collections of interviews. Sometimes it delights me when someone tells a story in a different way. I've had several versions, a man telling me the story of his life in a different way. You realize that all of these are true. The word 'composite,' that's the way we look at our lives. Unfortunately, I'm afraid all biographies and autobiographies are fiction."

He added: "I believe what I said in the Flood book; it's more truthful than factual."

Before the disclosure, Ross raised the prospect with Mitchell of a fourth Mr. Flood story, which would end with the old man simply disappearing without a trace. However, by that point the writer, feeling uneasy enough about how far the ruse had played out, was "appalled" by the idea of continuing. He also was beginning to fear that when the truth *did* eventually come out, the entire thing would be written off as a hoax and then perhaps cast doubt on his previous work. This would have been especially worrisome given the well-kept secret about his gypsy composite. As it was, Mitchell for years afterward took pains to assure questioners that his other nonfiction pieces were, indeed, entirely factual—knowing, of course, that in at least one other instance, that wasn't true.

In any case, when the book version of *Old Mr. Flood* appeared with its disclaimer about Mr. Flood, there was no apparent anger or sense of deception. Some reviews didn't even mention it, while others, like the reviewer in the *Herald Tribune*, seemed to condone it. "As a reporter of the New York scene whose integrity equals his human insight and admirable command of a disciplined prose that is never loosely journalistic or falsely literary, Joseph Mitchell informs his readers that this portrait of Mr. Flood is not one man but a composite of several venerable Fulton Fish Market habitués," the review said. "His purpose has been to make the stories 'truthful rather than factual.' Having become acquainted with Mr. Flood when he first appeared in the pages of *The New Yorker* we are reluctant to accept a multiple image. In his person and his philosophies, in his speech and in every detail of his deportment, old Mr. Flood remains intact and indivisible."

In our own times, however, Mitchell's Mr. Flood has occasionally been cited and criticized, usually in the wake of some instance of high-profile journalistic fabulism, such as that committed by Jayson Blair or

Stephen Glass, and there surely would have been even more such assertions had people known about Mitchell's invention of Cockeye Johnny Nikanov. But it's a questionable tactic for today's critics to apply modern standards to past actions rather than the practices of the time. Of course, the other key distinction between Mr. Flood and contemporary journalistic inventions is that Blair, Glass, and their ilk were deceiving their own editors and publications, while in Mitchell's case, his editor not only knew about the deception but actually encouraged it.

It should also be remembered that, at the end of the day, Mitchell was really creating literature. Philip Hamburger called the autobiographical nature of the Mr. Flood pieces "fiction of the highest." Mitchell "was projecting himself fictionally into old age, and it's a masterpiece. There are no two ways about it. And I don't think that it makes a bit of difference whether there was a Mr. Flood or there wasn't a Mr. Flood. Just as it doesn't make a difference whether there was a Nicholas Nickleby or a David Copperfield."

CHAPTER 9

THE BOTTOM OF THE HARBOR

"I DIDN'T REST SO good last night," [Mr. Poole] said. "I had a dream. In this dream, a great earthquake had shook the world and had upset the sea level, and New York Harbor had been drained as dry as a bathtub when the plug is pulled. I was down on the bottom, poking around, looking things over. There were hundreds of ships of all kinds lying on their sides in the mud, and among them were some wormy old wrecks that went down long years ago, and there were rusty anchors down there and dunnage and driftwood and old hawsers and tugboat bumpers and baling wire and tin cans and bottles and stranded eels and a skeleton standing waist-deep in a barrel of cement that the barrel had rotted off of. The rats had left the piers and were down on the bottom, eating the eels, and the gulls were flopping about, jerking eels away from the rats. I came across an old wooden wreck all grown over with seaweed, an old, old Dutch wreck. She had a hole in her, and I pulled the seaweed away and looked in and I saw some chests in there that had money spilling out of them, and I tried my best to crawl in. The dream was so strong that I crawled up under the headboard of the bed, trying to get my hands on the Dutch money, and I damn near scraped an ear off."

—From "The Bottom of the Harbor," 1951

. .

ONCE—AND APPARENTLY *only* ONCE—JOSEPH MITCHELL summoned the courage to climb to the highest reach of the Statue of Liberty, its torch. Having swung treetop to treetop as a boy adventurer and ascended still-rising skyscrapers as a newspaper reporter,

Mitchell was not one to be intimated by heights. Even so, after clambering up the five hundred or so steps just to get to the lady's crown, Mitchell nervously worked his way up the forty-foot nearly vertical ladder that ran inside her narrow, upraised arm. At the final rung, he stepped out from darkness into sunshine and a view unlike any other in the world—the majestic entirety of New York Harbor at his feet. Daintily, he moved about the tiny balcony surrounding the torch, gazing for miles in every direction; with a stiff wind whipping about, his knees wobbled and an unfamiliar queasiness rose in the pit of his stomach. Access to the torch had been closed to everyone but maintenance workers since a terrorist scare in 1916, but there was another, unstated reason—human beings simply were not meant to be up here, suspended more than three hundred feet above the sea. But occasionally a persuasive working journalist could still gain access and, despite his nerves, Mitchell relished what this privileged vantage point afforded him. Below him, freighters and tugboats and ferries and scows crisscrossed the watery concourse, in slow motion. Miniature ocean liners waited patiently at the Manhattan piers, and miniature battleships sat under repair at the Brooklyn Navy Yard. He could follow the East River to the Williamsburg Bridge and beyond, and due north the view was straight up the Hudson to the horizon. Turning to the west he saw the meandering rivulets of the Meadowlands. To the south was the Verrazano Narrows, the harbor entrance separating Staten Island from Brooklyn, and then the Atlantic beyond. After a few minutes Mitchell could feel the arm swaying, and he pulled back from the thin railing and took his descent—but not before the sheer immensity and glory of the harbor was imprinted on him forever.

Amid the boxfuls of yellowed newspaper clippings, writing scraps, journal notes, pamphlets, and other miscellany that Mitchell left after his death, there was one especially telling artifact. It was a lengthy article about the workings of New York Harbor, which he had cut out from the February 1937 issue of *Fortune* magazine. In an accompanying double-page spread, a map annotated the scores of bays, channels, inlets, and marine landmarks that made up the harbor—a two-dimensional version of what Mitchell saw with his own eyes. The article covered the commercial aspects of the harbor in great detail, from the comings and goings of those stately liners to the bustling Brooklyn docks to Staten Island's oyster grounds and the Fulton Fish Market. The article is heavily underlined; it's clear Mitchell read it closely and set it aside for some future use.

In fact, Mitchell would devote the next phase of his writing life to a series of stories from and about the New York waterfront, pieces that dealt with the harbor's impact on the lives of the city's residents but also with its larger, metaphorical implications for all people, wherever they lived. They are stories that, taken together, established a defining Mitchell motif. In one sense this body of work can be seen as a logical extension of the themes Mitchell developed in "Old Mr. Flood." Certainly the tales grew out of his interest in the waterfront, first culti-

Therese caught her husband in a rare recreational pose, no suit or hat in sight, during a vacation in Rhode Island.

vated years before at the fish market, and no doubt his Depression-era experience as a merchant seaman further whetted his curiosity about lives that revolved around the water. Then, too, the "Rats" story, by happy chance, had nudged Mitchell in this direction.

After several years devoted almost exclusively to the "Old Mr. Flood" series, the next piece Mitchell published centered on a character almost Mr. Flood's equal in terms of his crustiness, idiosyncratic personality, and firm views on life. But this time the protagonist, Ellery Thompson, captain of a hardworking fishing boat, was as real as the wrecks that littered the fishing grounds off his home base of Stonington, Connecticut.

The Profile, entitled "Dragger Captain," appeared in *The New Yorker* in two parts in January of 1947. Thompson is captain of the *Eleanor,* a trawling boat, or "dragger," which pulls nets to snare its catch—primarily flounder destined for New York's restaurants. At age forty-seven, he has three decades of fishing behind him and is widely considered the ablest captain in Stonington. With so much hard-won experience, he can tell from the weather at sunrise if a day is going to be worth putting out to sea, and he knows how to drag a line close to the submerged wrecks without snagging it. Most important, he has an almost mystical intuition as to where the fish are. His two crewmen tell Mitchell that over time Thompson has achieved a kind of flounder consciousness. "He only sleeps four or five hours," one says. "The rest of the night he lies in bed and imagines he's a big bull flounder out on the ocean floor."

Mitchell came to know Thompson through mutual acquaintances at the Fulton Market, where the captain sold his catch. It's easy to see why the rumpled sailor appealed to the natty planter's son. For one thing, Thompson, while not formally educated, is cerebral in his way, and he seems to have his priorities in order—which is to say, they align perfectly with Mitchell's. "He abhors hurry," Mitchell writes. "He thinks that humanity in general has got ahead of itself. He once threatened to fire a man in his crew because he worked too hard." At another point, he says of Thompson, "He is deeply skeptical. He once said that the older he gets the more he is inclined to believe that humanity is helpless. 'I read the junk in the papers,' he said, 'and sometimes, like I'm eating in some eating joint and I can't help myself, I listen to the junk on the radio, and the way it looks to me, it's blind leading blind out of the frying pan into the fire, world without end.'"

It turns out that a tragedy underlies Thompson's dark outlook—the terrible death of his younger brother, Morris, a fellow dragger captain. During the worst days of the Depression, Morris took his boat out to fish in a gale, against his better judgment, because he needed the money. A huge wave swept him over the side and he drowned. Thompson and his father went out as soon as they got word and began to drag for his body. As Mitchell recounts, "On the morning of the third day"—the Christian imagery unmistakable, if not redemptive in this instance—"when they had almost decided to quit and go in, it came up in the net."

Despite this traumatizing experience, Thompson manages to meet life less with bitterness than with a droll world-weariness. He is, in fact, a near-ideal Mitchell protagonist. The captain is eloquent, he is highly skilled at a man's trade, he is a pilothouse philosopher—and for good measure, he cooks up a tasty lobster. Mitchell explains that when other captains catch lobsters in their fishing nets, they ship the best of them to the market for sale. Thompson, however, keeps the best lobsters for himself and his crew, boiling them expertly and storing them on ice to indulge in whenever the mood strikes. He holds forth on any number of subjects, with great humor. For instance, somewhere along his life's journey Thompson became a self-taught painter, specializing in portraits of the *Eleanor* and the fishing boats of friends and acquaintances, the vessels invariably braving angry skies and storm-tossed waves. Much to everyone's surprise, Thompson's paintings became popular, first with the kind of people looking for nautical-themed art for vacation homes, then among more-serious collectors who made the trek out from New York to acquire them. The collectors "never fail to inform [Thompson] that he is a primitive," Mitchell writes. "This word used to anger him. He now understands its significance in relation to painting, but he pretends that he doesn't. Last summer, a woman from New York told him that she knew dozens of painters but he was the first primitive she'd ever met. 'I'm not as primitive as I have been,' Ellery said. 'Nowheres near. Back before I got the rheumatism, I was without a doubt the most primitive man in eastern Connecticut.'"

In reporting his story, Mitchell spent long hours fishing with Thompson and his crew, as they laboriously set out the dragging nets and later reeled them back in to see what had fetched up. Much of Mitchell's time on the *Eleanor* coincided with the visits of two oceanographers who were using the boat as a kind of floating laboratory. Like Mitchell, the scientists had gravitated to Thompson because of his reputation as the most knowledgeable man in the Stonington fleet, the better to help them assess the health of commercial fishing in and around Long Island Sound. Again, much like Mitchell, who became something of an authority on everything from anthropology to architecture in pursuit of his work, Thompson embraced the oceanographers' research so completely that he became a virtual collaborator and as conversant in the Latin names for the fish he caught as the scientists were.

Because they spent so much time together for the Profile, and because of their congruent worldviews, Mitchell and Thompson became friends. Their connection was further cemented by the fact that "Dragger Captain" provided them a tantalizing if brief promise of Hollywood fame and fortune.

After the story was published, Mitchell was approached about turning it into a film script. He was open to the idea, and so was Thompson, to whom Mitchell promised 10 percent of any proceeds that might result. It seems there was a deal struck for an option—basically a lease on the movie rights for a set period of time in exchange for a modest payment—and much correspondence between the two ensued as Mitchell kept the captain apprised of the prospects. Occasional notes in the gossip columns fueled their hopes. "I'm enclosing a clipping, in case you missed it, of the Hedda Hopper column I mentioned in my telegram, in which she said that Warner Brothers had 'acquired' the Dragger Captain Profile and would develop it for Gary Cooper," Mitchell wrote in May of 1948. "This report was repeated in movie columns in the *Herald Tribune* and the *Times*. I was quite excited about it. . . ." But in following up for himself, Mitchell learned that the report grew out of "studio commissary gossip" and that "the only truth in it is that a writer has been assigned to try and work out a script on dragger fishing, using the Profile as background, which, of course, we knew already." In the end it was all just Hollywood fairy dust; neither Gary Cooper nor anyone else ever appeared in a movie version of "Dragger Captain."

IT'S NOT CLEAR WHY—LIKELY as not it had to do with Mitchell's conflicted feelings about the work—but the slim volume *Old Mr. Flood* was not published as a book until 1948, three years after the culminating piece appeared in *The New Yorker*. Its appearance marked the writer's tenth anniversary of joining the magazine. As had been the case with *McSorley's*, his earlier anthology, *Old Mr. Flood* reinforced in the literary community Mitchell's status as a writer of uncommon craftsmanship and imagination. Few observers, however, were noting that his productivity was continuing to abate. After *The New Yorker* published the final installment of the Mr. Flood pieces in August 1945, it would be a full sixteen months before Mitchell's byline appeared again, with "Dragger Captain." An even starker gauge of Mitchell's ebbing output: In 1939, his first full year at the magazine, the eager-to-please young writer published fourteen pieces; that's the same number he would produce from 1944 until his death half a century later.

Of course, the stories Mitchell *was* turning out now were considerably longer, more shaded and complex in tone, more creatively ambitious, and more detailed in structure than those at the beginning of his career; they were, in other words, more technically demanding and simply harder to write. Mitchell was further burdened by a strain of perfectionism as compulsive as any other aspect of his personality. As a young newsman he wrote quickly because of nonstop deadlines and a newspaper's need to fill an entire issue each day. If the results seldom satisfied him, all he could really do was strive to be better with the next story. At *The New Yorker*, given leave to work at his own pace and with no real deadlines pressing in on him, Mitchell was free to indulge an obsession for his writing to be just so, and this self-imposed pressure only mounted with age and growing acclaim.

Mitchell's perfectionism also led him to ground his stories in authoritative research, and lots of it. Always a voracious reader for pleasure, he now devoted a great deal of his reportorial time to poring over books in the service of his current projects—the more esoteric the subject, it seems, the better. (Mitchell's papers include a 1978 letter complimenting the author of *The Story of Brick,* "a fascinating book to anyone interested in the history of brickmaking. . . .") His small apartment was chockablock with volumes, floor to ceiling. "Books, so many books, an unbelievable number of books," recalled his daughter Nora. "He read them all. Of course, he was always reading lots of them at the same time. He had them stretched out through the apartment."

Still, in pursuit of a story, Mitchell's main tools were the reporter's classic ones—strong legs, acute observation, and unparalleled listening skills, not to mention the patience to engage in serial interview-conversations with his subjects. All this work, especially the interviews, yielded reams of original material. "I [wrote] with a kind of shorthand. An afternoon's conversation would fill up several of those notebooks," Mitchell explained to Norman Sims. Depending on the nature of the story, these interviews could play out over weeks, months, or even years as Mitchell patiently stalked his quarry, fueled by coffee and a bottomless curiosity. After each conversation, Mitchell would transcribe those notebooks full of his idiosyncratic shorthand into thick stacks of single-spaced typescript.

There was an almost scientific method to Mitchell's persistence with his subjects, and he did think about it in those clinical terms. "I've interviewed people so much that I know what I'm hearing better than the ordinary interviewer," Mitchell continued with Sims. "Fortunately, I've been able to get them interested and not throw me out. They get goddamn tired sometimes and say, 'No, no, no, I don't want to.' But then they call me up and say come on back. So I think I do have an ability to know what I'm hearing the way an archaeologist knows what he is seeing when he picks it up out of the dirt. I have some good idea what it is. I like to think of it as an archaeological digging into the minds of these people."

With his stacks of notes at the ready, then, Mitchell would get down to his real labor—the writing. And labor it truly was, as can be readily seen from the few draft examples Mitchell left behind. Seated at the sturdy Underwood typewriter that he would use his entire *New Yorker* career, Mitchell would patiently cast and recast sentences, sometimes dozens of times, changing just a word or two with each iteration until an entire paragraph came together and seemed right. He would move through his drafting of the story in this slow, painstaking fashion, at certain points (in that pre-computer era) using a scissors to cut these passages apart, sometimes sentence by sentence, and physically rearranging them to get a better feel for the narrative rhythm. In so doing he often used paper clips to hold the sentence strips together, and these constructions would come to resemble a long, flexible washboard or a kind of primitive girdle. All this fussing was exceedingly time-consuming, even for a magazine writer, which helped to establish Mitchell's growing reputation for deliberation. "If you're going to have lunch with him and you go in and pick him up," recalled Philip Hamburger, "you would see that he had [paper] scraps. He had been cutting out sentences. . . . It was obvious that the act of writing was, for Joe, a difficult one."

Only a person completely dedicated to words, even addicted to words, would go to such lengths with them. In Mitchell's case, it was an addiction that sprang from his mother's early encouragement of the reading habit. The condition was nurtured by listening to the great talkers everywhere around him while he grew up in Robeson County, be they family members or characters from the community's fields, warehouses, churches, and stores. For instance, Mitchell said that every time he heard the hymn "There Is Power in the Blood," he was reminded of his childhood and a Fairmont tenant farmer named Alonzo. In addition to being a farmer, Alonzo was a skilled butcher and "jackleg preacher." And as he butchered a lamb or calf, Alonzo would sing from the hymn: "There is power, power, wonder-working power in the blood of the lamb. . . ." Before he bent to his work, however, Alonzo earnestly blessed the animal and gave thanks for its use. Said Mitchell, "He butchered according to Leviticus." Mitchell's ear was further developed in the streets and backrooms of New York City on the newspaper beat, a true-life Damon Runyon universe of cops, hustlers, gamblers, street preachers, bartenders, and barflies.

These aural influences were augmented by his extensive reading, which in time he came to appreciate as master classes in assembling a narrative. As seen, Mitchell devoured all types of writers and genres; in various interviews and writings he references Chaucer, Stendhal, Thomas Mann, Flaubert, Rabelais, Kafka, Twain, Flannery O'Connor, Henry James, Dante, Shakespeare, and the authors of the Bible, to name but a few. Tellingly, the names are essentially all writers of fiction (well, depending on where one stands on Scripture). Still, beyond Stephen Crane and other realists in the "street" tradition, few of his influences are especially discernible in Mitchell's own writing. Like any writer of consequence, once Mitchell got past his apprenticeship, he managed to shape a style all his own.

That style was naturalistic, unforced, and elegant, the kind of prose that non-writers might have assumed was easy but that professionals knew was anything but. Mitchell prized permanence, endurance, and beauty, whether those qualities came together in a carefully constructed cast-iron building or a Profile. In fact, he routinely talked about writing in structural terms—how a well-told story required a substantial foundation, high-quality materials, a logical "flow," and interesting adornments. And that is how he went about his work. Mitchell fashioned long, languid sentences that built layer upon layer, achieving a satisfying richness—not dissimilar to many Southern novelists who were his contemporaries. His authoritative and liberal use of facts framed his tale, even as his careful sentences relentlessly propelled it along. Mitchell stories may not have much plot, as such; the "action" more typically involves human beings revealing themselves to us, bit by bit, usually in their own words, until we become privy to their innermost feelings and impulses.

While Mitchell was telling one story on the surface, much of his deliberation owed to the effort he made to achieve an extra level of meaning with his pieces—what he sometimes called their "underground stream" of meaning. It was this less-obvious meaning, he felt strongly, that marked the best literature and brought people back for second or third readings. And certainly no other writer "sounded" quite like Joseph Mitchell. His clear, foursquare style merged with his penchant for infusing historical context to create an appealingly gauzy effect, a feeling the novelist Thomas Beller once described simply as "Mitchell time." "Mitchell invented a temporal dimension for his stories, a strange and twilit place," Beller explained, where "a density of historical fact and the feeling of whole eras fading from view are sharply juxtaposed with scenes of cinematic immediacy related in the present tense."

Mitchell's was also an indisputably American voice. It's ironic, then, that his paramount literary influence, and the one he most openly admired, was James Joyce—neither American nor a writer of nonfiction. Indeed, one can rightly be considered a photographic negative of the other: Joyce worked in fiction, Mitchell nonfiction; Joyce characters were often real people given a thin fictional veneer, while Mitchell brought fictional techniques to telling the stories of real people; Joyce prose was dizzyingly complex and enigmatic, Mitchell prose direct and clear. Yet at the most fundamental level Mitchell and Joyce were artistic brothers, because both examined the lives of their home cities' most humble citizens, in the most modest precincts, to convey universal truths.

Beyond that artistic connection, Joyce resonated with Mitchell on any number of personal and psychological levels. As someone who always considered himself an exile, Mitchell felt a kinship with Joyce's need to leave Ireland in pursuit of his muse. Then there was their mutual delight with word origins, wordplay, and puns. While Mitchell didn't follow Joyce's impish lead in sprinkling his stories with puns, in his personal life he reveled in them. Sometimes when Mitchell was invited to an event he preferred to duck, he politely told the callers he was sorry but he was just headed off to Buffalo. That led him to tell friends that if he ever wrote his autobiography, it would be entitled "A Man Called Me . . . But I Was in Buffalo." More seriously, Mitchell brought a lexicographer's zeal to documenting unique words, phrases, and usages, particularly from his native region. A heavy rain is a "frog-choker"; to "dingdong" someone is to nag them to death. "He got his legs crossed" meant he was in financial trouble, but if things improved he might get "almost back up to broke." "He may out-nice you, but she will out-sad you," observed one acquaintance. "If she does that again, I'll snatch her baldheaded," said another.

Joyce's main influence on Mitchell, however, was simply inspiration. At one point in the early seventies, Mitchell noted in his journal that he hadn't read many new books of late, that the older he got the more he preferred rereading works that he knew from experience spoke to him. "The novel that I get down most often is *Finnegans Wake*," he wrote. "I keep my place in it, and I gradually read it straight through, and I read it over and over, just as one of my grandmothers used to read the Bible. I am now reading it for the seventh time. I feel toward it much as a very old man might feel toward an overcoat he has bought and knows that he most likely won't ever buy another: it will last me."

While drafting a story, Mitchell would closet himself in his warren along the staff writers' row of the twentieth floor of *The New Yorker*'s offices, a bleak venue that Hamburger famously dubbed "Sleepy Hollow." Gardner Botsford, a longtime *New Yorker* editor who handled many of Mitchell's stories, described Mitchell's office as an austere space, uncluttered and with everything in its place. His desk held a glass full of "needle-sharp pencils." He sat in an uncomfortable-looking wooden swivel chair, bent over his typewriter while he composed. As he did, Mitchell listened for the music of his passages as intently as he listened for rhythms in his characters' confessionals. Nonfiction writing "has to have a lyricism," he would explain. "By lyricism I don't mean it has to be *poetic* by any means. I do believe the most commonplace words are the ones that in the end have the most power. . . . The commonplace words are the strong ones. It reminds me of those old paving stones the fishermen use to weight the nets. Those words are like stones. I'll search endlessly for the right small words of a few syllables that hold something up. A foundation."

When at last Mitchell had the story where he wanted it, he typed up a final version for submission to his editors. The payoff for all his labor was copy that, even within the finicky precincts of *The New Yorker,* was legendarily pristine. "I'd insert maybe three commas," Botsford recalled of reading a Mitchell manuscript. "[He] took forever to write a piece, but when he turned it in, the editing could be done during one cup of coffee."

SOMETIME IN THE MIDDLE of 1948, Mitchell started reporting a story about a tightly knit Brooklyn-based group that had fascinated him for years. The Caughnawaga community of Native Americans was "a band of mixed-blood Mohawks," widely respected in the construction trades for their skill as high-steel workers. Mitchell, with his fascination for buildings, had long been cognizant of the unique role the Caughnawaga played in the creation of the city's signature bridges and skyscrapers—a culture operating high above New Yorkers but not really of them. In September of 1949 he told their story in "The Mohawks in High Steel," a Reporter at Large piece notable not only for its fascinating storyline but also for its non-patronizing treatment of Native Americans at a time when that was highly unusual. Indeed, a *New Yorker* colleague (and a polymath of a different kind), Edmund Wilson, was so taken with the story that he used it as the introduction to his book *Apologies to the Iroquois.* Mitchell describes life on the Caughnawaga reservation a few miles upriver from Montreal, Canada, and in its satellite colony in the North Gowanus neighborhood of Brooklyn.

Mitchell again focuses on one person to help convey the story of a culture. This time, he is "a man of fifty-four whose white name is Orvis Diabo and whose Indian name is O-ron-ia-ke-te, or He Carries the Sky." Diabo quit his rivet gang because of crippling arthritis. A regular at the Nevins Bar and Grill, Diabo, like Mitchell, is a man with one foot in two separate worlds and a bit unsteady for the straddle. One day Mitchell finds him drinking gin instead of his usual ale.

"I feel very low in my mind," he said. "I've got to go back to the reservation. I've run out of excuses and I can't put it off much longer. I got a letter from my wife today and she's disgusted with me. 'I'm sick and tired of begging you to come home,' she said. 'You can sit in Brooklyn until your tail takes root.' The trouble is, I don't want to go. That is, I do and I don't. I'll try to explain what I mean. An Indian high-steel man, when he first leaves the reservation to work in the States, the homesickness just about kills him. The first few years, he goes back as often as he can. Every time he finishes a job, unless he's thousands of miles away, he goes back. If he's working in New York, he drives up weekends, and it's a twelve-hour drive. After a while, he gets married and brings his wife down and starts a family, and he doesn't go back so often. Oh, he most likely takes the wife and children up for the summer, but he doesn't stay with them. After three or four days, the reservation gets on his nerves and he highballs it back to the States. He gets used to the States. The years go by. He gets to be my age, maybe a little older, maybe a little younger, and one fine morning he comes to the conclusion he's a little too damned stiff in the joints to be walking a naked beam five hundred feet up in the air. . . . He gives up high-steel work and he packs his belongings and he takes his money out of the bank . . . and he goes on back to the reservation for good. And it's hard on him. He's used to danger, and reservation life is very slow; the biggest thing that ever happens is a funeral. He's used to jumping around from job to job, and reservation life boxes him in. He's used to having a drink, and it's against the law to traffic in liquor on the reservation; he has to buy a bottle in some French-Canadian town across the river and smuggle it in like a high-school boy, and that annoys the hell out of him."

Then again, it's on the reservation where Diabo (pronounced DIE-bo) can find the traditional foods he longs for: o-nen-sto, or corn soup, and boiled Indian bread made with hominy and kidney beans. Diabo even finds comfort resting in a graveyard:

"There's hundreds of high-steel men buried in there. The ones that were killed on the job, they don't have stones; their graves are marked with lengths of steel girders made into crosses. There's a forest of girder crosses in there. So I was sitting on Uncle Miles's stone, thinking of the way things go in life, and suddenly the people in the long-house began to sing and dance and drum on their drums. They were singing Mohawk chants that came down from the old, old red-Indian times. I could hear men's voices and women's voices and children's voices. The Mohawk language, when it's sung, it's beautiful to hear. Oh, it takes your breath away. A feeling ran through me that made me tremble; I had to take a deep breath to quiet my heart, it was beating so fast. I felt very sad; at the same time, I felt very peaceful."

Harold Ross, having seen "The Mohawks in High Steel" in galleys prior to publication, was the first—though scarcely the last—to praise it. "I would report that I've read the story on the Indians, and that I consider it wonderful," Ross told Mitchell in a letter that July. "Not only am I gratified at being a party to the publication of such a distinguished piece of writing, but, personally, it takes a great load off my mind: I've been nagged about those Indians in Brooklyn for ten years, and have been lobbying for a story on them most of that time. I never expected one as brilliant as this, but you cast your bread on the waters and sometimes a miracle occurs."

"Mohawks" doesn't rest on Diabo the way "King of the Gypsies" and the Mr. Flood stories rested on their protagonists; Diabo, in fact, doesn't even turn up until the concluding pages of the piece. Yet it would seem that Mitchell once again was less than forthright about one of his key characters.

A review of both the reservation record and Mitchell's research for "Mohawks" (it is one of a handful of stories where some of his original reporting notes survive) strongly suggests that Diabo was either a third composite figure or quite possibly a pseudonym for a veteran construction-gang leader of that period, a man named Paul Horn. By 1949, Horn, a well-known member of the Caughnawaga, had worked in high-steel construction for almost twenty-five years, in many states. He had helped erect the Chrysler Building, the George Washington Bridge, and dozens of other New York landmarks. At the time he also was an elected official of the Brooklyn local of the International Association of Bridge, Structural and Ornamental Iron Workers, the union representing the Caughnawaga and other high-steel workers.

Horn lived most of the year in Brooklyn but spent summers back on the reservation in Canada. He was said to be unusually garrulous for a Caughnawaga, most of whom tended to be more guarded with outsiders.

Diabo was, and remains, a common surname among the Caughnawaga, who today are more familiarly known as the Kahnawake. Paul Horn, in fact, *was* a Diabo. His father, Peter Diabo, had the Indian name O-na-ka-ra-ke-te, which means He Carries the Horn, and at some point he simply changed the family name to Horn. (Recall that the Indian name of Mitchell's character Orvis Diabo is O-ron-ia-ke-te, or He Carries the Sky.)

Early in his reporting Mitchell conducted a long interview with Horn, and in subsequent interviews Mitchell spoke to many people *about* Horn and his family. But there is no Paul Horn in the story. On the other hand, there are no interviews with an "Orvis Diabo" reflected in Mitchell's reporting notes, and no one he interviewed mentioned an Orvis Diabo. During an interview with a Brooklyn minister who had worked among the Caughnawaga for years, the subject turned to Indian names generally; Mitchell typed the note "O-ron-ia-ke-te: He Carries the Sky," then later scribbled the word "Orvis" in pencil next to this entry. There is no explanation for this, and it is the lone occasion that name appears in the notes.

Of course, it's not known if the Mohawk files Mitchell left behind constitute the entirety of his story notes, though they appear comprehensive; an Orvis Diabo interview may yet be out there somewhere. But an extensive search turns up nothing to suggest that a Caughnawaga named Orvis Diabo, subject of a famous *New Yorker* story, ever existed. Nor does the name register with Kahnawake officials today. The reservation isn't large; the population numbers about eight thousand now, and when Mitchell wrote his story it was less than three thousand. People there know one another. But the Kahnawake membership office has no record of Orvis Diabo and has never heard of him. Nor has the reservation's library archive. Nor has Ronald Boyer, a deacon at the St. Francis Xavier Mission Church on the reservation. Now in his mid-seventies, Boyer was a high-steel man himself, helping to erect, among other structures, the Verrazano-Narrows Bridge. Boyer knew Paul Horn, and because of his ministerial work he knows most of the people on the reservation, but he has never heard of Orvis Diabo. None of the Kahnawake asked about this matter had ever even heard of "Orvis" being used as a first name.

If the Diabo character *was* in essence Paul Horn, it's unclear why Mitchell changed his identity or altered other personal details, such as his age (Horn was forty-six at the time of the story, whereas Diabo was said to be fifty-four). It's possible that because Horn was an important union official—and at the time the only Native American to hold such a position in that local—he may have been wary of the attention from a high-profile magazine article. Beyond that, he was a somewhat controversial figure back on the reservation. The Caughnawaga, who had been converted centuries earlier by Jesuits, were mostly Catholic, with a minority of Protestants. But in the early twentieth century they saw a revival of native religious practice, centered on the traditional Iroquois longhouse. The reservation had a main longhouse, and its adherents were ardent in their observance and use of ritual. Horn and several other Caughnawaga established separate longhouses there, however, and these were considered by many to be more of a hobby activity than a true spiritual undertaking, and thus a trivialization of the longhouse tradition.

Unlike the case of Old Mr. Flood or Cockeye Johnny Nikanov, there doesn't seem to be anything in Mitchell's notes or files, or in *The New Yorker*'s archive, to shed light on the Orvis Diabo backstory or on who might have known about it.

On three different occasions in a span of five years, then, Mitchell had either invented key characters or at least blurred their reality. So were any other of his protagonists inventions? Given that Cockeye Johnny was, one is tempted first to turn to Mitchell's 1955 sequel—a longer and equally textured piece about the gypsy culture, entitled "The Beautiful Flower." (Mitchell retitled it "The Gypsy Women" when it was republished years later.) The entertaining account delves deeply into the lives and techniques of the gypsy women who ran sophisticated con games—most notably one they called the *bajour*. And while the piece does reference in passing Cockeye Johnny, it actually was written as a Profile about Daniel J. Campion, a New York Police Department captain who oversaw the Pickpocket and Confidence Squad (and who almost certainly was the model for "Detective John J. Sheehan" in the original story). The gypsy women's story is told entirely through Campion's narration, and he was decidedly a real person—a longtime friend and old newspaper source of Mitchell's, who would continue to see and correspond with him for years afterward. Similarly, the best known of Mitchell's other subjects, both before and after Cockeye Johnny and Mr. Flood—characters like Joe Gould, Ellery Thompson, Mazie Gordon, Lady Olga, and George Hunter—were well known to, or documented by, many others besides Mitchell. His "minor" protagonists, such as Commodore Dutch and Santa Claus Smith, were flesh and blood, too. In any case, Mitchell's remaining papers yield no suggestion that any other of his familiar subjects didn't exist in reality.

However Mitchell had rationalized his approach with the composites, in reality what he was doing was bending the boundaries of non-fiction to the point where these particular stories were more accurately seen as fact-based fiction. And then, just as curiously, he pulled back. Mitchell would always be proud of the Flood, Mohawk, and gypsy stories, especially as to their literary craft and impact. But from his later defensiveness about the Flood trilogy and the fact that he never disclosed what he had done with the Nikanov or Diabo characters, it seems clear that Mitchell carried some regret about taking this tactic as far as he did.

AND WITH THAT, MITCHELL returned to the waterfront and began pulling together a story from threads he had been gathering for many years. "The Bottom of the Harbor," which appeared in *The New Yorker* in the first week of 1951, was a portrait of the waters that surround the city's five boroughs but considered from a sort of upside-down perspective. The picture wasn't pretty, but it made for a dazzling travelogue.

As with "Rats," this story was less about any one human character than it was a portrayal of an entire ecosystem—one that man-made pollution was quickly ruining. It represented another statement on Mitchell's part about what he considered the significant cost of twentieth-century "progress" on quality of life. It also made "Bottom of the Harbor" one of the earlier stories in the mainstream press to warn about the systematic degradation of the natural environment. By this time, health authorities had put the harvesting and consumption of clams and oysters in widespread areas off-limits because of contamination. Meanwhile, certain of the region's fisheries were declining, and entire industries were being put at risk. And as filthy as the water was, Mitchell says, the bottom of the harbor "is dirtier than the water. In most places it is covered with a blanket of sludge that is composed of silt, sewage, industrial wastes and clotted oil." All of this Mitchell conveys in the story's opening pages so as to be unambiguous about his intent.

But having established how appalling these conditions are, Mitchell moves on to describe a marine life that remains stubbornly, defiantly abundant. He dwells on the remarkable symbiosis between man and marine life, such as when he discusses the harbor's robust eel population thriving among the hundreds of shipwrecks littering the bottom. One Sunday afternoon Mitchell tags along with a "rogue" oyster digger, who grew up with the oyster beds and understands when it's safe to harvest them, despite the prohibition against it. The man eventually tongs up five dozen of the shellfish. He opens several that are between four and seven years old, and he eats them. "Every time I eat harbor oysters, my childhood comes floating up from the bottom of my mind," he tells Mitchell.

Mitchell is halfway through the story before he introduces a named character—a state conservation officer named Andrew Zimmer, who is well known to the fishing communities that he is paid to oversee in and around New York. Day and night, Zimmer trolls the watery byways, looking for illegal harvesters and other miscreants. His twenty-eight-foot skiff is unmarked and looks like every other lobster boat out on the water, yet it is familiar enough to all the baymen, who refer to it as the "State Boat." During a break from Zimmer's patrolling one chill morning, he and Mitchell stop at a Sheepshead Bay restaurant for some oyster stew. There he introduces Mitchell to a friend named Leroy Poole, the owner of a party boat, who obsesses about, even dreams about, the harbor. Mitchell uses Poole as a vehicle to bring the story back around to where it began—warning of the despoiling of this outwardly robust yet surprisingly fragile marine environment and how pollution and overfishing are threatening their way of life. As with other of Mitchell's characters, Poole becomes a kind of stand-in for the writer himself. "Sometimes I'm walking along the street, and I wonder why the people don't just stand still and throw their heads back and open their mouths and howl," he complains. Zimmer asks him why. "I'll tell you why," he replies. "On account of the God-damned craziness of everything."

Next for Mitchell was almost a sister piece to "Bottom of the Harbor," in that it dealt with a landmark South Street seafood restaurant that many harbor denizens, especially the workers in and around the Fulton Market, were intimately acquainted with. Sloppy Louie's was operated by its no-nonsense owner, Louis Morino. *The New Yorker* called this story "The Cave" when it appeared in June of 1952, but when it was republished in later collections Mitchell retitled it "Up in the Old Hotel."

A short, stocky man, Morino immigrated to America as a teenager after growing up in a fishing village in the north of Italy, and he worked his way up in the restaurant business. Now in his sixties, "he has an owl-like face—his nose is hooked, his eyebrows are tufted, and his eyes are large and brown and observant," Mitchell writes. "He is white-haired. His complexion is reddish, and his face and the backs of his hands are speckled with freckles and liver spots. He wears glasses with flesh-colored frames. He is bandy-legged, and he carries his left shoulder lower than his right and walks with a shuffling, hipshot, head-up, old waiter's walk. He dresses neatly. He has his suits made by a high-priced tailor in the insurance district, which adjoins the fish-market district."

Sloppy Louie's was a longtime favorite for those connected to the fish trade but also for professionals who worked in nearby office build-ings. It featured fresh seafood cooked simply but impeccably, in a plain, almost refectory-like setting. Mitchell himself had been going there for the better part of a decade. He and Louie were friends, and the restaurant had already made an appearance in his "Old Mr. Flood" trilogy, during the reporting of which Mitchell had several long talks with the restaurateur. Sloppy Louie's occupied the ground floor of a six-story building that fronted the fish-market sheds, and Louie used the second floor for storage and for his waiters to change. Above that, however, the windows to the street were boarded up. And it turns out those upper floors were largely inaccessible inside, as well, because there were no stairs and the only way up involved moving a manual elevator so ancient that no one knew if it *could* be moved or was even safe to try. In a prior life the building had been the Fulton Ferry Hotel, but whatever was in the upper floors constituted a mystery—one that

Mitchell and Louis Morino, one of his favorite talkers,
outside Sloppy Louie's restaurant.

had nagged at Louie for years. The dark space above his establishment amounted to a kind of "cave" that he longed to explore.

Mitchell's Profile begins as a fairly straightforward account of Louie, his life, and his restaurant. But in stopping by one day for breakfast and engaging Louie in conversation, Mitchell learns of the building's curious history—and Louie's obsession with what's contained in those upper floors. So the account gradually shifts to a kind of detective story. In fact, the story is structurally anchored by two protracted monologues by Louie. The first occurs as he recalls an elderly but refined woman he came to know some years before, a Mrs. Frelinghuysen, whose vivid memories transport Louie back in time to prewar New York and eventually link him to one of the city's most venerable families, the Schermerhorns, who, it turns out, still own his building. Once he discovered this fact, Louie recalls, "I went back inside and stood there and thought it over, and the effect it had on me, the simple fact my building was an old Schermerhorn building, it may sound foolish, but it pleased me very much. The feeling I had, it connected me with the past. It connected me with Old New York." The second lengthy monologue, unfolding soon after the first, is Louie's recitation of the history of the building, which he became determined to excavate once he learned its impressive provenance.

Because of the inherent danger in the antiquated and long-unused elevator, which was designed to rise with a rope-and-pulley system, Louie had been unsuccessful at talking anyone else into giving it a try. Now he asks Mitchell if he is game. The natural-born explorer leaps at the chance. With considerable effort, they rouse the ancient elevator to life and access the third-floor reading room of the old hotel. "It was pitch-dark in the room," Mitchell writes. "We stood still and played the lights of our flashlights across the floor and up and down the walls. Everything we saw was covered with dust. There was a thick, black mat of fleecy dust on the floor—dust and soot and grit and lint and slut's wool." There are no treasures evident, just the most banal kind of detritus—bedsprings and stacked bed frames, brass spittoons, empty whiskey and seltzer bottles. Mitchell is keen to continue up to the fourth floor and see if they would have better luck. But Louie, who had hoped to turn up at least some hotel registers or other historical documents, becomes almost despondent in his disappointment. "There's nothing up here," he says. "I don't want to stay up here another minute. Come on, let's go."

"This climax is a tremendous letdown, and it is meant to be," the critic Noel Perrin observed of the story. "They have broken through to the past, and all they find is trivial debris. For once the past had seemed retrievable—but when you reach out to seize it, you find nothing but dust and decay." For Mitchell, whose longing for the past was every bit as strong as Morino's, the ending was also an example of the dark humor he so enjoyed, for in this instance the ultimate joke was on them.

IN A JOURNAL NOTE set down a quarter century after "The Cave" first appeared, the writer provided a rare peek into the kind of dramatic and emotional ignition required to make a Joseph Mitchell story happen. Back in late 1950 or early 1951, he said, he had the notion of doing a Profile about Morino, and he undertook some initial conversations with him to that end. But he eventually began to think better of the project, Mitchell said, since "articles about old restaurants were getting to be pretty old hat, as far as *The New Yorker* was concerned." Then, by happy chance, came the spark.

> Sometime in the winter of 1951, Louie and I made the trip up in the old elevator or hoist. As I remember it, we went only to the third floor, but we may very well have gone up at least one more floor before he decided he had had enough. After Louie and I got out of the cage, I got back in and made a trip up by myself, and, as I remember it, I stopped and got off at every floor. The elevator experience made a deep impression on me and revived my interest in doing the Profile, but nevertheless I decided to postpone working on it for a while. Then, some months later, after thinking about it a good deal off and on, I decided to write

about the trip up in the elevator with Louie and not about Louie per se or the restaurant per se. I decided to leave out what I myself had found out about the upper floors and confine the story entirely to the trip up with Louie.

Beyond revealing much about Mitchell's creative process, this note also demonstrates how Mitchell was quite open to, in essence, editing the experience to suit his purposes—by sharpening the episode's focus and heightening its literary impact. In the same way, "Up in the Old Hotel" is noteworthy for its vivid examples of one of Mitchell's favorite techniques, which he was employing to even greater effect in these later stories: This is to let Louie, his protagonist, declaim in long, expansive monologues.

No doubt that, even as they were enjoying the story, some *New Yorker* subscribers were curious as to how Mitchell could possibly capture such disquisitions, some of which go on for pages. Mitchell, as has been shown, was an intense listener, and beyond that he had an incredible memory. In one journal note Mitchell discussed his "freak memory"—that while on the one hand he never seemed to be able to get down the multiplication tables, he had the ability to "remember conversations word for word." Mitchell felt part of that paradox owed to the fact that a person's speech has a distinct rhythm, which he somehow was able to key in to. Whatever was behind this talent, *New Yorker* contemporaries like Philip Hamburger attested to it. Of course, Mitchell mostly relied on the shorthand notes he took during his lengthy interviews, which he typed into fuller, cleaner form back in his office. In this way he worked like many reporters. Capturing lengthy quotation *was* an art form, unquestionably, but it could be done quite accurately with enough practice.

Like any accomplished nonfiction writer, Mitchell understood and appreciated the raw power of quotation in storytelling. When a character is speaking in a story, there is no one else—not even the author (or so it would seem)—standing between him and the reader. That makes for a strong and visceral connection, one that plugs the reader directly into the character's thinking, emotions, and motivation for action. That's why it is just as important for writers of nonfiction as it is for novelists.

Unlike most other journalists, however, Mitchell routinely stitched together disparate conversations and compressed them into what comes across in the story as a single protracted monologue. That is why the speeches in Mitchell's stories are so unusually long and so seamless. For Mitchell, this was simply a matter of being comfortable forgoing a literal recounting in order to attain a more fundamental truth. "Something that Louie said after we came down from up in the hotel, I might have had him saying while we were up there," Mitchell later would say of this tactic. "I don't think you ought to go around making up quotes, but I do think it's all right to move them around in the chronology." Because he had known Morino for so long and was a regular at the restaurant, it's certain that the speeches in "Hotel" were constructed from multiple conversations over a number of years, even though the story itself turns on a single visit by the writer. "There's a way of being over-precise and over-documentary," Mitchell elaborated. "I don't want to make up anything, but sometimes there are juxtapositions that a writer has to make. Something that's said at the man's table when we're having breakfast, I may quote him when we're out on the boat, but I see nothing wrong in any way about that. I feel a great responsibility as a reporter or as a writer. I want to get it right."

Mitchell's "waterfront" stories were connected by more than a place or a physical theme. In each, the past becomes an almost palpable presence. But in a sense, these excursions were more like warm-ups for a story Mitchell was slowly working on that would go deeper into the past, and in a more surprising way, than any he had done before.

CHAPTER 10

MR. HUNTER

"To TELL YOU THE truth, I'm no great believer in gravestones. To a large extent, I think they come under the heading of what the old preacher called vanity—'vanity of vanities, all is vanity'—and by the old preacher I mean Ecclesiastes. There's stones in here that've only been up forty or fifty years, and you can't read a thing it says on them, and what difference does it make? God keeps His eye on those that are dead and buried the same as He does on those that are alive and walking. When the time comes the dead are raised, He won't need any directions where they're lying. Their bones may be turned to dust, and weeds may be growing out of their dust, but they aren't lost. He knows where they are; He knows the exact where-abouts of every speck of dust of every one of them. Stones rot the same as bones rot, and nothing endures but the spirit."

—From "Mr. Hunter's Grave," 1956

. .

ONE AFTERNOON BACK IN THE SPRING OF 1947, MITCHELL'S WAN-derings took him to the far southern precincts of Staten Island and the tiny community of Sandy Ground. He had heard that the place was founded by free blacks in the middle of the nineteenth century, but he didn't know much about it beyond that. Walking the quiet neighborhood streets, he came upon an elderly African American man sitting on a porch. Mitchell introduced himself and struck up a conversation.

The man was James McCoy, a retired oysterman. He was eighty-four years old. McCoy was orphaned at birth in Norfolk, Virginia, and as a boy he was sent north to work the oyster boats of southern Staten Island. He labored for a couple of dollars a day, said McCoy, who, Mitchell made a mental note, had six fingers on his right hand. It was a tough existence for any youth, especially one without family. As he put it, "You had to make every edge cut that would cut." He used to enjoy raising sweet potatoes, but with years of overplanting you couldn't raise a decent sweet potato in Sandy Ground anymore, a handy little metaphor for the general decline of the place. As for the oysters that afforded him a living, McCoy said he never ate them. But he did like clams.

Who else might I see to learn more about the history of Sandy Ground? Mitchell asked. Look up the minister of the African Methodist Episcopal Zion Church, McCoy suggested. He lives over on Bloomingdale Road, just a few blocks away, where he boards with the head of the church's trustees—a man named George H. Hunter.

Mitchell thanked McCoy. He immediately made the short walk to Hunter's house and knocked on the door. No one was home.

So, instead, Mitchell made his way over to the church's cemetery.

GRAVEYARDS CAN BE FORBIDDING places, to be approached with a certain trepidation if they are approached at all. But in the Southern culture, these are not necessarily the impulses cemeteries arouse. Many Southerners, who as a people seem to possess an organically deeper appreciation of history (and mystery) than the general population does, consider cemeteries less termination points than way stations, emotional touchstones whose inhabitants remain as "alive" as if they were about to stroll out from behind a nearby cedar tree. Certainly Mitchell grew up in such an environment.

He spoke and wrote often, and fondly, of his lifelong attraction to cemeteries, and they pop up so routinely in his stories as to be ancillary characters. He also wrote eloquently about how the customs of his extended family when he was a boy in North Carolina deeply influenced his perspective on cemeteries. Mitchell's clan visited the local churchyards in pleasant, regular pilgrimages after Sunday services;

these sociable outings were comparable to conventional visits with relatives, with the notable exception that, here, the "hosts" were long dead. As such, cemeteries were places the impressionable young Mitchell came to associate with affection and humor and observation; they were much less about death than life. "[E]very time I read the Anna Livia Plurabelle section [of *Finnegans Wake*] I hear the voices of my mother and my aunts as they walk among the graves in old Iona cemetery and it is getting dark," he wrote many years later.

This explains why Mitchell's habitual wanderings when he was an adult took in many cemeteries. And here was yet another reason for his eternal appreciation of New York; the city, great in numberless ways, is one of the world's best for cemetery lovers. There are so many of them, developed over such a long period of time and with person-alities as diverse as the numerous ethnic groups that established them; they represent ever-evolving American history texts. Too, cemetery-trolling was a passion that afforded Mitchell the opportunity to in-dulge numerous of his enthusiasms at once—history and genealogy; geography; architecture; masonry and the decorative arts; and horti-culture. In particular, Mitchell was a great student of wildflowers, and cemeteries, with their uneven caretaking, were ideal places to find beautiful examples of these, as well as their poor cousins, exotic weeds. When he headed off to a cemetery, Mitchell usually had a field guide to plants with him, and he often made notes of what he saw there. If he came across a plant he couldn't find in his guide, he would often snip it and tuck it away to be identified when he got back to his apart-ment and different reference works.

Given its long history and relative (for New York) expanse, Staten Island was one of Mitchell's favorite destinations for cemeteries. That pursuit is what took him to Sandy Ground in the first place.

Now and again over the next few years, Mitchell would return to the island's southern tip and the Rossville–Sandy Ground area. He continued to record the unique flora he found there, but he also began researching the region's history and its genealogy—the centuries of farmers and fishermen who had lived and died along the Arthur Kill, the narrow passage separating Staten Island from New Jersey. These were primarily Dutch and English and Huguenots. And then there was this tiny community, Sandy Ground, which had been colonized a century earlier by free black émigrés from the Eastern Shore of Maryland, who were lured to work the oyster beds then flourishing all around Staten Island. Mitchell consulted local historians and clergy familiar with the area—but only as able. His research was tucked between writing and reporting his "active" stories of that time. At Sandy Ground, Mitchell was doing the kind of exploratory investigation he often engaged in when he was intrigued by a story idea but not sure if it would pan out. With one thing and another, it wouldn't be until early June of 1955 that the writer actually sat down to talk with George Henry Hunter.

The day he did, he found the old man sitting in the front row of the A.M.E. Zion Church, off to himself. It was warm enough already that the church had distributed paper fans throughout the pews, courtesy of a local funeral home. George Hunter at that point was eighty-six years old, dignified, articulate, erect of bearing, and clear of thought. As they sat there, Hunter began to slowly unspool for Mitchell the story of his own life and how it came to be intertwined with the history of Sandy Ground. He told of how he was the son of a slave who had escaped to her freedom in New York State just ahead of the Civil War; how she brought her boy to Sandy Ground at age thirteen; how his stepfather was an oysterman and a drunken brute whom George despised; how he left home to be a cook on a codfish boat, then became a hod carrier and eventually learned the brickmason's trade.

As they talked, Mitchell and Hunter crossed Bloomingdale Road to Hunter's house, a two-story frame dwelling set apart from its neighbors by being so well tended and by the array of decorative lightning rods on the roof. Hunter showed Mitchell around the house and took evident pride in how immaculate it was; long a widower, he did his own cleaning. His own cooking, too. He especially enjoyed baking pies and cakes. He showed off the remains of a devil's food cake he'd baked a few days earlier when he hosted the church choir for dinner. In the pantry was an intact chocolate layer cake; Hunter said the choir ate so much of the main meal that they'd had little room left for his

George Hunter in a portrait by Therese. The Mitchells visited him often in the years after The New Yorker *published "Mr. Hunter's Grave."*

desserts. In the dining room, several ornate placards with religious mottoes hung on the wall. The first read: JESUS NEVER FAILS.

Hunter continued with his personal history: How he had been an alcoholic as a young adult, then beat the affliction and turned his life to the Lord. How he began his own business building and cleaning brick cesspools and made a success of it. How he married the prettiest girl in Sandy Ground, lived contentedly with her for over thirty years, and deprived her of nothing until she died. How he remarried a few years later, again happily, only to see his second wife pass away also. At the time Hunter himself was confined to bed with a bad heart. When his wife was returned to their home for the wake, Hunter's friends carried him in their arms downstairs so he could see her.

By the time that first meeting was over, Mitchell knew he had a viable story about the life and slow death of the Sandy Ground community. And he knew George Hunter would be the vehicle for that story.

From Mitchell's reporting notes, it's known that the writer interviewed Hunter on at least seven different occasions, from that initial meeting, in June 1955, through the spring of 1956. Several times Therese accompanied her husband and made portraits of Hunter, which she later presented to him as a gift. When Mitchell was back for a third interview, on a Sunday in late September, Hunter led the writer on the short walk over to the church cemetery, the oversight of which fell to him as head of the church's board of trustees. Weeds and vines had largely overtaken it, and Hunter carried a sharp hoe to hack the vegetation away from the stones as they went along, grave by grave. Here and there he pointed out key members of the Sandy Ground community and people who had figured prominently in his life. At last they came to a section of the cemetery devoted to Hunter's own family. His two wives were buried there. But the freshest grave belonged to his son, William, who had recently died after a hard life.

By now Mitchell knew he had not only a good story but something much richer—a larger tale about the human impulse to persevere. In being steered by chance to George Hunter almost a decade earlier, Mitchell stumbled on to what would turn out to be one of the most enduring and defining stories of his career. "Mr. Hunter's Grave" appeared in *The New Yorker* on September 22, 1956. In a story of fifteen thousand words, Mitchell managed to pull together almost all the great themes he'd been writing about, and thinking about, for a quarter century.

THE STRUCTURE OF "MR. Hunter's Grave" is deceptively simple, and, but for the title, the early going gives no indication of the sober subjects it will eventually traverse. As with so many of his pieces, Mitchell sets up the story as a visit, and the action, in Joycean fashion, is compressed into the course of a single warm summer afternoon—Mitchell using that third visit as his narrative framework. He opens the story by explaining how his cemetery wanderings brought him to tiny Sandy Ground in the first place, then goes into its history. For more than fifty years the black oystermen had thrived in brutally laborious jobs, and with their success Sandy Ground itself experienced a kind of prosperity. The hamlet developed with much more of a Southern feel and pace than a Northern one. Dozens of tidy white frame homes, neatly built and maintained, arose on spacious lots. People visited one another on inviting front porches. Residents put out large gardens, to feed themselves and to ferry fresh produce—particularly the luscious strawberries the island was known for—to Manhattan's markets. Sandy Ground at that time afforded its residents an almost impossibly edenic life, especially for people of color in a highly segregated world. And it was a life that tended to revolve around the one fixture in the residents' lives other than the oyster beds—the A.M.E. Zion Church.

By the turn of the century, however, the rest of New York began to see what the Sandy Ground oystermen had known for some time: With the explosion in the region's population and its commercial activities, including severe overfishing, the waters in and around New York Harbor were now highly polluted. Yields from the oyster beds atrophied, and questions arose about the safety of the shellfish. Finally, in 1916, in the wake of a typhoid epidemic that was linked to Staten Island oysters, the beds were shut down and the inevitable downward spiral of Sandy Ground began. As its residents scrambled for nonfishing opportunities, the population declined. By the time Mitchell discovered it, Sandy Ground had reached a dilapidated and parlous state. "The way it is now," Hunter laments, "Sandy Ground is just a ghost of its former self. There's a disproportionate number of old people. A good many of the big old rambling houses that used to be full of children, there's only old men and old women living in them now. And you hardly ever see them."

Hunter is one of the last holdouts. Mitchell had been told the octogenarian's memory was still acute, and indeed as he talks he summons long-passed names, stories, and personalities with gripping detail. Mitchell, as is by now his custom, lets Hunter talk for pages of unbroken monologue. As the two men set off for the Sandy Ground cemetery, in the narrative version of their actual graveyard tour, Hunter segues into his personal history, including a spell of alcoholism that was a kind of crucible for him. "I turned into a sot myself," he says. "After I had been drinking several years, I was standing in a grocery store in Rossville one day, and I saw my mother walk past outside on the street. I just caught a glimpse of her face through the store window as she walked past, and she didn't know anybody was looking at her, and she had a horrible hopeless look on her face." About a week later, he continues, he bought a bottle of whiskey and was opening it when something happened.

"I knew what whiskey was doing to me, and yet I couldn't stop drinking it. I tore the stamp off the bottle and pulled out the cork, and got ready to take a drink, and then I remembered the look on my mother's face, and then a peculiar thing happened. The best way I can explain it, my gorge rose. I got mad at myself, and I got mad at the world. Instead of taking a drink, I poured the whiskey on the ground and smashed the bottle on a rock, and stood up and walked out of the woods. And I never drank another drop. I wanted to many a time, many and many a time, but I tightened my jaw against myself, and I stood it off. When I look back, I don't know how I did it, but I stood it off, I stood it off."

Embracing religion, the newly sober young man would go on to become active in the A.M.E. Zion Church, memorize much of the Bible, and engage ministers in Talmudic contemplations on the meanings of certain passages. ("We discuss what I call the mysterious verses, the ones that if you could just understand them they might explain everything—why we're put here, why we're taken away—but they go down too deep; you study them over and over, and you go down as deep as you can, and you still don't touch bottom.") His cesspool business prospered, he had the long marriage to a woman named Celia, and they had their son, Billy.

At this point in the story, subject and interlocutor arrive at the cemetery. As they do, Mitchell's slow reveal of Hunter's life darkens considerably. Celia dies of cancer, as does his second wife, Edith. Hunter then opens up about Billy. As a young man, Billy joined the family business and got married, and Hunter relates how proud all this made him. But then Billy began to drink. At first, recalling his own battle, George Hunter stifled his worry and said nothing. But in time, as Billy sank deeper into alcoholism, his father tried to intervene. "I asked him to stop, and I begged him to stop, and I did all I could, went to doctors for advice, tried this, tried that, but he wouldn't stop. It wasn't exactly he wouldn't stop, he couldn't stop." Finally Billy, too, was diagnosed with cancer; he died a year before the story takes place. Hunter recalls the funeral service and the beautiful floral wreath that marked his son's grave and then later coming across the wreath as the flowers were dying. With that, Hunter reaches into his wallet and takes out a patch of fabric, which he had retrieved from the wreath. Unfolding a ribbon, he shows it to Mitchell. Inscribed on it, in gold letters, are the words BELOVED SON.

Finally the two men reach his family's plot, which is far better tended than the rest of the graveyard. He points out Celia's grave. Edith's stone is nearby. Mitchell can see that Hunter has put his own name on this second stone; only the final date remains to be carved into it. He tells Mitchell it was his intention to be buried in the same grave with Edith—not next to her, but literally in the same spot, his casket interred just above hers. He goes on to explain that as ground had become more precious, he had begun to encourage the practice of using the same burial site for two caskets. ("That's perfectly legal," Hunter says, "and a good many cemeteries are doing it nowadays.") The process merely requires that the initial grave be dug eight feet deep instead of six, leaving room above it for a second, later casket. But because Hunter was indisposed with his bad heart when Edith died, he had relied on others for the arrangements. He made the cemetery's gravedigger, John Henman, promise he would dig Edith's grave eight feet deep. Henman said he would. Thus Hunter ordered the gravestone, with both names.

Here is how Mitchell has Hunter conclude the story:

"Well, one day about a year later I was talking to John Henman, and something told me he hadn't done what he had promised to do, so I had another man come over here and sound the grave with a metal rod, and just as I had suspected, John Henman had crossed me up; he had only gone six feet down. He was a contrary old man, and set in his ways, and he had done the way he wanted, not the way I wanted. He had always dug graves six feet down, and he couldn't change. That didn't please me at all. It outraged me. So, I've got my name on the stone on this grave, and it'll look like I'm buried in this grave."

He took two long steps, and stood on the next grave in the plot.

"Instead of which," he said, "I'll be buried over here in this grave."

He stooped down, and pulled up a weed. Then he stood up, and shook the dirt off the roots of the weed, and tossed it aside.

"Ah, well," he said, "it won't make any difference."

"Mr. Hunter" is a moving-enough story on its face, but its true power and enduring appeal owe to the fact that it is such an affecting allegory, on mortality specifically and the human condition generally. "He knew that everything had fallen apart in his lifetime, the [Sandy Ground] estates had gone to ruin and families had disappeared," Mitchell recalled. "He looked at it in a very worldly, sad way. I couldn't have looked for that man and found him." Or as he observed to Norman Sims in talking about "Mr. Hunter" more than thirty years after it appeared, "The revelations that keep coming from his mind astonish me. I think, my God, here's Lear. Here's Lear on Bloomingdale Road in Staten Island!"

It took Mitchell many visits to receive those revelations and amass the trove of detail that went into the story's soliloquies. Part of that investment was Mitchell establishing a deep bond (indeed, a genuine friendship that lasted until Hunter's own death) with his subject, getting their relationship to a level of comfort where the older man would speak without self-consciousness. But part of the time involved the reporter's search for what Mitchell often described as the "revealing remark." "I couldn't really write about anybody until they spoke what I consider 'the revealing remark' or the revealing anecdote or the thing that touched them," Mitchell would explain. "If you read that Profile of Mr. Hunter, he tells in there about his mother, about seeing her in the window of a store one time. She was passing in the street. He saw her face and how sad it was. By seeing it in that way, he saw it in an unfamiliar juxtaposition that revealed something to him. I've often deliberately tried to find those things. It's not in the way a psychoanalyst does, I'm sure. But you're trying to report, at the beginning without knowing it, the unconscious as well as the consciousness of a man or woman. . . . Once I had what I considered the revealing remark, I could use that to encourage them to talk more about that aspect of their lives. They were able to talk, like Mr. Hunter could talk about his first wife's death, about his son's death, about his stepfather who he hated and who I think hated him. That way I could go far deeper into the man's life than I could any other way. It isn't necessary to fabricate anything if you have patience. In my case, it wasn't patience, because I was genuinely interested in finding out these things."

As he had with Louie Morino and other of his protagonists, Mitchell spliced together Hunter's speeches from related segments of these multiple conversations. Spending so many hours with his subject, Mitchell was not only learning about his history but also absorbing his patterns of speech. By weaving these initially disjointed remarks into long monologues, Mitchell was creating a more powerful narrative driver. The notes for "Mr. Hunter's Grave" provide insight into how he did this. Consider an important point that occurs halfway through the story, when Hunter relates his mother's slave background. The following three Hunter quotations come from three different interviews:

> *My grandmother was a slave and my mother was a slave. My mother was five years old when her mother was sold and she never saw her again, never saw her or heard from her. She was*

sold to some man in Georgia. My mother was living in Alexandria, Virginia, when she ran away and came north. She used to say they gave her one pair of shoes a year and if they wore out she had to go barefoot, snow on the ground or not.

My mother was a slave and her mother was a slave. My mother's name was Martha Jennings, she was born in the Shenandoah Valley, Virginia. It's likely she took the name of the people who owned her. . . . My mother worked for her mistress, took care of her. They went on a visit to Alexandria, Virginia, and that's where she ran away, I don't know who helped her or how, but she finally landed up in Ossining.

My mother was eighty-eight when she died. Martha Jennings was her maiden name.

And here is a portion of Hunter's speech in the story, constructed from the above passages as well as from additional details about Martha Jennings that Mitchell learned along the way:

To tell you the truth, my mother was born in slavery. Her name was Martha, Martha Jennings, and she was born in the year 1849. Jennings was the name of the man who owned her. He was a big farmer in the Shenandoah Valley in Virginia. He also owned my mother's mother, but he sold her when my mother was five years old, and my mother never saw or heard of her again. . . . Just before the Civil War, when my mother was eleven or twelve, the wife of the man who owned her went to Alexandria, Virginia, to spend the summer, and she took my mother along to attend to her children. Somehow or other, my mother got in with some people in Alexandria who helped her run away. Some antislavery people. She never said so in so many words, but I guess they put her on the Underground Railroad. Anyway, she wound up in what's now Ossining, New York, only then it was called the village of Sing Sing, and by and by she married my father.

In the main, the source material for the thrust of Hunter's speeches is there in Mitchell's notes. Then again, judging only from those notes, the speeches were essentially re-imaginations, streamlining and liberally embroidering the original quotations. So just how much license *did* Mitchell take? It's hard to say with any certainty. For one thing, we don't know whether Mitchell's saved notes reflected Hunter's literal speech—or even whether they were intended to. Perhaps they were more like lengthy reminders of what the subject was talking about at the time, which Mitchell always intended to flesh out from memory. (Adept as he was at note-taking, Mitchell wasn't a human tape recorder, and he wouldn't have transcribed literally *everything* Hunter said in any case.) We also don't know whether some of Mitchell's notes for "Mr. Hunter's Grave" were destroyed or lost or simply haven't surfaced yet.

Still, Mitchell's reporting materials raise other important questions. There are no references to some of the story's most philosophical passages, such as Hunter's observation that "I'm no great believer in gravestones. . . . When the time comes the dead are raised, [God] won't need any directions where they're lying," or when Hunter discusses the "mysterious verses" of biblical prophecy, where no matter how deeply you plumb "you still don't touch bottom." (In one interview note, Hunter does talk about reading Proverbs, however, and he allows that in "some parts of the Bible, I'm all at sea.") Nor, for that matter, is there any record in the notes of Hunter's "revealing remark" about seeing his mother in the store window. These omissions, of course, don't prove Hunter *didn't* say them; they only prove a mystery.

Then, too, the notes reveal that while the key events in "Mr. Hunter's Grave" did happen, Mitchell sometimes altered their circumstances, as he did in telling Louie Morino's story. For example, one of the clerics Mitchell consulted about the area's history was the Rev. Raymond Brock, rector of St. Luke's Episcopal Church in Rossville.

Brock was very familiar with the A.M.E. Zion Church and talked to Mitchell about George Hunter. While Mitchell was preparing his story, he asked Brock if he could set their meeting in St. Luke's Cemetery, which was one of the graveyards Mitchell knew from his early visits. Brock agreed that would make for a better read and gave his permission, and indeed in the story it is Brock, not James McCoy, who steers Mitchell to Hunter. In another instance, according to his notes, Mitchell first came across the BELOVED SON ribbon while in Hunter's house on his second visit there; it was spread atop a bureau in his bedroom. On a table beside Hunter's bed lay his late son's wallet. While it's possible that Hunter had for a time carried the ribbon in his own wallet, it doesn't appear he pulled it out for Mitchell in the poignant manner the writer described.

What does it all mean? Especially in light of the license Mitchell admitted taking with his characters' dialogue, one cannot compare the "Mr. Hunter" notes to the finished story without concluding that there is a generous dollop of Mitchell himself in Hunter's speeches. While Mitchell stayed faithful to the spirit and tang of Hunter's observations, it seems clear that much of the old man's language was Mitchell's own.

Of course, today's *New Yorker*, or any mainstream publication, would never knowingly permit such liberties with quotation; they would take a dimmer-yet view of composites being billed as "nonfiction." But transparency in reporting is a relatively young ethic; it developed gradually, primarily across the second half of the twentieth century, as journalism evolved from a workaday job to a more respected profession, and many of the early *New Yorker* nonfiction writers— having come directly from anything-goes newspaper city rooms— could be quite creative in their latitude.

"At *The New Yorker*, and in nonfiction writing in general, the lines between fact and invention had traditionally been quite blurry," writes Ben Yagoda, an authority on long-form journalism and author of a comprehensive history of *The New Yorker*. The magazine had run composites prior to *Mr. Flood*, for instance, and in 1952—just three years after Mitchell's Mohawk story—his running mate Liebling pub-

lished a multipart Profile of one "Col. John R. Stingo," a colorful race-
track figure who in real life was a *New York Enquirer* columnist named
James A. Macdonald. Liebling invested so much of his own words and
worldview into Stingo that when the series was published as a book
entitled *The Honest Rainmaker,* the jacket copy conceded that it was
difficult to say "how much . . . is gospel and how much is unashamedly
apocryphal." Even deep into William Shawn's reign as editor, the
magazine endured several high-profile instances in which nonfiction
writers were shown to have taken the kinds of liberties that had been
commonplace in *The New Yorker*'s adolescence.

Those early *New Yorker* tactics definitely included conflation and
"sweetening" of speeches. For instance, one of the earliest of the magazine's standout journalists, Morris Markey, wrote long dispatches
that quoted his subjects at suspicious length. Harold Ross openly gave
his writers a wide berth on this score, as long as the speeches retained
the owner's spirit and context and didn't insult common sense. But
even Ross had his limit. Yagoda relates a 1948 incident in which Ross
criticized a Joel Sayre article for an improbably long speech of several
thousand words. "[This] manifestly is not quote at all," wrote Ross,
"but just Sayre writing. He's ostensibly quoting one of his women
characters. It doesn't sound any more like a woman talking than I
sound like Betty Grable."

There's one other pertinent distinction in such examples as George
Hunter or Louie Morino: These were friendly and flattering portraits,
in which, it can be argued, no real harm was done with the rearranging
and massaging of the protagonists' speeches. The same would not be
true if the subject was controversial or the treatment sharp, which
would raise the suggestion of personal bias on the part of the writer,
but such pieces were not in Mitchell's repertoire. In a philosophical
sense, one might compare how Mitchell approached a story like "Mr.
Hunter's Grave" to a present-day filmmaker attempting to faithfully
depict a historical event—but within a two-hour window. In the service of practicality and dramatic impact, the director might consoli-
date characters, compress events, or alter known speeches in their
specifics, if not in thrust. The difference is that the movie would be

characterized as being "based on" or "inspired by" real events; "Mr. Hunter's Grave," like all of Mitchell's later *New Yorker* work, was simply tagged as nonfiction.

Mitchell certainly didn't think there was anything malign or unprofessional about what he was doing. As he said, he truly believed the latitude taken with a character's speech and certain surroundings were in the service of a greater good. The core "truth" of the story was important; its interior factuality was not.

Pantheon Books editor-in-chief Dan Frank, who worked with Mitchell near the end of his life and who is an unabashed Mitchell fan, offered an insightful view of the writer's approach to his characters, including their monologues. "Yes, there was something literary or artificial in Joe's depictions. But that did not make his portraits less faithful," he said. "The most contrived aspect (at least to my ears) of course were the lengthy speeches that he would give his characters. They are simply too well constructed, with too many sentences that only Joseph Mitchell could have written. But if he had gone the opposite route and been faithful to their actual speech, one would be on the slope toward oral history—and also would have undermined Joe's intent to infuse these figures with the 'uniqueness,' the particularity that he saw in them."

Speech is character. In an age before the ubiquity and national reach of television flattened out our regional dialects and homogenized our usages, Mitchell managed to capture the unique flavor and patois of his subjects. Further, surviving letters to him from Hunter and such other late Mitchell subjects as Ellery Thompson and Daniel Campion tend to reinforce that the writer accurately captured their individualistic expressions in their stories. Nor did any letters appear to dispute the fundamental accuracy of what he quoted them saying, which is arguably the bottom line. There's no apparent record of any of his characters objecting to how they were quoted. They appreciated that they came across on the page as articulate, with the common digressions and tics of speech cleaned up, and that Mitchell had faithfully conveyed what they had said. Mitchell's subjects recognized themselves in their speeches.

———

LITERARY LICENSE ASIDE, THERE is no question that the success of "Mr. Hunter's Grave" owes much to the fact that, as with many of his protagonists, there was so much of Joseph Mitchell in George Hunter to begin with. In time, Mitchell came to realize that this synchronicity—this overlap of his own interests and outlooks with those of his subjects—was no accident, that to some extent he was self-selecting, albeit in a way that allowed the writer to bring greater acuity to the work. "If you find [a subject] you have no connection with, you start out with a laborious matter right at the beginning," Mitchell said. "The insights you have about yourself *may* contribute to the insights you have about the other person, or they may not. There is a structure there of looking for an insight. Mr. Hunter could not have been out of a background any more different than mine—well, anyway, our backgrounds were pretty different. But I could understand him and he could understand me. Gradually, I got out of him what I needed, but you never know."

What Mitchell "got out of him" was a story that resonated with readers on all the fundamental levels that literature must. Indeed, in telling the story of Sandy Ground and George Hunter, "Mr. Hunter's Grave" is full of allusions of mortality and time passing, some pronounced—it does take place in a cemetery, after all—but others quite subtle, such as when Mitchell relates Hunter's offhand observation that bones left over from the dinner table make excellent fertilizer for his rosebushes. He takes pains to note the slow deterioration of Sandy Ground's formerly proud houses; the wilting flowers of Billy Hunter's funeral wreath; the eroding features of even relatively recent stone grave markers; and the weeds, of course, everywhere overtaking those tombstones. Man simply cannot keep up, and at the end of the day it's all out of our hands, anyway. "We don't know what the hell is going on around us," as Mitchell would later explain, "whether we're being propelled or whether we think we have free will about making our own lives, or whether we're like mice in a laboratory. We think we can see through things and we may be directed to see through things."

The literary merit of "Mr. Hunter" was appreciated immediately upon publication. A typical observation—and one Mitchell was especially glad to get—came from the respected British critic John Davenport, who sent the author this handwritten note:

> I've been reading your pieces in *The New Yorker* for a good many years; recently, too few of them, it seemed to me. Now in the issue of September 22nd comes 'Mr. Hunter's Grave.' It is wonderfully, superlatively good. I would not inflict fan-mail on you except for reasons of pure vanity: I knew it was yours before I'd finished the first column on page 50. There was no need to check the signature on page 89. [At the time, *The New Yorker* still ran bylines at the end of articles instead of at the beginning.] It makes me happy to think that I introduced Dylan Thomas to your work with *McSorley's Wonderful Saloon.* He had a great admiration for you, as you must know, for he told me he had met you; a pleasure denied me, though we have several common friends. With many thanks. . . .

Should the reputation of "Mr. Hunter's Grave" suffer for the license Mitchell employed in telling it? As with any aspect of art, that is up to the appraiser. What can be said with a degree of confidence is that had Mitchell (or anyone else, for that matter) written the piece adhering to what Hunter literally said and in the rigidly accurate sequence in which events occurred, the result would have been a compelling human-interest story but not much more. With the imagination he applied, Mitchell produced an enduring piece of literature, the kind of work without which we'd be the poorer.

Several months after "Mr. Hunter's Grave" was published, its protagonist sent Mitchell a letter about "the wonderful story you gave in the magazine *New Yorker.*" For weeks afterward, George Hunter said, people were writing him and stopping by his home to congratulate him. Friends couldn't get original copies of that issue and so were passing them around to one another. Hunter's penmanship is tall and precise, and his manner is as dignified but direct as the speech Mitch-

ell captured in the story. After his opening pleasantries, he comes to
the real point of his letter.

> We are observing the 106th anniversary of our church next
> Sunday, Dec. 16th, '56, from 10 o'clock. . . . We have pastors
> from every church to speak. So I and our congregation will be
> looking for you, and the people who know about that kind of
> business tell me that you were well paid for that story, but that
> is none of my business. The only thing I am interested in is my
> church and I feel that you should give the church a nice dona-
> tion. Please do not count me anything.
>   May God bless you and your family.
>
>   Sincerely yours,
>   George H. Hunter

Two weeks later, *The New Yorker* sent the A.M.E. Zion Church a
check for fifty dollars.

CHAPTER 11

A RIVER IN A DREAM

I OFTEN FEEL DRAWN to the Hudson River, and I have spent a lot of time through the years poking around the part of it that flows past the city. I never get tired of looking at it; it hypnotizes me. I like to look at it in midsummer, when it is warm and dirty and drowsy, and I like to look at it in January, when it is carrying ice. I like to look at it when it is stirred up, when a northeast wind is blowing and a strong tide is running—a new-moon tide or a full-moon tide—and I like to look at it when it is slack. It is exciting to me on weekdays, when it is crowded with ocean craft, harbor craft, and river craft, but it is the river itself that draws me, and not the shipping, and I guess I like it best on Sundays, when there are lulls that sometimes last as long as half an hour, during which, all the way from the Battery to the George Washington Bridge, nothing moves upon it, not even a ferry, not even a tug, and it becomes as hushed and dark and secret and remote and unreal as a river in a dream.

—From "The Rivermen," 1959

· ·

WITH MITCHELL'S SUCCESS, HE AND THERESE OCCASIONALLY discussed finding a bigger apartment—one where, at the very least, they could have their own bedroom. But invariably after looking at other places they decided to stay put. They preferred familiarity to comfort, even if it came with complications. For instance, Nora, by now a teenager, sometimes brought home boyfriends. But her home was such a cracker box that her parents went to almost comic lengths to be inconspicuous. Elizabeth, eight years younger than Nora, had her own room to disappear into. For his part, Mitchell might go off to Nora's bedroom and turn in early. That left Therese, who would typically sit in the cramped kitchen (separated from the living room by only a swinging door), trying to mind her own business. But if this was a steady boyfriend and Therese knew they desired more privacy, she would closet herself in the bathroom and, using the commode for a chair, read for hours. "I really don't know how they did it," said Nora.

Therese Mitchell, daughter of Scandinavian immigrants, and Joseph Mitchell, who could trace his North Carolina roots to the Revolutionary War, brought markedly different yet complementary styles to their parenting. Whereas Therese was a true free spirit, her husband was regimented, the train conductor, the benign disciplinarian. Therese would "saunter down the street whistling 'Bloody Mary Is the Girl I Love,'" recalled Nora, while Mitchell would shush his daughters' speaking ill of someone lest others on the crowded sidewalk overhear. "He was in charge of Christmas cards, hanging pictures, seeing that our homework was done and making final decisions on all major purchases," Nora wrote. "She figured out tips, created elaborate recipes, avoided PTA meetings. . . ."

Aside from his book research, Mitchell generally didn't bring his work home, which he considered a place reserved for family and friends. He certainly never wrote there. As with all parents, Therese and Joseph Mitchell made their most important imprint on their children with the example of their own relationship. Nora and Elizabeth grew up witnessing the small, easy rituals that suggest a contented marriage is also a satisfying friendship. "Sixteen (or twenty or forty) years with the wrong woman," Joseph would sing as he brought Therese coffee or kissed her in the tiny kitchen. "It's good enough for the likes of you" was her invariable response. After dinner they often read, he sitting on one end of the living room couch, she lying across the length of it, her feet in his lap.

The Mitchell daughters were decidedly products of their parents' combined temperaments and talents. Firstborn Nora had the bigger personality; she was quicker to act on an impulse and more rebellious as an adolescent than her younger sister would be. While Elizabeth was quieter, she had her father's gift of observation and missed very little. City kids, they were both intelligent and intuitive, and they went to a series of excellent (mostly private) schools in New York (although Elizabeth's high school years were spent at a boarding school in Pennsylvania). They had less interest in grades, however, than in the tumultuous world around them. As such, both grew up with strong social consciences that would eventually inform their careers—Nora as a probation officer specializing in juvenile offenders, and Elizabeth in her work with those suffering from severe mental illness.

Their father was as fastidious in his domestic habits as he was in his writing. He cleaned fruits and vegetables with soap before preparing them. He washed his raincoat and seersucker suits in the shower. He whisked the lint off his daughters' clothes before letting them go outside. He donned a coat and hat to take out the garbage. "He spent hours brushing his teeth and flossing and gargling and carrying on," Nora recalled. He reflexively straightened pictures on the wall if they were crooked. He loved vacuuming the family's small apartment, and nothing quite set him on edge like a dirty bathtub.

Mitchell's daily routine was equally tidy. Each morning he would sit on the couch and spread the day's papers on the floor before him, reading with a razor blade in his hand to slice out those stories he wanted to save. He always polished his shoes and he always made the family breakfast. When the girls were young, he always walked them to school; Nora recalls that for several years their route took them past a women's detention center, sometimes as the new arrivals were just rolling up from night court. He would return from work at 6:00 P.M.—often as not, on the dot. "He was so canonical that his key in the lock usually coincided with the Church of the Ascension bells, and as a result I usually burst out crying whenever I hear church bells," Nora once wrote.

They adored living in the Village, with its quirky neighborhoods and byways, its funny angles, its shops and clubs and churches and family restaurants and dives all coexisting contentedly. It truly *was* a village then; neighbors knew everyone and watched out for one another, especially the children. But the Mitchells took full advantage of the wider city's cultural offerings. One weekend they might visit the Museum of Modern Art and the Russian Tea Room; another would be the Cloisters; another would see them traipse off to Staten Island in search of spring wildflowers.

He "was more attached to home and place than anyone I ever knew or heard of," said Nora. "He knew the significance and provenance of

Mitchell with young Nora and Elizabeth in Central Park.

every arrow and pottery shard, the names of every native weed, flower, snake, bird and fish, the family names and serpentine connections of everyone within fifty miles. . . ." After Mitchell joined *The New Yorker* and had an increasingly pliant work schedule, his homecomings to Fairmont became longer and more frequent. That continued after Nora and Elizabeth were born. The family spent a sizable portion of each summer in North Carolina, usually traveling south by train—an exciting adventure in itself—and occupying their own compartment with double-deck berths. At other times of the year Mitchell would go to Fairmont by himself, to talk over the family business and simply to stay connected. "He . . . spoke to his family every Sunday [on the telephone], wrote and received hundreds of letters and always knew if the camellias were blooming, if the tobacco had been put in and if the tomatoes were still coming," Nora said.

After enough trips, Mitchell's daughters began to understand that their father's polite patience and courtly manner were earmarks of a Southern gentleman. But he also had an irritable side, and he made no effort to hide it from his family. As was evident from his stories, there was much about the modern world that rankled him. "He generally thought people were pretty horrible," Nora remembered. "He hated the board of education. He hated psychologists. He had a big list of people he didn't like." And when he *was* forced to speak of these distasteful human beings, a favorite Mitchellism was "goddamned son of a bitch"—as in, "Goddamned sons of bitches let their dogs go to the bathroom all over the sidewalk and then go home and listen to *Vivaldi!*" or "Goddamned sons of bitches ruin good fish by putting *paprika* on it!" Mitchell was frequently thwarted by machinery, and Nora particularly recalled one occasion where he kicked a balky gumball machine in a subway station. "I told him . . . how that traumatized me," she added, "and he apologized and felt terrible."

Mitchell's professional acquaintances sometimes felt his ire, as well. When his British publisher brought out *The Bottom of the Harbor,* Mitchell was understandably peeved that the word "harbor" was changed to the British spelling "harbour" on the cover and jacket copy yet the American spelling was retained throughout the text. He surmised, no doubt correctly, that the British publisher had simply photographically reproduced the American-edition text to save money. But Mitchell found the naked inconsistency maddening and insulting to readers. "As I said, either 'harbour' or 'harbor,' it doesn't make the slightest difference to me," he vented in a letter to his agent, "but God damn it, not both."

Now and again friends also saw the edgier, impetuous, even darker side of Mitchell. All his life he enjoyed socializing over drinks, and his list of favorite New York haunts was long—Costello's, McSorley's, Bleeck's, Chumley's, the White Horse, the Cortile, and many others. There were times when Mitchell would get so deep into his cups that he might forswear drink for months or even years. When he *was* drinking, however, Mitchell generally kept his wits about him—but not always, and what might happen then was anyone's guess. A friend recounted a night in the late thirties or early forties when Mitchell suddenly appeared at a favorite bar near the Village, walked without a word past several acquaintances to the back of the room, sat in a chair facing the wall, and loudly began singing the hymn "There Is a Green Hill Far Away." The owner, who knew Mitchell well, came back and told him to cut it out because he was beginning to startle the other patrons. "Listen, Nick," Mitchell snapped, "when I feel like I want to sing a hymn I'm gonna sing that hymn and I'm gonna sing it the way I want to sing it. This time I got the urge to sing a hymn to myself, so I sung it." The owner told Mitchell he was crazy. Mitchell agreed—and said what he usually said when so accused, that it was all because, as a boy on the farm, he'd been hit on the head by a cow.

Then again, Mitchell when drinking could abruptly turn raucous or vulgar, irritable or sometimes simply maudlin—could "suddenly become a different person," according to Philip Hamburger. He recalled once when he and Mitchell and several friends were in a bar, and had been there awhile. In the course of the evening's conversation, a fellow *New Yorker* staffer—"a very fine writer, but a son of a bitch," Hamburger said—pronounced that a woman of their mutual acquaintance was ugly. This affront enraged Mitchell, and he loudly berated the man in front of everyone. "The very notion that anybody would call a woman ugly made Joe wild," Hamburger said. At other times, excessive drinking prompted Mitchell to hold a room with lengthy soliloquies from *Ulysses* or *Finnegans Wake*.

By all accounts, such mischief abated considerably once Mitchell became a father and reined in the late-night salooning. Besides, by this point the writer was quietly dealing with a more pronounced concern than the occasional bender among friends. From his journal notes, it's clear Mitchell at this time was experiencing regular bouts of depression, which would plague him, in varying degrees of severity, for the rest of his life. Mitchell had always been prone to melancholia and tended to have a glass-half-empty perspective on things, anyway. ("You know, you're a pretty gloomy guy," Harold Ross once told him.) But what he was beginning to experience now was clinical depression. The predisposition to depression ran in his family, and Mitchell's distress over the changes transforming New York only served to fuel the attacks. Over the years his doctors prescribed a number of medications to mitigate the condition. These worked well enough for Mitchell to mask his depression from his daughters, who used to tease their father about his well-known hypochondria but didn't realize until years later what a serious and chronic illness he battled for so long.

Indeed, except for the stray outburst triggered by a dirty bathtub, Mitchell's children remember kindness and patience as the central qualities of their relationship with him. Nora recalled an example from when she was college age. After receiving a classical education at the Lenox School, a private and then all-girls prep academy on the Upper East Side that didn't have many Greenwich Village kids, Nora went on to Vassar. But after a year there, her indifference to exams caught up with her and she dropped out. She dreaded what her father might say when he came to retrieve her, but there was no ranting or recrimination. Instead, Mitchell simply quoted Ecclesiastes about the race not going to the swift or the battle to the strong, "but time and chance happeneth to them all." And that, Nora said, "is generally the way he reacted to our vicissitudes"—not with condemnation but with patient support.

IN APRIL OF 1959, Mitchell published the last of his stories centered on the region's waterways, "The Rivermen." The story related the life, history, and traditions of the little community of Edgewater, New Jersey, which was wedged into a narrow strip of land between the Hudson River and the Palisades, just across from the George Washington

Bridge. Edgewater had long been connected to the shad-fishing industry, and it still was, though it was down to only several dozen shad fishermen and represented a way of life that was receding like an ebb tide. In the Edgewater of Mitchell's telling, modern commerce is literally crowding out the past, seen symbolically in the large aluminum factory that has been built in a U-shape in order to preserve Edgewater's ancient cemetery; indeed, the only way to access the latter is to go through the gates of the former. The critic Noel Perrin, writing an appreciation of Mitchell many years later, would note his "genius for finding real-life metaphors," citing as an example this passage from "The Rivermen," which focuses on the rosebushes growing in that graveyard:

Coarse, knotty, densely tangled rosebushes grow on several plots, hiding graves and gravestones. The roses that they produce are small and fragile and extraordinarily fragrant, and have waxy red hips almost as big as crab apples. Once, walking through the cemetery, I stopped and talked with an old woman who was down on her knees in her family plot, setting out some bulbs at the foot of a grave, and she remarked on the age of the rosebushes. "I believe some of the ones in here now were in here when I was a young woman, and I am past eighty," she said. "My mother—this is her grave—used to say there were rosebushes just like these all over this section when she was a girl. Along the riverbank, beside the roads, in people's yards, on fences, in waste places. And she said *her* mother—that's her grave over there—told her she had heard from *her* mother that all of them were descended from one bush that some poor uprooted woman who came to this country back in the Dutch times potted up and brought along with her. There used to be a great many more in the cemetery than there are now—they overran everything—and every time my mother visited the cemetery she would stand and look at them and kind of laugh. She thought they were a nuisance. All the same, for some reason of her own, she admired them, and enjoyed looking at them.

'I know why they do so well in here,' she'd say. 'They've got good strong roots that go right down into the graves.'"

That final image is strongly redolent of "Mr. Hunter's Grave," which "The Rivermen" has much in common with. As he did with George Hunter, Mitchell centers his story on a spry, colorful, and colorfully spoken, town elder—in this case, seventy-four-year-old shad fisherman Harry Lyons—to capture a way of life that the author reveres for its simplicity, community, and constancy (the rhythms of the annual fishing cycle), as well as for the healthy symbiosis between mankind and nature. At one point Mitchell describes a traditional shad bake, a community picnic in which the large fish are boned, butterflied, nailed to white-oak planks, and mop-basted with butter as they broil slowly over open coals—and in so doing again reminds us that food is as vital to the memory's nourishment as to the body's. In that sense "The Rivermen" is a strongly romantic story, and pleasant, and a reader can almost feel the afternoon sunshine as he joins Mitchell on the deck of Lyons's shad barge and reawakens the past.

In the end, however, "The Rivermen" is perhaps even more elegiac than "Mr. Hunter's Grave," to the extent that it is overtly a lamentation, a discourse on the end of things. That strain is woven throughout the piece, but Mitchell nakedly drives it home in the story's conclusion. In fact, he delights in beginning this final section with a particularly vivid example of his graveyard humor. As young girls skip rope along the town's riverbank, they sing a nonsense song: "The worms crawl in/The worms crawl out/They eat your guts/And spit them out." Soon after, Mitchell relates a scene in which one of Lyons's friends, Joe Hewitt, who is visiting at the time, studies a photograph that Lyons has tacked up in his shad barge. The picture shows a large group of Fulton Market fishmongers at one of Lyons's shad bakes. It was taken only a few years prior, but Hewitt—in the photo himself—remarks on how many of the men have since died. His gloomy commentary becomes a veritable litany. "This one's alive," he says. "This one's dead. This one's alive. At least, I haven't heard he's dead. . . . This man's alive. So's this man. Dead. Dead. Dead. Three in a row. Alive. Alive. Alive. Dead. Alive. . . ."

The following spring, Little, Brown published a book that collected Mitchell's six waterfront pieces: "The Rats on the Waterfront," "Dragger Captain," "The Bottom of the Harbor," "Up in the Old Hotel," "Mr. Hunter's Grave," and "The Rivermen." Entitled *The Bottom of the Harbor*, the book was received warmly, even rapturously. "The memorable things in *The Bottom of the Harbor* are the portraits of men of strong character," Brooks Atkinson wrote in *The New York Times Book Review*. "Mr. Mitchell gives them his undivided attention. He does not criticize or evaluate them; he does not patronize them in any way. . . . If this book were a collection of feature articles, the character and technique of the author would not be a matter of importance. But *The Bottom of the Harbor* is literature." Half a century later, many critics still consider *The Bottom of the Harbor* the apotheosis of Mitchell's career, the point at which a master in complete control of his work has found the timeless themes equal to his talent.

When *Harbor* appeared in early 1960, Mitchell was fifty-one years old. Throughout the decade of the fifties, he published only five stories in *The New Yorker*, albeit some of the most consequential pieces he would ever write. During that span, the protective cocoon of *The New Yorker* meant he hadn't had to navigate many professional changes—with one significant exception.

Harold Ross, founding editor of *The New Yorker* and the man who had recruited Mitchell, appreciated both his dark moods and humor, and encouraged his idiosyncratic subject matter, died from lung cancer at the end of 1951. For almost two decades, Ross had made a point of staying connected to Mitchell, and the writer found the editor's mix of wit, empathy, and constant encouragement energizing. On one occasion Mitchell derived particular pleasure from telling Ross something about his own family that the editor hadn't known. By chance, Mitchell had come to learn that one of Ross's uncles back in Colorado had helped bankroll the rise of an eccentric religious figure of that period, Bishop Alma White, leader of the Pillar of Fire movement. Ross—

whose soft spot for shamans and spiritual charlatans matched Mitchell's—was delighted by this revelation. "One day [Ross] put his head in my office, as he used to do every now and then, and asked me how I was getting along," Mitchell recalled. "I was bogged down in some Profile or other, and getting nowhere, and I said that I was ready for Bellevue. 'You ought to go over and ask Bishop Alma to pray for you,' he said."

It was true that Ross, per his reputation, maddened many a *New Yorker* writer, often as not through his queries written on working galleys of their stories. These were legendary for both their number and fractured syntax (Ross's most fabled habit was scribbling "Who he?" in the margin whenever a new character caught him off guard). In 1957, as James Thurber was preparing a series of articles about Ross, he asked if Mitchell was the writer who once got a story galley back from the editor with a staggering one hundred forty-four queries on it. Mitchell replied that Thurber had the wrong man; he suspected the actual recipient was the "other" Joe—Liebling. Then Mitchell passed along a related anecdote. "When I first came to *The New Yorker*," Mitchell wrote Thurber, "Joe and several others were quartered in a suite of offices down on the eighteenth floor. There was no name on the door, and one day, after a wrangle with Mr. Ross over queries, Joe hired a sign painter to paint WHO HE? in gold letters on the glass part of the door. A few days later one of the elevator operators said that another tenant on that floor had asked him what in the name of God kind of product did the WHO HE? company put out." All his life Mitchell maintained great affection and respect for Ross, his champion and occasional co-conspirator. He was also one of the *New Yorker* staffers who felt the editor's genius was willfully underappreciated, because he was so easy to caricature (as he felt Thurber did) and left so much comic material in his wake.

Not long after Ross's death, his second-in-command and longtime managing editor for factual matter, William Shawn, was named editor of the magazine. The diminutive and preternaturally serene Shawn couldn't have been more different from Ross as a person, but he was just as stubborn and as an editor he was committed to the same principles of excellence. He knew better than anyone what a treasure *The New Yorker* had in Mitchell. And since Mitchell had worked directly with Shawn for as long as the writer had been at the magazine, the change at the top of the masthead actually meant little in terms of Mitchell's routine.

Another aspect of Mitchell's job that didn't change much during the fifties was his salary. According to pay stubs, Mitchell earned one hundred fifteen dollars a week from 1945 until 1953, when he received a twenty-five-dollar raise. In real spending terms, his annual salary of about seven thousand three hundred dollars in 1953 was the equivalent of about sixty thousand dollars today. In what was then a considerably more affordable New York City, that was a respectable enough salary. But top writers at other magazines were earning much more, and *The New Yorker* had a well-deserved reputation in the industry for penury. Mitchell's journal notes recount an occasion on which Liebling invited *The New Yorker*'s owner, Raoul Fleischmann, to lunch at the Algonquin. Both men were having a pleasant time until Liebling announced that it happened to be the twenty-fifth anniversary of his joining the magazine. Fleischmann instantly stiffened. "Mr. Liebling, if you're expecting any increased emolument because of that"—which of course he was—"you're mistaken."

Mitchell understood. After the 1953 adjustment, his pay would stay the same for the next eleven years—no doubt reflecting in part the declining productivity. Still, if it hadn't been for some annual income from Joseph's portion of the North Carolina farming proceeds, the Mitchell family—with one breadwinner and two daughters in private schools—would have had a harder time getting by than it did.

While Mitchell privately groused about his pay—the issue would become even more acute for him a few years down the road—it was one reason he didn't feel particularly guilty about his infrequent appearances in the magazine and doing much as he pleased with his workdays. Mitchell spent hours upon hours wandering the city, constantly curious about it, cataloging its small details that added up to a magnificent whole. His journals are replete with examples. One day, for instance, he was at the Fulton Market visiting with a vendor named

Joe Carter, proprietor of Joseph H. Carter, Inc. On a post in front of Carter's stand was this sign:

J H C
I N C

On this occasion a group of dieticians had stopped during a tour of the market to talk with Carter. A woman who noticed the sign asked, "Mr. Carter, what do those letters mean?" Carter replied, "They mean 'Jesus H. Christ, I need cash.'"

Unlike the walks of his apprenticeship in the early thirties, Mitchell could now be unhurried. He particularly indulged his lifelong love of older buildings, with their architectural curlicues and weathered embellishments that reminded him of the physical idiosyncrasies in aging people. He articulated this passion in his unfinished memoir:

Ever since I came here, I have been fascinated by the ornamentation on the older buildings of the city. The variety of it fascinates me, and also the ubiquity of it, the overwhelming ubiquity of it, the almost comical ubiquity of it. In thousands upon thousands of blocks, on just about any building you look at, sometimes in the most unexpected and out-of-the-way places, there it is. Sometimes it is almost hidden under layers of paint that took generations to accumulate and sometimes it is all beaten and banged and mutilated, but there it is. The eye that searches for it is almost always able to find it. I never get tired of gazing from the back seats of buses at the stone eagles and the stone owls and the stone dolphins and the stone lions' heads and the stone bulls' heads and the stone rams' heads and the stone urns and the stone tassels and the stone laurel-wreaths and the stone scallop-shells and the cast-iron stars and the cast-iron rosettes and the cast-iron medallions and the clusters of cast-iron acanthus leaves bolted to the capitals of cast-iron Corinthian columns and the festoons of cast-iron flowers and the swags of cast-iron fruit and the zinc brackets in the shape of oak leaves propping up the zinc cornices of brownstone houses and scroll-sawed bargeboards framing the dormers of decaying old mansard-roofed mansions and the terra-cotta cherubs and nymphs and satyrs and sibyls and sphinxes and Atlases and Dianas and Medusas serving as keystones in arches over the doorways and windows of tenement houses. There are some remarkably silly-looking things among these ornaments, but they are silly-looking things that have lasted for a hundred years or more in the dirtiest and most corrosive air in the world, the equivalent of a thousand years in an olive grove in Greece, and there is something triumphant about them. . . . To me, they are sacred objects. The sight of a capricious bit of carpentry or brickmasonry or stonemasonry or blacksmithery or tinsmithery or tilesetting high up on the façade of a building, executed long ago by some forgotten workingman, will lift my spirits for hours.

In 2009 photographer Steve Featherstone showcased the ornate beauty of Mitchell's "found objects." Mitchell collected everything that struck his aesthetic fancy, from hotel pickle forks to bricks to the bygone doorknobs shown here.

When he had opportunity, Mitchell would lug some of these "sacred objects" home to the Village apartment. The inveterate collector couldn't help it; his habit, carried over from childhood, gave him immense pleasure even into old age.

If a building was condemned and about to be torn down, Mitchell considered it fair game and might try to pry off, say, an interesting set of brass address numbers or a decorative rosette. It was his way of literally hanging on to pieces of a disappearing past. Later in his life, he recalled an occasion when he and Joe Cantalupo discussed purloining some balcony sculptures, to preserve them, from a building that was about to be razed near the foot of the Brooklyn Bridge. By the time Mitchell circled back to the building, however, he discovered that "someone had beaten [us] to the punch." (He was happy to learn later that the statues had found their way to a Brooklyn museum.) On this point Mitchell's barkeep friend Tim Costello offered another apt observation: "If [Mitchell] ever disappears, start looking for him under fifty foot of brick, with a rusty fire escape on his chest and a pleased smile on his face."

In truth, most of the artifacts Mitchell carried home were considerably less exotic, their significance less archaeological or architectural than anthropological. These included bottles and boot hooks, drawer pulls and pickle forks, and the brightly colored glass insulators from old electrical poles. Boxes of bottles and nails and bronze hardware from apartment buildings and hotels were stored under the beds and sofas and other furniture that crowded the family's apartment. His "antiquarianism was obsessive," said Hamburger. Then there were his beloved bricks; always the bricks. "He had enormous collections of old bricks. He was fascinated by bricks," Hamburger said. He recalled a cocktail party where Mitchell learned that a guest was from a family "very prominent in manufacturing bricks. Now, this was manna from heaven. So, he gets her in the corner and he spent the whole evening talking about bricks—kinds of bricks, special bricks, the color of the soil, the way in which the bricks were made, how they would get this stuff off the Hudson. That kind of thing just grabbed him."

The thread that best connected all Mitchell's disparate finds was their essential beauty. Underscoring that aesthetic, a 2009 Duke University exhibit entitled "The Collector: Joseph Mitchell's Quotidian Quest" featured photographs by Steve Featherstone of various Mitchell *objets* that pop from the page in almost three-dimensional detail—brass keys and brass hinges and brass doorknobs and brass drawer pulls and brass buttons and blue bottles and green bottles and broken bottles enclosed in glass jars. Photographed with some of the items are Mitchell's handwritten notes of explanation. One photograph, for example, includes a vertically bisected screw and a note on *New Yorker* letterhead that reads, "mutilated screw that came out of the MUNICIPAL BUILDING doorknob—see if I can find one to replace it."

CHAPTER 12

JOE GOULD REVISITED

[GOULD] TOLD PEOPLE HE MET in Village joints that the Oral History was already millions upon millions of words long and beyond any doubt the lengthiest unpublished literary work in existence but that it was nowhere near finished. He said that he didn't expect it to be published in his lifetime, publishers being what they were, as blind as bats, and he sometimes rummaged around in his pockets and brought out and read aloud a will he had made disposing of it. "As soon after my demise as is convenient for all concerned," he specified in the will, "my manuscript books shall be collected from the various and sundry places in which they are stored and put on the scales and weighed, and two-thirds of them by weight shall be given to the Harvard Library and the other third shall be given to the library of the Smithsonian Institution."

—*From "Joe Gould's Secret," 1964*

· ·

IT IS TYPICAL FOR THE RELATIONSHIP BETWEEN A JOURNALIST AND his subject to end once the latter's story is published. That had been anything but the case with Mitchell and Greenwich Village iconoclast Joe Gould, protagonist of Mitchell's "Professor Sea Gull" piece. After the Profile appeared in 1942, the author of *An Oral History of Our Time* inserted himself into Mitchell's life and would stay there for more than a decade—to Mitchell's endless chagrin.

In the wake of the popular story, Gould—emboldened by his new fame—had been savvy enough to appreciate that Mitchell, too, was profiting from their "partnership," in terms of his ascendant literary reputation. He also knew that the writer's highly developed sense of guilt would not let him simply walk away from New York's favorite Bohemian once their editorial business had been transacted. Staffers at *The New Yorker* quickly came to dread Gould's appearances to pick up mail and reader contributions to the Joe Gould Fund; they usually knew he was there before they saw him, because the stench of his clothes preceded him. "The sound of his voice began to make me wince," Mitchell later confessed. Gould became a black hole for the writer, devouring his time and energy. The visits were especially grinding if Gould was hungover, as was not unusual. "In this state," Mitchell wrote, "he was driven to talk, he was determined to talk, he would not be denied, and I would be lucky if I got him out in an hour and a half or two hours, or even three. He would sit on the edge of an old swivel chair in a corner of my office, his portfolio on his lap, his clothes smelling of the fumigants and disinfectants used in flophouses, rheumy-eyed, twitching, scratching, close to hysteria, and he would talk on and on and on. His subject was always the same—himself. And I would sit and listen to him and try my best to show some interest in what he was saying, and gradually my eyes would glaze over and my blood would turn to water and a kind of paralysis would set in."

What no one, not even Mitchell's *New Yorker* colleagues, knew was that the writer had a special reason to find Gould's presumptuous behavior galling. Over the course of reporting the Profile, Mitchell found himself increasingly skeptical about Gould's oral history. It was a given that it existed, because many people had seen elements of it, the newspapers had done stories about it, and Gould himself was seldom without the weather-beaten portfolio carrying whatever writer's notebooks were in progress. Naturally, Mitchell wanted to see the material himself and repeatedly asked Gould for the notebooks. When Gould complied, the ones he shared contained essays he had written, and they were usually iterations on the same handful of themes, such as the death of his father, a physician, or a mock-serious treatise on the dangers of consuming tomatoes. What they *weren't*, however, were true oral histories—which is to say, the recorded comments or monologues or overheard conversations of other people. These developments began to concern Mitchell. His anxiety was only compounded by what seemed to be elaborate evasions when the writer pushed Gould to see material that went beyond the essays. The bulk of his history was locked away for safekeeping in remote locations, Gould would explain, such as on a farm out on Long Island, and might not be retrievable until the end of World War II. It all gave Mitchell a growing queasiness about the entire undertaking. After all, as indisputably interesting as Joe Gould might be, he scarcely would have merited a full-blown Profile without the extraordinary undertaking of the oral history. Still, based on what Mitchell *had* seen and on the testimony of various other credible sources, he was comfortable enough to write the Profile.

And that would have been that but for Gould's subsequent peskiness and his taking advantage of Mitchell's good nature. Mitchell figured that in time Gould would drift away, but he didn't. Desperate to

Joe Gould would become a nuisance to Mitchell, but what most unsettled the writer was how much of Gould he saw in himself.

extricate himself, Mitchell began introducing Gould to book editors of his acquaintance, hoping the prospect of actually publishing the oral history would be enough of a distraction for Gould that it would purchase Mitchell some peace. When Gould blew off one such meeting, Mitchell set up another. Then a September 1943 meeting with Charles A. Pearce, of Duell, Sloan and Pearce, went awry because of Gould's various equivocations and, finally, his startling declaration that the oral history should be published only after his death. With that, Mitchell loses all courtly restraint.

> I was exasperated. As soon as Pearce was out of the room, I turned on Gould. "You told me you lugged armfuls of the Oral History into and out of fourteen publishing offices," I said. "Why in hell did you do that and go to all that trouble if you've always been resolved in the back of your mind that it would be published posthumously? I'm beginning to believe," I went on, "that the Oral History doesn't exist." This remark came from my unconscious, and I was barely aware of the meaning of what I was saying—I was simply getting rid of my anger—but the next moment, glancing at Gould's face, I knew as well as I knew anything that I had blundered upon the truth about the Oral History.

Thus did Mitchell discover that the multimillion-word *Oral History of Our Time* in essence existed only in Gould's febrile imagination. Mitchell was awash in emotions. He was incensed; he felt betrayed, embarrassed, used—and not a little panicky. He had just written a major Profile predicated on the oral history; would he and *The New Yorker* now have to take it all back? For a fleeting moment the writer considered following through and demanding of Gould an explicit answer to Mitchell's accusation—but he didn't. In part, this was to keep from shattering what little remained of Gould's dignity. But it was also true that, at that juncture, Mitchell didn't really want to hear Gould's answer. For if Mitchell *did* know with certainty there wasn't an oral history, he would have to do something about setting the matter straight, with all the attendant embarrassment, or worse. In any case, Mitchell didn't press Gould for confirmation of his suspicions, and Gould didn't volunteer it. Both men simply understood that, in an instant, things between them were different.

Before long, Gould's health worsened, and an anonymous female patron staked him to a small hotel room of his own, providing some stability and an escape from the flophouses. He stopped dropping by *The New Yorker*, and he and Mitchell came to see each other only sporadically. But over time Gould lost his patron, and then his health, and then his mind. In 1953, Mitchell learned that Gould was in a state mental hospital, suffering from senility as well as a host of physical maladies. In 1957, he died there. Mitchell, who had kept abreast of Gould's steady decline through friends and hospital contacts, got the news in a phone call. After hearing the particulars of Gould's final days, Mitchell thought to inquire whether Gould happened to leave behind any papers. "None at all" was the reply.

AT THE TIME OF Gould's death, Mitchell was busy reporting "The Rivermen." And Joe Gould's secret might well have stayed buried with the vagabond himself but for Mitchell's pack-rat habits—and a still-nagging sense that Gould had pulled one over on him. Two decades after he had worked on the original Gould Profile, Mitchell was in his office one day going through old files when he came across the notes and related materials that he had gathered in preparing it. Many, perhaps most, reporters would have long since consigned such matter to the rubbish bin. But here were his original reporting notes, typescripts of Gould's protean monologues, news clippings and drawings and photographs and Gould letters and poems. There were notes on seemingly insignificant events and actions, such as when Mitchell first proposed the Gould story to his editors—June 10, 1942, a Wednesday morning. The notes also convey how thoroughly Mitchell dove into a Profile assignment—not to mention the extent to which Gould had been adopted by the Village cultural establishment. As Mitchell recounted:

Ever since my first interview with Gould, I had been tracking down friends and enemies of his and talking with them about him. Most of these people had known Gould for a long time and either were regular contributors to the Joe Gould Fund or had been in the past. In fact, several of them—e.e. cummings, the poet; Slater Brown, the novelist; M. R. Werner, the biographer; Orrick Johns, the poet; Kenneth Fearing, the poet and novelist; Malcolm Cowley, the critic; Barney Gallant, the proprietor of Barney Gallant's, a Village night club; and Max Gordon, the proprietor of the Village Vanguard, another Village night club—had been giving him a dime or a quarter or a half dollar or a dollar or a couple of dollars once or twice a week for over twenty years. Each person I saw had suggested others to see, and I had looked up around fifteen people and spoken on the telephone with around fifteen others.

Mitchell initially intended to keep the secret about the oral history just that—"let the dead bury the dead," as he put it, echoing George Hunter. But in his old files, Mitchell found a letter from Gould in which he referenced a portrait that the painter Alice Neel had done of him in the early thirties. Mitchell followed up with Neel, who invited him to her studio and showed him the Gould portrait. The subject was nude, sitting on a bench in a steam bath. The shocking aspect of the tableau, however, was not the dearth of clothing but that Neel had painted Gould with more than the requisite number of male genitalia. When Mitchell pressed about this, Neel said that Gould was proud of the painting and visited it often. "I call it 'Joe Gould,'" she said, "but I probably should call it 'A Portrait of an Exhibitionist.'" She paused for a moment, then explained. "I don't mean to say Joe was an exhibitionist. I'm sure he wasn't—technically. Still, to be perfectly honest, years ago, watching him at parties, I used to have a feeling that there was an old exhibitionist shut up inside him and trying to get out, like a spider shut up in a bottle. Deep down inside him. A frightful old exhibitionist—the kind you see late at night in the subway. And he didn't necessarily know it. That's why I painted him this way."

As he contemplated Neel's remarks, Mitchell began to reconsider the emotional relationship he still maintained with Gould—who, while deceased, had never really left the writer. He realized that in the wake of Gould's death "I had replaced the real Joe Gould—or at least the Joe Gould I had known—with a cleaned-up Joe Gould. . . . By forgetting the discreditable or by slowly transforming the discreditable into the creditable, as one tends to do when thinking about the dead, I had, so to speak, respectabilized him." Once he got Gould back into proportion, Mitchell added, "I concluded that if it was possible for the real Joe Gould to have any feeling about the matter one way or the other he wouldn't be in the least displeased if I told anything at all about him that I happened to know. Quite the contrary."

Of course, Mitchell also knew that he had a damn good yarn to tell, and with the publication of "The Rivermen" he'd been seeking his next story. There was perhaps one final motivation for him to revisit Gould, which Mitchell conveys in what is almost—but not quite—a throwaway line from the piece: "I believe in revenge."

Whatever the rationale for changing his mind, Mitchell plunged into Joe Gould the sequel. A number of factors combined to make it the steepest challenge of his professional life. The sheer complexity of the reporting and the need to go into so much of the backstory of the 1942 Profile—the sequel was five times longer than the original—meant that the preparation of the article was inordinately time-consuming. "I have been working on [it] for over a year," Mitchell wrote an admirer while in the throes of composition, "and was under the impression that I had it almost finished, but here lately, little by little, I began to realize that it wasn't anywhere near finished, it was not only far too long it was all lopsided, and that I would have to do a lot of revising and rewriting, and I was about ready to give up and go on down to the Bowery. 'What the hell's the use?' I asked myself yesterday morning. 'Who reads these damned stories, anyway?'"

At this same time Mitchell was shuttling back and forth to North Carolina due to his mother's failing health. Betty Mitchell—the quiet woman who inculcated in her firstborn an appreciation for literature and then gave him the support he needed to leave home in search of his writing destiny—died in June of 1963, at the age of seventy-seven. This period was an emotionally and physically exhausting one for Mitchell, and his conflicted feelings about Gould only exacerbated the writing challenge. It exacted a toll on Mitchell. By that November, he wrote to a friend back in North Carolina that he was nearing the end of "a *New Yorker* Profile that I've been working on for what seems like the last three hundred years."

Then, just when Mitchell could have used a piece of good news, he got perhaps the worst yet.

IT'S HARD TO OVERSTATE what A. J. Liebling and Joseph Mitchell had meant to each other over the years. One gets a glimpse from a letter their mutual friend and colleague St. Clair McKelway sent Mitchell in the late fifties. It was summer; McKelway was in London, and Liebling was visiting. Any correspondence was welcome from the amusing and peripatetic McKelway, who could drop from sight for months at a time and whose flamboyant bipolar condition and attendant paranoia only made him all the more interesting. But this particular letter had a special resonance for Mitchell. "You'd love London, I think, as much as I do," McKelway wrote. "I feel about it somewhat as I felt about New York when I first came there in 1925 to work on the *World*, only now, at this age, I find certain limitations of mine enable me to enjoy things about London I possibly would not have had time for when I was twenty." McKelway reported on some of the things he and Liebling had been up to during the latter's visit. "Joe and I miss you. Having dinner last night at Scott's, a kind of local Dinty Moore's, but older, Joe said, 'God damn it, Mac, I wish I was rich. I would send an escort for Mitchell and have him brought over here for three months so we could walk around and talk to him.'"

Liebling's transatlantic wistfulness captures the deep affection and camaraderie between the two Joes. Mitchell and Liebling had known each other their entire professional lives, and neither man relished anything more than the other's company—be it while walking the city, debating favorite books over a cup of coffee, eating in a trusted restaurant, or having a nightcap (or three) at Costello's. And talking, always talking—these were two of the magazine's greatest talkers: Liebling, the native New Yorker who was garrulous coming out of the womb, and Mitchell, the courtly and once-shy Southerner who could, when enamored of a subject, engage in long flights of discourse as if he were a character out of Thomas Wolfe. Mitchell's daughters remember Liebling as a kind of eccentric uncle. He was a frequent visitor at their apartment, and he adored Therese's cooking (as did all the Mitchells' friends). A treasured bit of family lore recounts how, one morning when Liebling had come around for breakfast, he pulled a volume from Mitchell's bookcase in the living room, contentedly read for a while, then marked his place with a slice of leftover bacon.

Throughout the postwar forties and into the fifties, the long period during which Mitchell became increasingly selective about his story pursuits and steadily reined in his production, Liebling kept turning out an almost heroic stream of Reporter pieces, Profiles, and criticism—

Therese Mitchell took this photograph of A. J. Liebling and his third wife,
the writer Jean Stafford, during a visit to the Lieblings' Long Island home.

all of it infused with a winking drollery and sharp judgments. (In an appreciation published on the centennial of Liebling's birth, *The New York Times* caught his spirit perfectly with its headline: HE SPREAD HIMSELF THICK.) For the Rabelaisian Liebling, the very act of writing had a theatrical quality about it, and he was an approving audience of one. "You could hear Liebling—not only his typewriter going, but his own amusement, his self-appreciation," recalled Philip Hamburger. "And you could hear him chuckling and laughing and actually doubled over." Still, when the story was done, there was no one whose judgment mattered more to him than Mitchell, and vice versa.

In time, however, decades of overindulgent eating and drinking, and his resulting corpulence, caught up with Liebling. Chronic health issues began to slow him down, and he started experiencing periods of depression—something new to him but familiar enough to Mitchell. By the early sixties, the torrent of Liebling stories for *The New Yorker* had been reduced to a trickle.

Mitchell could see plainly enough the parlous state of his friend's health. Nonetheless, he was shaken to his core when, in December of 1963, Liebling was rushed to the hospital with what was diagnosed as viral pneumonia. The following week brought a series of spiraling complications, until Liebling at last died of congestive heart failure. He was fifty-nine years old. The shock of this turn and the deep imprint it left on Mitchell are evident in a letter he wrote to Liebling's widow, Jean Stafford, more than a decade later. Said Mitchell, "Every Christmas since 1963 has been shadowed for me by recollections of those deeply disturbing and for that matter deeply puzzling days up at Doctors Hospital and Mount Sinai (and particularly by recollections of that bleak, cold-to-the-bone, new-snow-on-top-of-slush afternoon that Joe was moved from Doctors to Mount Sinai). . . ."

At Liebling's funeral, Mitchell offered the eulogy. The service was held at Frank E. Campbell's celebrated funeral home at 81st and Madison, and Mitchell told the mourners that he and Liebling had come there together on a number of occasions—one time in particular, he recalled, for the funeral of an old newspaper colleague. In accord with the deceased's wishes, Mitchell said, literally no words were spoken at the service. "Everybody sat for a while with his own thoughts," he continued. "Some music was played, and then it was over. I was shocked by this, and, as Joe and I walked up the street afterwards, I said so, but Joe said that he wasn't. I have forgotten his exact words, but he said something to the effect that it was the only funeral he had ever attended that he completely approved of."

It had been a season of loss for Mitchell. Within months he had experienced the death of his mother and that of a best friend who, more than anyone else, was also a professional muse to him. They represented two polestars in his life. The sudden severing had the effect of quickening, and deepening, the spells of depression he was prone to anyway. And the blows came just as Mitchell was desperately trying to wrestle the difficult Joe Gould story to a conclusion. The timing almost certainly darkened the already-dark tenor Mitchell intended for the sequel.

THROUGH THAT WINTER AND spring, Mitchell willed himself forward, channeling his grief into his writing. "Joe Gould's Secret" finally appeared in *The New Yorker,* in two long installments, in September of 1964. Once again, Mitchell had managed to produce a story that, in its tone, direction, and surprising conclusion, no other *New Yorker* writer ever had.

From the opening lines, Mitchell's revisit takes a much harsher line with Gould than the genial original. "He was nonsensical and bumptious and inquisitive and gossipy and mocking and sarcastic and scurrilous," Mitchell says of his subject. He reports that sometimes Gould resorted to petty thievery, even from his own friends, to survive. Readers familiar with the first Profile—and there were many—would have sensed immediately that, for some inexplicable reason, Mitchell's once-affectionate attitude toward Gould had changed, even to the point of anger.

That anger gradually becomes understandable as Mitchell spends the first half of the sequel describing his complicated relationship with Gould and his growing sense that all was not as it seemed with the oral history. By two-thirds of the way through the piece, when Mitchell reveals Joe Gould's secret—that the oral history does not really exist—the reader fully grasps that the puckish misfit of "Professor Sea Gull" is a manipulative and self-deluding figure who warrants, it would seem, only pity.

Yet at this point Mitchell executes an emotional pirouette. Rather than condemning Gould for his elaborate charade, Mitchell begins to reconstruct all the reasons why he had admired him in the first place. Everyone has masks, Mitchell says, so in that way Gould was no different from the rest of us. But what *did* set him apart was that he had the courage to reject convention and societal (even familial) expectations, in order to live the life he felt called to. Joe Gould fielded the world's indignities with wit and resourcefulness. And he carried with him an idea—not a trifling idea, but one so epic and audacious and stubborn that it had to be admired on its face. Besides, as Gould had explained to Mitchell, it wasn't a question that the oral history didn't exist, exactly; it was all up there in his head. He simply hadn't had the opportunity to transcribe it, if you will.

This last point in particular resonated with Mitchell. After exposing the truth of the oral history, he launches into a sidebar that is as remarkable as it is jarring. Mitchell spends more than one thousand words detailing the big novel of New York City that he got it into his head to write when he was a newspaperman in his early twenties. Highly autobiographical in nature, it was to be a great, roiling ocean of a novel, and Mitchell discusses at length the characters, the main plot, the subplots, the settings, the mood. He even recounts actual speeches by some of the characters. Here his protagonist—a young, Southern-born, Baptist-raised newspaperman who considers himself an "exile"—emerges with some friends from a Harlem nightclub and encounters an elderly black street preacher, who would figure prominently in the tale:

Like the Baptist preachers the young reporter had listened to and struggled to understand in his childhood, the old man sees meanings behind meanings, or thinks he does, and tries his best to tell what things "stand for." "Pomegranates are about the size and shape of large oranges or small grapefruits, only their skins are red," he says, cupping his hands in the air and speaking with such exactitude that it is obvious he had had first-hand knowledge of pomegranates long ago in the South. "They're filled with fat little seeds, and those fat little seeds are filled with juice as red as blood. When they get ripe, they're so swollen with those juicy red seeds that they gap open and some of the seeds spill out. And now I'll tell you what pomegranates stand for. They stand for the resurrection. The resurrection of our Lord and Saviour Jesus Christ and your resurrection and my resurrection. . . ."

This was extraordinary; it really did seem the entire novel was all right there—in Mitchell's head. "But the truth is, I never actually wrote a word of it," he confesses. "Even so, for several years I frequently daydreamed about it, and in those daydreams I had finished writing it and it had been published and I could see it. I could see its title page. I could see its binding, which was green with gold lettering." Put another way, Gould's oral history was no less real than Mitchell's novel—and Mitchell's novel was no more real than Gould's oral history. It was a sobering, even courageous admission from a writer, and it explained Mitchell's expiation of any lingering resentment for Gould and any lingering guilt he felt for playing along with the fiction of the oral history years after he knew the truth. "Those recollections [about the novel] filled me with almost unbearable embarrassment," Mitchell continues, "and I began to feel more and more sympathetic to Joe Gould."

Mitchell's comparison of his unwritten novel to Gould's unwritten oral history is an explicit nod to a point that many observers over the years have made: There were many startling similarities between Joe Gould and Joe Mitchell. Both came from small towns; both were raised in successful, influential families; both were expected to go into the family business; both considered themselves disappointments to their strong-willed fathers; both felt the gravitational pull of New

York; both felt like eternal exiles; both made their life's work the telling of other people's stories. As one of Mitchell's friends and *New Yorker* colleagues, the critic Stanley Edgar Hyman, noted, over the course of the two pieces the writer has merged with his subject. "Then we realize that Gould has been Mitchell all along, a misfit in a community of traditional occupations, statuses, and roles, come to New York to express his special identity; finally we realize that the body of Mitchell's work is precisely that Oral History of Our Time that Gould himself could not write."

Three decades later another critic, Christopher Carduff, proffered a similar, but more menacing, notion: that Gould "is Mitchell's nightmare vision of himself: he's the over-educated, over-reaching, seized-up artist-journalist as Madman. In this final Profile, Mitchell's graveyard humor yields to horror as the distance between reporter and subject closes."

Late in his life, Mitchell talked openly about his connection to Gould. "To me a very tragic thing [about the Joe Gould Profiles] is the story of so many people who bit off more than they could chew—and I'm one of them, you know," he told Norman Sims. At another point in their discussion, when Sims asked why Mitchell found Gould so compelling, he replied, "Because he is me."

In a coda that Mitchell surely would have appreciated, a collection of Gould's writings—apparently unknown to Mitchell—was found "hiding in plain sight" in the Elmer Holmes Bobst Library at New York University. It turned out that Gould gave the journals to the painter Harold Anton for safekeeping. Anton tried to find a publisher for them but, not succeeding, sold them. The journals in turn were acquired by the library. The content in the collection of eleven dime-store composition books "bolsters rather than contradicts Mitchell's suspicions about the Oral History," according to a news account about the discovery. The pages and pages of "blotchy, messy script" give a detailed, if mundane, accounting of Gould's life from 1943—interestingly, the year Mitchell confronted Gould—to 1947. "The diary's 1,100-odd pages are first and foremost a record of baths taken, meals consumed, and dollars cadged," said the report. "It's clear that Gould's favorite subject was himself." Gould documented his peculiar routine almost every day. The entry for August 4, 1943, begins: "Queen Elizabeth's Birthday. Bugs got on a rampage. As a consequence I got up late."

The notebooks also reveal that Joseph Mitchell was a reliable, and generous, contributor to the Joe Gould Fund.

CHAPTER 13

INTO THE PAST

ONCE, WALKING ACROSS THE George Washington Bridge around sunset, about a third of the way over, I was caught in a wind-and-rain storm so fierce that I thought it would blow me off, and I lay down flat on the walk for half an hour or so, when some policemen in a patrol car saw me and rescued me. Sometimes I dream about this, only, in the dream, I am not on the George Washington Bridge, I am riding through a storm on top of an airplane. I am somehow or other sitting on top of an airplane riding through a storm.

—From Joseph Mitchell's journal, circa early 1970s

. .

FOR MANY A NEW YORKER, THE SINGLE BEST THING ABOUT THE CITY is the cultural buffet. Artists themselves, Joseph and Therese knew the layouts of the major museums as well as they knew the subway lines. They regularly took in book readings and photographic exhibitions and neighborhood chamber concerts. They adored the movies, mainstream or art-house. They were enthusiastic theatergoers. Mitchell was particularly taken with the stage, which might be expected of a writer who could recite Shakespeare and Joyce from memory and for whom elaborate monologues were the pistons of his own stories. And as has been seen, several of those stories enticed producers to approach him about adapting them for stage or screen.

One of the first times that happened was back in 1942, when, only a few months ahead of his initial piece on Joe Gould, Mitchell turned out his "composite" Profile of Johnny Nikanov. In the years afterward,

Mitchell remained in touch with New York's gypsy community, and he was an active member of the international Gypsy Lore Society. Then in 1955 he had revisited the subject with the Profile of Daniel J. Campion, a New York police captain who oversaw the unit that tried to keep up with the city's confidence men and women. Campion was the city's top authority on gypsy families and their elaborate scams. He was Mitchell's tour guide for a mesmerizing journey into the lives of the gypsy women who ran sophisticated con games. One of these games, the *bajour,* involved separating a victim from her savings after the fortune-teller removed a "hex" from it. (*Bajour* victims were almost exclusively women, who opened themselves to the scam after having their futures read.) The story, primarily conveyed in several extended Campion speeches, was a smart and readable bookend to Mitchell's first gypsy piece.

For several years after the second piece, Mitchell was again approached by producers, who wanted to use his gypsy tales as the basis for a Broadway musical—and, as was evident in his fierce response to Sidney Sheldon's uninvited attempt to do the same, Mitchell closely guarded his authorial rights. As usual, most of the promising-sounding inquiries fizzled out. Then a producer named Edward Padula persuaded a Texas banker-cattleman-impresario named Harris Masterson to invest four hundred thousand dollars in the idea, and suddenly the project was a go. In June of 1964 the new musical comedy *Bajour* was announced. Its star would be Chita Rivera, the singer and dancer perhaps best known for her role as Anita in *West Side Story.* And playing the role of "Cockeye Johnny Dembo"—the musical's stand-in for Cockeye Johnny Nikanov—was Herschel Bernardi.

Explaining the show's development to his father, Mitchell wrote, "My share in the proceeds, if and providing it is a success, will be comparatively very small, but if a musical comedy is a hit it can bring in so much money that even a small share can amount to something. Of course, if it isn't a success, I won't get anything out of it, nor will anyone else, and the Texas banker will lose his $400,000." Given how long the project had taken to go from idea to adaptation, Mitchell tried to keep any enthusiasm in check. But a letter to friend Rose

Wharton in October of that year made it clear that he had been bitten by the Broadway bug. "One day the producer called me up and asked me to come to some of the rehearsals and I tried to put him off," Mitchell said, "but a few afternoons later I went over to the theatre, intending to stay for just half an hour or so, and before I knew it I was hooked. I stayed all afternoon, and next afternoon I slipped away from the office and went again."

He and Therese rode up to Boston for a tryout performance, where they reveled in the opening-night excitement. As he told Wharton:

> Afterwards, we went over to the Ritz-Carlton with the producer and his staff and some of the cast to wait for the reviews. As the reviews came in, one by one, the press agent stood up and read them aloud. Two were slams, one was yes-and-no, and two were enthusiastic, and it was fascinating to watch the reactions of the actors and actresses. And I was amazed at my own reaction—instead of feeling uninvolved, I found that I felt quite passionate about it. After all, I didn't write it, and it was none of my doing, but it *was* based on my work. And now, back in New York, I find myself walking three blocks out of my way every morning on the way to work in order to pass a big billboard advertising *Bajour*. My name is the smallest name on the billboard, you have to stand up close to see it, but it's there, and I do enjoy seeing it.

Bajour opened on Broadway on November 23, 1964, at the Shubert Theatre in New York. Mitchell had prevailed on his father, now widowed a little more than a year, to come up from Fairmont for the Broadway opening. But middling reviews and not especially memorable songs made it challenging for *Bajour* to attract a profitable audience. The producers tried a variety of measures to keep interest in the show up and costs down to survive into spring, when it was hoped the April resumption of the New York World's Fair would boost Broadway attendance generally. But *Bajour* closed on June 12, 1965, after a respectable run of two hundred thirty-two performances.

———

THE ADRENALINE RUSH OF being in the center of a Broadway production helped Mitchell counter the despair he was still experiencing after
the deaths of his mother and Liebling. So, too, did the praise he continued to garner from all quarters about the Joe Gould sequel. In recent years *The New Yorker* had run some of the most powerful,
high-impact nonfiction in its history, including Rachel Carson's "Silent Spring" and Hannah Arendt's "Eichmann in Jerusalem." Yet from
a reader standpoint, "Joe Gould's Secret," which unfolded one surprise
after another, was one of the magazine's most talked-about stories in
memory. Fans included Mitchell's fellow staffers. "No one on the
eighteenth floor is doing anything else but talking about the Profile
today and agreeing that you are our finest writer, by far," one young
colleague wrote him when the story appeared. Other critics agreed
when, in the fall of 1965, *Joe Gould's Secret*—consisting of the original
1942 Profile and the two-decade-hence reprise—was brought out in
book form by Viking. "Joseph Mitchell is one of our finest journalists,
unique in his compassion and understanding for the haunted little lost
men such as Joe Gould," declared the novelist Dawn Powell, who
knew Gould well. "He transforms a forlorn, intolerably pathetic gentleman panhandler into an engaging, Dickensian orphan rogue."

But it would be a later review and career assessment, by Mitchell's
friend and colleague Stanley Edgar Hyman, that really began to put
Mitchell's full body of work into a more literary context. In a piece
that harkened back to Malcolm Cowley's appreciation three decades
earlier, Hyman, writing in *The New Leader,* essentially asked the question: In focusing on Mitchell's journalistic acumen, have we sold him
short on his art? He rushed to answer his own question. "Mitchell is a
formidable prose stylist and a master rhetorician," he wrote, adding
what would become an oft-repeated summation of the storyteller: "He
is a reporter only in the sense that Defoe is a reporter, a humorist only
in the sense that Faulkner is a humorist."

Like all artists, Mitchell works in broad and enduring themes—
and he had been for some time, Hyman argued. As proof, he circled

back to Mitchell's stories collected in *McSorley's Wonderful Saloon* two decades before. "*McSorley's* was enthusiastically reviewed and had a considerable sale, but no one seemed to notice that the forms of reporting were being used to express the archetypal and the mythic: that Mazie might run a Bowery movie house but is an Earth Mother nevertheless; that Cockeye Johnny Nikanov, the king of thirty-eight families of slum gypsies, is simultaneously a Winter King; that McSorley's looks very like an ale-house but is in fact a Temple." Hyman went on to trace how Mitchell's rural Southern childhood helped shape his recurring themes—finding humanity in the world's less fortunate, the loss of Eden. He discussed the abundance of resurrection images in Mitchell's stories and noted that his Profile of the Mohawks "has already become a classic of imaginative ethnography." But now Mitchell had perhaps reached his apotheosis in Joe Gould, Hyman said. On the surface it would seem a kind of comic account of a colorful loser, but "read less superficially, the book is a pathetic and moving account of a 'lost soul' who had been an unloved boy." And it is written "in the bubbling, overflowing manner of James Joyce. Mitchell sees Gould 'sitting among the young mothers and the old alcoholics in the sooty, pigeony, crumb-besprinkled, newspaper-bestrewn, privet-choked, coffin-shaped little park at Sheridan Square.'"

If Hyman's appreciation was a bit overwrought, it was widely read and discussed, considerably nudging along the growing realization that Mitchell—long recognized as a first-rate journalistic talent—was in fact a first-rate writer of literature whose chosen medium happened to be nonfiction. It was an especially apt time in American letters for someone like Hyman to put Mitchell into this broader perspective. The period was witnessing the emergence of a movement that would come to be termed "the New Journalism." In the fall of 1965, only a few months before Hyman's piece appeared, Mitchell's own magazine serially published Truman Capote's *In Cold Blood*, the seminal example of the so-called "nonfiction novel." Gay Talese, Michael Herr, Joan Didion, Tom Wolfe, and other young, prodigiously talented practitioners were bringing a new cheek to their nonfiction stories, a contemporary (and often cynical or satiric) attitude, and a personal voice.

Consistent with the other social and cultural tremors shaking America in the middle and late sixties, the New Journalism was a reaction to the staid, entrenched conventions of the print media. The youngsters were thumbing their noses at their "square" elders as surely as the rockers and realists and postmodernists in other artistic fields. The New Journalists were at least as attentive to their writing as to their subjects—often to a highly self-conscious degree. Indeed, as with Tom Wolfe, that self-consciousness could be the point.

Eventually some critics—including some of the New Journalists themselves—claimed the achievement of something new in pushing nonfiction writing into the realm of literature. But astute observers, like Hyman, countered that *New Yorker* writers like Mitchell, Liebling, Lillian Ross, and John Hersey actually had been well out ahead of them. Or as a later *New Yorker* nonfiction master, John McPhee, succinctly put it, "When the New Journalists came ashore, Joe Mitchell was there on the beach to greet them."

Not that Mitchell, for his part, had much use for such debate. Years later, in recalling his early days at the magazine with fellow newspaper transplants like Liebling, Meyer Berger, and Richard O. Boyer, Mitchell explained how they talked constantly about what they wanted to accomplish. It was less about inventing a new form, he said, than it was about finding a fresh way of interpreting what they considered the most fascinating and complex city in the world. They certainly respected antecedent efforts at a New York realism, such as Stephen Crane's *Maggie: A Girl of the Streets,* but now that style felt "stilted." They sought more-naturalistic voices and approaches, and for inspiration they scoured the new publications then popping up in Europe. Of course, this was happening at a time when Harold Ross was quietly but deliberately opening up *The New Yorker* to different approaches to nonfiction. "We never thought of ourselves as experimenting," Mitchell said. "We were thinking about the most direct way we could write about the city, without all that literary framework. To speak directly." Mitchell would never be comfortable with any label of his work, which he simply considered foursquare writing that he hoped was revealing of the human predicament. He also may have resisted categorizing because he knew, unlike the general public, the extent to which he bent journalistic rules in his stories. Yet as he said in a cryptic but emphatic journal note, probably sometime in the early seventies: "I was a reporter, and then I became a magazine writer, and then I became at least in my own eyes simply a writer AND I PROFOUNDLY DESPISE SUCH TERMS AS NEW JOURN, CREATIVE JOURN."

That capital-letter disdain, however, didn't keep acolytes and English majors from pestering him about the New Journalism. And in time, as Mitchell surveyed the growing, and enduring, imprint that he and his *New Yorker* counterparts had made on American letters, his attitude did soften. Near the end of Mitchell's life, a graduate student pursuing a dissertation specifically inquired if the writer, back in the forties or fifties, felt that any other reporters took the same pains he had to learn so much about his subjects, or to go into such detail, or to quote at such length, or to make every sentence pull so much weight. Did he believe that John Hersey, with his epic account of the bombing of Hiroshima, and Lillian Ross, with her provocative Ernest Hemingway Profile and novelistic portrait of film director John Huston, were truly breaking new journalistic ground? Hadn't Mitchell already done that? The writer replied:

I didn't have a whole lot of interest in that hullabaloo some years ago in re is there a New Journalism and if so who were its pioneers, and afterwards my interest dwindled to no interest at all. Several times, through the years, I have been asked questions about the matter by interviewers, and, having a vague, uneasy feeling that I *should* know something about it and genuinely wanting to be helpful, I disregarded my lack of knowledge as well as lack of interest and went ahead and answered the questions, and then, later on, reading what I had said, I was appalled by the shallowness and the haphazardness and in some cases the looniness of my remarks, and consequently, sometime ago, after one of these experiences, I made a solemn vow or at least a vow never to answer questions about journalism new or old ever again unless I am on the witness stand under oath and the judge orders me to or unless a gun is being held to my head, and therefore I am obliged to say that I am sorry but I can't help you with answers to your questions. However and nevertheless and be that as it may, I wish you luck in finding the answers, for at this late day I am beginning to feel that I would really like to know what they are myself.

On the other hand, Mitchell the lifelong lover of literature had a more sanguine view of the literary establishment, and, propelled to some extent by evaluations like Hyman's, Mitchell's name began to be mentioned in the same conversation with the best purveyors of American literary fiction. That judgment was validated in 1970, when Mitchell was inducted into the National Institute of Arts and Letters. Chartered by Congress, the institute honored top artists in music, painting, sculpture, architecture, and writing. Membership was limited to two hundred fifty (an elite subset of fifty of these constituting the Academy of Arts and Letters). So it was that Mitchell took his place among a who's who in the American arts that ranged from Aaron Copland and Samuel Barber and Georgia O'Keeffe to Alexander Calder, Robert Penn Warren, and Eudora Welty. A handful of *New Yorker* colleagues were in the pantheon already—William Maxwell, E. B. White, and S. J. Perelman, for instance—but others in Mitchell's reportorial cohort were not. Indeed, the letters inductees were mostly novelists, playwrights, critics, poets, historians, and biographers. John Hersey and Janet Flanner (*The New Yorker*'s longtime Paris correspondent) were among the few working journalists represented when Mitchell was tapped. Induction into the institute was an imprimatur from the cultural establishment. But owing to the institute's limited membership and the inevitable politics that enveloped its pronunciations of merit, the question of who got in and who didn't often provoked hard feelings, including among some *New Yorker* writers who felt they were no less worthy than the honorees. Others simply considered the organization elitist and self-important and (ostensibly) paid it no heed. No one, however, seemed to begrudge the honor to Mitchell, whose body of work spoke with uncommon eloquence. Indeed, Mitchell was proud of the recognition and always took seriously his involvement with the institute's affairs.

Still, there is a price when one is officially designated a national treasure—the air grows thinner, the public's expectations become all the more elevated. As it was, Mitchell held himself to an impossibly high standard, a bar that, intentionally or not, he had steadily raised in the previous two decades of *New Yorker* writing. Now, with the world heaping praise on him, it was starting to have a kind of paralyzing effect. With such stories as "Mr. Hunter's Grave," "The Rivermen," and "Joe Gould's Secret," Mitchell had unquestionably taken his writing to the level of art. With all this pressure, how could the master keep producing . . . well, masterpieces?

One summer when Mitchell was back in North Carolina, he and his father went down to a pond that A.N. had built, where an alligator had subsequently taken up residence. The elder Mitchell named the animal Bill, and "he fed that alligator everything he could think of to feed him," Mitchell would recall. A.N. would get day-old bread from the grocery or, when he wanted to offer a special treat, pineapple upside-down cake. This particular summer A.N. hadn't seen Bill for some time, and there was talk along the swamp that someone had killed an alligator; A.N. thought perhaps it had been Bill. Then, while the father and son stood at the pond in conversation, the alligator suddenly appeared—and Joseph was a little startled at his father's visceral delight in seeing the prodigal reptile. "Hello, Bill! I'm glad to see you, Bill!" A.N. gleefully called out. As Joseph remembered it, "I had the strangest thing, it's very hard to explain—a spasm of jealousy. . . . This is probably the only case in medical history of a sibling rivalry with an alligator!" Mitchell laughed as he told Bill's tale, but there was some underlying truth to his envy over affection that, it seemed, could be elicited more readily by the animal than by the son.

In the wake of his mother's death and with his widowed father in

Men in hats: A. N. Mitchell, left, visits with his always
well-dressed sons Joseph, Harry, and Jack.

slowly declining health, Mitchell was now traveling to Fairmont every chance he could—typically in the spring and late fall or early winter, in addition to his traditional summer trip. A "quick" visit was at least a week, and he spent a month when he was able.

Ironically, it was his mother's death that helped free Mitchell to take these extended trips. He inherited one of the family farms that had been in her name, then had that heavily wooded property timbered out. The modest windfall afforded him a financial latitude he'd never before had. All his life Mitchell had harbored an anxiety, warranted or not, over where his next dollar was coming from. But with some independent means, "I became much braver than I had ever been before," said one journal entry.

Even when Mitchell *wasn't* in North Carolina, he worked hard to maintain the home connections. He kept up relationships with numerous friends and acquaintances there. He even had delivered to his New York apartment his home region's main newspaper, *The Robesonian*—

"a novel I have been reading a long time now," he once said of its typically provincial and quirky content. He scoured the paper, front page to obituaries, from the social notes (which always included the "New York Mitchells" when they were visiting Fairmont) to the latest elevation of the Lumbee River, from which measurement Mitchell could conjure in his mind's eye the current water level in the local swamps.

In truth, Mitchell considered himself first and foremost a North Carolinian. In a 1983 letter, he complimented a writer friend, Roy Parker, on a piece he'd written about Mitchell for a North Carolina newspaper. "I especially liked it because it linked me directly with where I come from and where I still belong—up until quite recently articles about me have always somehow seemed to indicate or imply or get across the idea that while I might possibly have been born in North Carolina I was really a New Yorker."

It was another way of expressing his lifelong sensation of exile—belonging to two worlds but not truly rooted in either. Mitchell referenced this notion frequently—in his journal notes, in letters to friends, in interviews later in his life. It became the central motif in his own story. "After I'm down in North Carolina awhile, I flee back up here [New York]," he told Sims. "And after I'm up here awhile, I flee back down there." On a page of journal notes, Mitchell scrawled, "Doomed to go back and forth between NY and NC, not feeling altogether at home in either place. Wanting one place when in the other." Elsewhere on the same page he writes that "most of the people I have known best ... have been exiled." In the note he cites such close friends as Louie Morino and Joe Cantalupo as examples, though he could just as easily have added the protagonists of innumerable of his stories, from Lady Olga to Joe Gould.

For Mitchell, Fairmont was and forever remained "a town in which I grew up and from which I fled as soon as I could but which I go back to as often as I can and have for years and for which even at this late date I am now and then all of a sudden and for no conscious reason at all heart-wrenchingly homesick. . . ." It was no secret to Mitchell's family how strong a grip the homestead continued to exert on the oldest son; they saw his joy every time he came through the front door. Nor did Mitchell ever rule out the possibility of returning one day for good, which continued to give them hope. "We always thought Joe would come back," acknowledged his youngest brother, Harry.

A.N. in particular never really stopped trying to lure Joseph and Therese. Family friend David Britt recalled that one of the properties the elder Mitchell acquired during the Depression was considered among the loveliest in Robeson County. "I have offered to give [Joseph] the McCall farm, which is the prettiest farm that I own, if he would come back down here and live on it with his family," A.N. told Britt. "Of course, it didn't work out."

When he *was* back home, Mitchell filled his days by catching up with friends and family, going over farm accounts with his father and brothers, and indulging in such simple pleasures as cutting rashers from a freshly picked watermelon (wielding a "long carving knife that has been sharpened so many times it has become narrow and limber") or foraging the fields for Indian artifacts. He welcomed the quotidian physical activities it takes to keep a farm running. One journal note relates a graphic example: what can happen when a cow becomes mired in a ditch. One day when Mitchell was in Fairmont, neighbors called to report a stench emanating from one of the far reaches of the family property. Mitchell, his father, and a number of their hands went out to investigate:

> We found a cow lying on her back, all four feet sticking straight up, in one of those narrow shallow ditches that are tributaries to the main ditch. . . . The maggots were working on her, and the smell was hideous, and it was hideous to think of her lying there lowing and lowing until she couldn't low any longer. She must've started across the ditch and made a false step and fallen on her back, and trying to get out she fitted herself tighter and tighter into the ditch. She had been dead so long in the hot weather that we couldn't pull her out with the tractor, we'd simply pull her apart.

In the end there was nothing for the men to do but bury the animal where she was, covering her with dirt and sand, and rerouting the ditch around her.

As the summer sun slid behind the swamps of Pitman Mill Branch, Mitchell was again keeping his father company, this time in side-by-side rocking chairs on the back porch, taking in the quiet. It was a ritual they had engaged in countless times. It was 1974, and by now Joseph's routine when he was back home had changed in one important respect—like his siblings, he functioned as a caregiver to a parent having great difficulty adjusting to the emotional and physical realities of old age. A.N. was ninety-three, his eyesight was dimmed by cataracts, he had to walk with the help of canes, and he needed more or less round-the-clock attention.

As darkness settled in, Mitchell patiently led A.N. to his small room. He helped the older man off with his clothes and into pajamas. He made sure A.N. took his medicine, then maneuvered him into bed. A little later, Mitchell himself turned in.

In the middle of the night Mitchell was awakened by the ringing of the small bell that A.N. kept at his bedside table. He went in to check on his father.

"See if the commode will flush," A.N. said. A bedroom closet had been converted into a private bathroom for his convenience. Mitchell flushed the toilet.

"It doesn't flush," A.N. said.

"Yes, it does, Daddy, it flushes all right."

"Must be my eyes," A.N. said with an aggravated sigh. He had tried to flush it but couldn't seem to work the handle. He got up with some difficulty and walked over to a small refrigerator, which Jack and Harry had installed so he more readily could get at the Coca-Colas he enjoyed. But in his determination A.N. had forgotten his cane; his son noticed this with some dismay, thinking it precisely the sort of innocent lapse that could lead to a fall.

"There's something wrong with it, too," A.N. said of the refrigerator. Mitchell went over and saw that the door couldn't fully close. Then he realized that his father had simply loaded too many Coke bottles into it and one was obstructing the door.

Mitchell resettled his father and returned to his own room. But with thoughts racing now, sleep wouldn't come; he opened up the Jerusalem Bible he kept there and, as he had all his life, began reading in Genesis and Exodus until his mind calmed. The middle-of-the-night exchange with his father had rattled him. As he noted, "It was the first time I ever saw him so confused."

Because Mitchell's siblings interacted with their father every day, the changes in A.N. were almost imperceptible to them. But to Mitchell, who saw him at longer intervals, they were pronounced and sobering. Watching mortality finally get its hooks into the man he'd long considered impervious to time was unsettling. Still, it wasn't entirely empathy behind this reaction. At this point, the writer was becoming an old man himself; he had just turned sixty-six.

One of the reasons I got so depressed helping Daddy get his clothes on and off and all that (although I did my best not to let him know or even sense that I was depressed) is that all those moles on his back and some of his other physical aspects as well as his mental confusion are all ahead of me—what I have to look forward to if I am lucky enough to last as long as he has. That and the general time-limit part of it. I can see him thinking: at the very best, I can only hope to live ten more years—although I guess, after sixty, all of us start thinking that way (or trying not to think that way). Boxed-in by time. As boxed-in as a prisoner on death row waiting for electrocution. Those moles: I have them already, and the liver marks on the back of my hands, and the coarsening of the skin on my face, and a certain lack of elasticity when I walk, and the forgetting of names (although I think that is due to all the Seconal and Valium and other medicines that I have been taking through the years, par-

ticularly Soma compound and the other strong headache medicines and duodenal ulcer medicines).

Despite A.N.'s fragility in his tenth decade on earth, he had lost
none of his vinegar. If anything, his physical and mental decline only
caused his patience to grow shorter, his tongue sharper. And he was
not at all reluctant to train his pique on his eldest. Joseph Mitchell's
frustration is palpable in a journal note as he recalled a conversation
with his father from a few years earlier, one concerning how over time
A.N. had divided the farm acreage among his children. Mitchell had
tried, delicately, to question the equity of some of the property alloca-
tions and how they would eventually impact his own children, but
A.N. cut him short. "Get it out of your heart what you've been thinking," he said angrily, and further instructed his son never to bring up
the subject again. "As always, it was impossible to talk logically or even
coherently with him," Mitchell wrote, noting A.N.'s "fury at even
being remotely questioned."

In fact, as much as Mitchell looked forward to visits home, the tension with his father was always just beneath the surface, waiting to
break through. Even a seemingly innocent conversation might do the
trick. For instance, if A.N. happened to mention that someone was
building a new home in the county—not unusual, given his passion for
real estate and knowing everyone else's business—Mitchell could be
sure it would lead to an admonition about the foolishness of renting an
apartment for one's home. Mitchell braced for these exchanges, which
he could see coming like the buildup of a summer squall, but that
didn't soften their impact. "I very rarely feel altogether at ease with my
father and haven't since I was a child," he wrote. "He is still able to
make an offhand remark and cut me to pieces."

On every such occasion, Mitchell was reminded why he couldn't
really be tempted by the prettiest farm in the family or the numberless pleasures of a springtime stroll in the woods. He would remember why he had wanted to leave home in the first place, all those years
ago, and he would begin looking forward to his return to New York as

much as he had looked forward to leaving it weeks before. He was in an emotional whipsaw, an exhausting cycle as predictable as the seasons.

UNFORTUNATELY, RETURNING TO NEW York no longer provided Mitchell the respite it once did. For many years now he had experienced distress at the changes reshaping his adopted city. But in the last decade, as he watched New York, his anxiety had turned to heartache; nostalgia morphed into palpable anger.

Like so many of the seminal figures in the history of *The New Yorker*, Mitchell had come to the great metropolis from other, mostly smaller, places. These non–New Yorkers were the people who gave the magazine its shape, tone, and purpose. Founding editor Ross was from the Rocky Mountain West. William Shawn was from Chicago by way of a small newspaper in rural New Mexico. Katharine White was from Boston, James Thurber was from Ohio, St. Clair McKelway was from North Carolina, and John O'Hara was from working-class Pennsylvania. That very "otherness" was key to *The New Yorker*'s freshness and inventiveness, in that all those creative people were exploring their curiosity about New York within the magazine itself. Unlike the natives, who tended to be blasé about the city, the transplants had no such compunction; they were fascinated by New York's every idiosyncrasy and crotchet. Outsiders like Mitchell brought with them the sense of discovery and wonder that were hallmarks of *The New Yorker* from the beginning.

They had all come to the city when New York was at its cultural and symbolic zenith, and grand public-works programs were pointing to a shining future, as if the entire enterprise were a living World's Fair. By the late sixties and early seventies, however, New York's glory days were long distant. The turbulent times were visiting on New York what Mitchell considered an almost biblical rash of pestilence. Crime, as in all major cities, skyrocketed. Motorists dodged potholes, and pedestrians ducked panhandlers. A huge homeless class developed and moved into the streets and subways. The city's finances were in shambles. Mitchell's beloved harbor was even filthier than when he'd documented it in 1951, and the air, if anything, was worse. Even his favorite fish-market haunt, Sloppy Louie's, burned in 1967 (though it would reopen the following year). The war in Vietnam, racial divisions and riots, generational rebellion, and then the Watergate scandal overlaid everything with a shroud of disillusionment. Maybe worst of all for Mitchell, New York had seemingly turned its back on its storied history and was bent on pulling down some of its most architecturally significant buildings. This all affected Mitchell profoundly. As he confirmed to his North Carolina friend Roy Wilder, Jr., in a 1972 letter, "I no longer have much enthusiasm for New York City, but I do have a kind of morbid interest in watching it go to pieces."

This sense of his city slipping its moorings was another factor exacerbating Mitchell's innate depression. With each passing year he felt more disconnected—not only from his place, New York, but from his time. He began to fixate on what he was losing. Mitchell's journal observations from this period sound very much like those characters in his stories who lament a world that is fast disappearing. "McSorley's, middle of the afternoon, sit at [a] table in back and have a few mugs of ale and escape for a while from the feeling that the world is out of control and about to come to an end." On that same page he notes, "Very likely that humanity is done for."

Eventually the depression-plagued Mitchell sought refuge from this outside welter the only way he knew how—by electing to "live in the past," as he explicitly and intentionally described it.

Living in the past: a deliberate retreat from the now, a flight from reality, a personal reversal of course—call it what you will. The point is that somewhere along the way Mitchell realized that a circuit had tripped in his mind, and he was now spending more time focused on what had gone before in his life—a space where the people so dear to him were all still alive, and the most satisfying times could be replayed at will—than he was confronting the frustrating present or an even worse future. It was Mitchell's way of coping emotionally with a world he felt was simultaneously overwhelming him and letting him down.

This new outlook was both facilitated and spurred by his keeping of journal notes, a routine Mitchell had recently begun. Sometime in the late sixties, Mitchell was consulting another doctor about his chronic depression, and he was advised that he might find it therapeutic to maintain a daily journal. From that point on—at times more faithfully than at others—Mitchell kept an eclectic, scattershot record of his day-to-day activities. Not a diary per se, it was more an ad hoc collection of notes, facts, observations, anecdotes, and arcana. Sometimes his recollections were typed out and more composed, but most often they were simply scrawls of dates, events, places he ate (and what the meals cost), books he bought (and what they cost), shows he attended (and what they cost), people he saw. Keeping track of such unremarkable things seemed to bring a satisfying order to a mind so troubled by the disorder he saw all about him. But the note-keeping also had the effect of sending him back into his memories. Mitchell's memories tended to be vivid, anyway—and in the throes of the black dog, they could be terrifying:

I know the exact day that I began living in the past. I didn't know it then, of course, but I know it now. The day was October 4, 1968, a Friday. . . . On that day, according to my diary, a dream woke me up around four A.M. In this dream, I was standing on the muddy bank of a stream that I recognized because of a peculiar old slammed-together split-rail bridge crossing it as being the central stream running through Old Field Swamp, a cypress swamp near my home in North Carolina. I had often fished in this stream as a boy. In the dream, I was fishing for red-fin pikes with a snare hook hung from a line on the end of a reed pole. I was watching a sandbar in some shallow water out in the middle of the stream that the sun was shining on, and I was waiting for a pike to show up over the sandbar where it would be clearly visible and where I could maneuver my line until I had the hook under it and could snatch it out of the water. I was intent on what I was doing and oblivious to everything else. And then I happened to look up, and I saw that the bridge was on fire. And then I saw that the mud on the opposite bank was beginning to quiver and bubble and spit like

lava and that smoke and flames were beginning to rise from it.
And then, a few moments later, while I was standing there, staring, fish and alligators and snakes and muskrats and mud turtles
and bullfrogs began floating down the stream, all belly-up, and
I realized that the central stream of Old Field Swamp had
turned into one of the rivers of hell. I dropped my pole and spun
around and started running as hard as I could up a muddy path
that led out of the swamp, but the mud on it was also beginning
to quiver and bubble and spit, so I plunged into a briar patch
beside the path and tried to fight my way through it, whereupon
I woke up. I woke up with my heart in my mouth.

LATE IN HIS LIFE, Mitchell summoned another memory—this one
more poignant than apocalyptic, involving one of his last moments
with his father. It was in late September or early October 1976, and
Mitchell had been back in Fairmont for a week or so. A.N. was ninety-
five at that point. They were again sitting on the back porch. The older
man was staring out to the yard and beyond. "I was very sure that he
was seeing in his mind the buildings that used to be out there in the
backyard—I remembered them all very well myself—but that had
been torn down one by one through the years as Fairmont grew from
a country village into something between a town and a city," Mitchell
wrote. There had been a small barn with a corncrib and hayloft in it,
and a larger barn farther out in the pasture, a smokehouse where they
used to cure hams and pork shoulders, a woodshed, a washhouse for
boiling clean the family laundry—all gone.

Suddenly A.N. sat up in his rocking chair and broke the silence.
"Son, it's your feet go first, your feet and your legs." Mitchell would
recall, "I had heard him say this several times during the past week and
I knew he didn't expect any answer or response from me. We continued sitting there, neither of us saying anything, until about fifteen
minutes had gone by, and then he roused himself again, and this time
he said something I had never heard before. 'Out on the farm, when I
was growing up,' he said, 'I went from shanks' mare to muleback to

horse and buggies, and after I moved to town I went from horse and buggies to Fords to Dodges to Cadillacs to rocking chairs.'

"I wanted to say something in response to this remark," Mitchell continued, "but I was so shocked by it—it was so bleak and so bitter and so true and so final and so unexpectedly revealing and so emotionally uncharacteristic of him—that I couldn't think of anything even remotely worth saying. We sat in silence for a few more minutes, and then he roused himself once again. 'Ah, well, son,' he said, 'I'm getting tired. I better go lie down for a while.'"

A.N. had taken ill in early 1975, and Mitchell and Therese went down to help tend to him. Throughout that year he had three separate operations, each of which Mitchell came home for. The last of these visits was in December. During this time Mitchell had been trying to write, but he'd had little luck with all the discombobulation. "In other words," he told Ellery Thompson, "I have been living in a state of confusion."

His father's decline was obviously on his mind when, in September of 1976, Mitchell wrote an uncharacteristically emotional letter that was published in the Fairmont weekly newspaper, *The Times-Messenger.* A full one thousand two hundred words, the letter actually was addressed to a North Carolina highway engineer, as what prompted Mitchell to write was a proposal to relocate part of Church Street in Fairmont to accommodate an expansion of the community's First Baptist Church. But that project would require the relocation of a number of graves in the adjacent cemetery, which Mitchell considered a desecration.

"The reason I have hesitated to write to you is that I am not a resident of Fairmont and it might at first appear that this matter is none of my business," he began. But he reminded people that he was born and raised there, still owned property and paid taxes there, and at some point intended to retire there. He was baptized in the Baptist church in question. "Ancestors of mine have been members of it since its earliest days," he wrote, "and my father and my two brothers and their families are members of it today. Furthermore, among the graves the church proposes to move are the graves of my grandfather and my grandmother and those of several other members of my family." Then he launched into the particulars of his objections:

First of all, I do not think that the present-day congregation and the present-day officers have the right—and I am speaking of moral and spiritual rights, not narrowly defined legal rights—to move these graves. If it were a matter of great importance to human safety—if the road, that is, was especially dangerous or in some way more dangerous than any other side road leading off a highway—that would be a different matter. . . . But what is involved is not a highway matter at all, in my opinion, but a matter of sacred trust. My grandfather and my grandmother could have buried their children in the old Mitchell-Griffin-Easterling cemetery out in the country from Fairmont, where my great-grandparents and my great-great-grandparents are buried, and they could of course have been buried there themselves, but they chose to bury their children and to be buried themselves in the cemetery of the First Baptist Church, a cemetery owned and administered by the church to which they belonged and in which they worshipped and to which they contributed. They chose the Baptist cemetery because they wanted to be close to the church and because they had every reason to think that their final resting places there would be permanent and undisturbed. In doing so, I think that they and the church entered into an agreement that might be described as an implied non-disturbance trust in perpetuity, and I do not think that the present-day congregation and the present-day officers can rightfully break this trust if their stated objective in doing so is merely to obtain more room for "necessary administrative offices and proper square footage for Senior Adults, Media Center, Parlor, and other facilities."

I would feel the same way if the people in the graves that the church proposes to move were in no way related to me. The old Baptist cemetery goes deep into the past of Fairmont and the surrounding countryside. It is one of the most historic places in the southern part of Robeson County, along with the cemeteries of Olivet and Iona and Ashpole. The men and women who are buried in it worked extremely hard and endured all kinds of hardships in helping to build up this part of North Carolina, and we are benefiting in one way or another from their work to this day. If it were not for them, we would not be here ourselves, let alone the church and the road. They cleared the land and drained the swamps, and they put up the turpentine distilleries and cotton gins and sawmills and grist mills and other enterprises, all of which are only memories now. I think they deserve our deepest respect and veneration. In any case, the least we can do is leave their graves alone. I was taught to honor my father and my mother and by extension my grandfather and my grandmother and all those who have gone before, and I firmly believe in doing so. I believe in preserving links to the past. I believe that these links give us something permanent to hold on to in our daily lives and make us feel more balanced and reconciled in relation to what may happen to us at any moment in the present and what will most surely happen to us sometime in the future. If the road is put through the cemetery, in ten years or so it will have to be widened or somehow changed, and in twenty years or so it will have to be changed again, and in time to come the old Baptist cemetery will be gone for good, like the old Court House in Lumberton. One more link with the past—with our own local past—will be gone, and spiritually we and our descendants will be the poorer for it, no matter how much more room we might have gained for administrative offices and Media Centers and Parlors.

For these reasons, I respectfully ask the Highway Department to reconsider its "agreement" with the church.

Mitchell was certainly capable of expressing strong emotion in private, but that had never been his custom in his public writing. This letter represented perhaps the most passion he had ever committed to print. Then again, he knew what few readers of the letter could have—

that he was on the verge of burying the one person over whom he had spent a lifetime sorting out his emotions, the person who had had more influence on him than any other. Consider a journal note Mitchell made around this time: "I am only now beginning to realize what I was writing about in those stories: my father as a Hudson River shad fisherman; my father as an Italian-American restaurant keeper; my father as an old Negro man." In the end the cemetery was not disturbed. This lengthy letter would turn out to be the last original piece of writing Mitchell ever "published."

A. N. Mitchell died that November. In the end, and even allowing for the enduring frustrations, the son felt that the many hours they spent together in the father's latter years brought them closer and, at least to some extent, eroded the disappointments the older Mitchell had held for so long. "I wanted his respect," Mitchell recalled years later, "and I believe I got it."

In the same journal note in which Mitchell connected his father to some of his most enduring and commendable characters, the writer typed another single phrase: "Ecce Puer," the title ("Behold the boy") of the poem James Joyce wrote after the confluence of his father's death and his grandson's birth. The last stanza reads,

> A child is sleeping:
> An old man gone.
> O, father forsaken,
> Forgive your son!

In the wake of A.N.'s death, the son became mired in an emotional funk that he couldn't seem to shake. "No matter how boring it may sound," he wrote to Ann Honeycutt the following March, "I've decided to be truthful and say that most of the time I seem to still be in the grip of the depression or the demoralization or whatever it might be called that took hold of me early last year when I realized that my father had given up and was getting ready to die. He died in November, and you'd think that I'd be able to get it out of my mind (or that particular aspect of it, anyway) by this time, but I can't seem to."

CHAPTER 14

INTO THE WILDERNESS

EXCEPT FOR MARON SIMON the rewrite man and Jimmy Flexner and Joe Alsop and, I think, Tex O'Reilly, and maybe a few others, you and I are the only ones still around. Stanley [Walker] is gone, of course, and so is Charlie McLendon (he was night city editor when we were there) who succeeded Stanley, and so is Lessing Engelking (he was assistant city editor under Stanley when we were there) who succeeded McLendon. Ogden Reid and Mrs. Reid are gone. And so is Armistead R. Holcombe the managing editor (Stanley called him the good gray blank), and so are the editorial writers Geoffrey Parsons and Walter Millis and Henry Cabot Lodge and Marcus Duffield, and so is Mr. Rogers the head of the morgue, and so is that nice cheerful Scandinavian girl Mae Nyquist who was his assistant and who was always so helpful to young reporters just starting out and who later became head of the morgue herself, and so are Ben Robertson (I think Ben was the first to go) and Ed Angly and Alva Johnston and Ishbel Ross and Lucius Beebe and Dick Boyer and Tom Sugrue and Tom Compere and Joel Sayre and Bob Peck and Bob Neville and Joe Driscoll and Beverly Smith and John T. Whitaker the city hall reporter who became a foreign correspondent and got mixed up with Mussolini's daughter Edda Ciano. . . . I hope this doesn't sound morbid to you.

—From a letter to a former New York Herald Tribune colleague, 1981

· ·

MITCHELL'S BLEAK OUTLOOK WAS HARDLY IMPROVED BY THE FACT that he was getting no traction whatever in what he'd hoped for some time now would be his next major writing project. The several ideas he pursued in the years since the second Joe Gould installment had all stalled. He toyed with adapting Gould's story for the stage. He considered a follow-up piece on George Hunter (the two men had stayed in touch after Mitchell's Profile; once, when Joseph and Therese visited in the mid-sixties on the occasion of Hunter's ninety-fifth birthday, they found him preparing to bake a pie). In the immediate aftermath of the Gould book, Mitchell seemed to be working intently on a major update about McSorley's, a piece that would go deeper into the saloon's colorful history. He amassed a trove of original material for that, such as wills tracking how the bar exchanged hands and the recollections of family members and principals, especially as to the later owners, the Kirwans. He and Therese even took a vacation in Ireland so Mitchell could piggyback some reporting on Old John McSorley's ancestry. One can readily imagine the appeal of the project for Mitchell. He knew McSorley's so well that reporting the story would not seem like starting from scratch. Besides, the Gould "sequel" had gone so well that the idea of revisiting another of his "greatest hits" might well have been attractive. Even so, Mitchell apparently could not find a suitable dramatic pretext for the story—at least to stand on its own—or build up enough momentum to overcome his inertia.

Still, as he felt his window of productivity shutting, Mitchell couldn't let go of the idea that had nagged at him for so long—that "big book" about New York City. At this stage of his life, the exact nature of the decades-old idea was hard for Mitchell to describe, when he tried to describe it at all, which given his secretive nature he seldom did except for occasional updates for his editors. What he had in mind was a work that would amount to "a summation of all I have ever written about the city," according to notes he assembled before one such meeting with William Shawn in the early seventies. But he would need something—a place, a person, an idea—to give the story definition. He thought for a while that McSorley's might be that connective tissue. He had a similar notion about the Fulton Fish Market, and over these same years he amassed folder after folder of market records, accounts of interviews and anecdotes, sketches of buildings, random musings, and other materials. But in time he rejected both those concepts; "they simply weren't representative enough," he said in one cryptic, and rare, journal note on the subject.

Instead, Mitchell eventually shifted his thinking to building his story around a larger-than-life character, and here he had two potential leads in mind. He had known both from his earliest days in New York, more than four decades ago. And both, as it happened, could be stand-ins for Mitchell himself. As with his shorter stories, being so comfortable and empathetic with his characters' personalities and motivations would make the formidable task more feasible.

The first of these was Joe Cantalupo, the carter from the Fulton Fish Market. The Joes had remained close since Cantalupo first took the young newspaper reporter under his wing (and, frankly, his protection, as Mitchell insinuated himself into a shadowy world not all that fond of nosy outsiders). In fact, Cantalupo had already spent a number of years helping Mitchell with his research on the market. Together they had turned up copious historical materials, including vendor checks and transaction documents dating back almost to the Civil War, and on many occasions Cantalupo had been a willing accomplice when Mitchell went on scavenging hunts in derelict buildings in the neighborhood. He was "distinctly a New Yorker," in Mitchell's estimation. Cantalupo's father had emigrated from Italy and begun the carting business near the end of the nineteenth century. The son would take it over and go on to run it himself for fifty years. In that time Cantalupo rose to be something of the "boss" of the market, a person of great influence because he knew everyone in the stalls, what they did there, and how they got there.

Despite his common roots, the hauler of the market's trash was worldly, well read, and thoughtful. He and Mitchell would sit over a meal at Sloppy Louie's and talk for hours. Cantalupo combined the qualities Mitchell loved about so many of his recent characters—he had the constancy of Louie Morino, the historical perspective of George Hunter, the homespun philosophy of Ellery Thompson, and the lifelong connection to the water of Harry Lyons. Mitchell particularly respected how, as an outsider, Cantalupo had gradually conquered a world long dominated by Yankees, and he did so in such a sly, amiable way that they didn't even realize it.

Physically Cantalupo was a great, hulking presence, and he could be intimidatingly gruff, a combination that made him seem like an

Mitchell with his lifelong friend Joe Cantalupo, who for the writer was a boisterous symbol of a New York that was fading away.

extra from a mob movie. But in truth he had a warm heart and a reputation around the Fulton area for integrity. And there was simply nothing he enjoyed more than eating. Friends tell of walking with Cantalupo to a luncheon meeting at a nice restaurant, only to have him stop along the way for a hot dog or a bowl of clams as a "warm-up." Kent Barwick, who worked closely with both Cantalupo and Mitchell for many years in various preservation efforts, recalls an afternoon in 1967 he spent with the two of them. It happened to be the last day of operation for the old Hoboken ferry, and they decided to honor the occasion by hopping the ferry, downing some clam steamers at a favorite seafood joint, then riding the boat back to Manhattan. Once back, Cantalupo allowed that it had been such an agreeable trip that they should do it again—which they immediately did. It was that sheer New York exuberance, so similar to Liebling's, that perhaps most endeared Cantalupo to Mitchell.

The importance of Cantalupo in Mitchell's life, and as a prospective character for his book, is clear from one particular note the writer made about him: "What I must establish as quickly as possible . . . as early in the story as possible: Joe Cantalupo became my guide to the fish market; a way of looking at the world; and an example of rising above it."

Mitchell's other narrative prospect was an equally close and venerable friend. Instead of being a prototypical New Yorker, however, this candidate was a classic New York émigré who, like Mitchell himself, had come to the city from the South and made it her own.

From the moment Mitchell met Ann Honeycutt, not long after he hit New York, the two became fast friends; they would remain so for

Ann Honeycutt in her late forties. Mitchell was one of the few men in her life she could count on.

the rest of their lives. Over the years Honeycutt transitioned from being the person some called "the girlfriend of *The New Yorker*" to simply one part of the big, rolling cast of characters who were, officially or unofficially, connected to the magazine. Worldly and witty, she was always excellent company. For many years she and Mitchell had lunch every few months with an editor at the magazine, Robert MacMillan, and one of its best-known cartoonists, Charles Addams. On one such occasion, Honeycutt noted with concern that Mitchell hadn't said much throughout the meal; he replied that he wasn't feeling well and was about to see the doctor. "Well, take it easy and don't let anything happen to you," she said—then, almost as an afterthought: "I depend on you. You're the one I call up when I have a hangover."

Mitchell had a certain gallant quality, and Honeycutt was not the only woman in his circle who counted on it. He played a similar role in the tragic later years of *New Yorker* writer Maeve Brennan (like Honeycutt herself, a former Mrs. St. Clair McKelway) and, more significantly, with Liebling's widow, Jean Stafford. In the last decade of Stafford's difficult life, the writer spiraled into a miasma of depression, alcoholism, and physical ailment. She might call Mitchell at any hour, mumbling in an alcoholic stupor or delivering a sharp rant. When she died, she named Mitchell executor of her estate.

Outwardly, Mitchell characterized his relationship with Honeycutt in fairly chaste terms. "I got to be like the younger brother, that's about the way it was," he recalled in an interview near the end of his life. "She was just a few years older than I was. It was a funny relationship, because she was like an older sister, but [also] like an aunt—she was always telling me what to do." But from the recollection of mutual friends and some of Mitchell's cryptic journal notes, it seems clear Honeycutt's feelings for him were about more than dependence, and Mitchell's for her were more than filial. Though there is no evidence suggesting their relationship was ever a sexual one, Mitchell—especially as a younger man—was hardly immune to her beauty and the charms that beguiled so many of his *New Yorker* colleagues. She was an impossibly romantic figure to him, the embodiment of that fizzy and fast-receding time in New York's history. "Listening to

Joe talk about her," said the magazine's former deputy editor, Chip McGrath, "you could hear the tinkle of ice in her glass, see the blotch of red lipstick at the tip of her cigarette." Indeed, one of the notes Mitchell made when he was gathering his thoughts about a prospective Profile of her suggested the depth of his feelings. Both of them implicitly understood they needed to keep things in check, he wrote. "We had without ever talking about it settled on a code of behavior. If either of us because of booze had overstepped this line, it would've been very embarrassing."

There was another thing that made Honeycutt irresistible to Mitchell, at least as a subject: She could tell a good story, and she had many to tell. One found in his notes underlines the point. After an evening out, Honeycutt invited her date back for coffee. She was in the kitchen getting the pot on and was about to rejoin the man in the living room—which in her apartment was accessed through her bedroom—when she found him lying in her bed, "strip stark naked." As she told Mitchell, "I went back into the kitchen and got a carving knife, one of those long, black-handled German carving knives that chefs use, and I went into the bedroom and I said, 'Do you see this knife? Take a look at this knife, and now I want you to get your clothes on and get out of here. I'm going into the kitchen to pour myself a cup of coffee and when I come back into this room if you're still here, I'll cut your balls off.' When I came back, there was no sign of him."

Of course, the final reason Mitchell was drawn so strongly to Honeycutt's story was that it paralleled his own: Southerner from the sticks makes her way to the big city between the wars to find fame, fortune, excitement, and—in her case, intermittently—love. Mitchell realized Honeycutt could provide him with an almost autobiographical approach for telling the New York story without its actually having to be autobiographical.

It's easy enough to see why *both* Cantalupo and Honeycutt were appealing prospects for Mitchell's prospective narrative, and, in fact, he never really let go of the idea of writing about either of them. Over the years he amassed an astonishing seven file drawers of resource materials about Honeycutt, consisting primarily of family history and legal files but also including caches of correspondence she maintained with Jean Stafford, Stanley Walker, and others in their mutual circles.

Yet for reasons known only to Mitchell, in the end neither subject, despite their obvious qualifications, exactly suited his writerly purpose. It's likely one of the hang-ups was simply that he knew both Cantalupo and Honeycutt *too* well; while that intimacy gave him special insight, it also made him more anxious than if he were writing about someone he wasn't so close to. Then, too, his enthusiasms tended to wax and wane. Mitchell's post-Gould pursuit of his next big project had only underscored the extent to which *his* New York was disappearing, and that in turn had the effect of stunting his ardor for the whole enterprise. As he wrote, "I began to be oppressed by a feeling that New York City had gone past me and that I didn't belong here anymore. . . ."

And so it appears that by the late sixties, the writer settled upon an important decision: If his capstone opus was going to have a protagonist, it would be Mitchell himself. Without question, Cantalupo, Honeycutt, and other friends and acquaintances would still figure in the book—but as characters only. Mitchell would have to "use myself as the center," he wrote in his journal.

For the self-conscious Mitchell, this was no easy decision. He had never written overtly autobiographical material, never even been comfortable with the idea. The early Mitchell stories that drew most directly on his personal experiences and family history had always been protected by the scrim of fiction. But with the passing of his mother (and soon enough his father), and with the encouragement of his patron, Shawn, the idea of autobiography seemed less daunting than it had before.

HAVING MADE THIS DIFFICULT choice, Mitchell took to the idea with some zeal, at least early on. By spring of 1970 he had pulled together a prospective opening for the book, a uniquely Mitchellesque love letter to the city that was far enough along that he was willing to share it with his editor. Almost as quickly as he got the material, Shawn telephoned Mitchell at home to praise it. According to Mitchell's note after their conversation, Shawn called it "some of the best writing about New York City I have ever read."

By this point in their lives, Mitchell and Shawn had a warm albeit complicated relationship. They were close, having worked together for Mitchell's entire career. Shawn had joined the magazine in 1933, the same year Mitchell began his freelance contributions to it; Shawn quickly was put in charge of the magazine's nonfiction writers, including Mitchell, until he succeeded Ross as editor. To each other they were Bill and Joe, but they were not intimate friends, as intimacy was not an emotion either man encouraged. Besides, Shawn was still the boss. His impeccable manners, legendary neurotic quirks (fear of elevators, bridges, and tunnels, to name but a few of pointed inconvenience to a resident of New York), and soft-spoken mien only punctuated the steely autonomy he exerted over every aspect of the magazine—including the professional and financial fortunes of its writing staff.

William Shawn displayed limitless patience waiting for the next Mitchell story, knowing it might never arrive.

He had earned that authority. Back in 1952, when Ross's highly successful magazine was bequeathed to his care, Shawn had nothing of his predecessor's public profile. The outside world didn't know what to expect of this quiet, introverted man. But Shawn quickly catapulted Ross's "comic paper" into a journal of unparalleled cultural influence. The magazine's reporting, always top-drawer, became broader, more openly political, and often personal. It was Shawn who sent political philosopher Hannah Arendt to Jerusalem for the Eichmann trial; who encouraged the sharp critical voices of Pauline Kael, Michael Arlen, Kenneth Tynan, and George Steiner; who published for his patrician audience James Baldwin's anguished, angry "Letter from a Region of My Mind." On the fiction side, Shawn cultivated stories that unmasked the desperation residing in the immaculate suburban homes of those same affluent customers. Readers responded, and so did advertisers. By the mid-sixties, the magazine was more profitable than it had ever been; *The New Yorker* was sometimes so fat with ads that it resembled a phone book. Shawn's critics would say it often *read* like a phone book, with too much text and tedium and too little of the old humor. But there was no denying that the diminutive Shawn now cast a long shadow on American letters and culture.

Given all they had been through together, and given that the editor was a nonpareil judge of writing talent, no one better appreciated Joseph Mitchell and what he had meant to the rise of *The New Yorker* than Shawn. Along with Ross, Shawn had provided Mitchell with the encouragement and flexibility he needed to pursue untraditional subjects. At the same time, Shawn *was* editor of a commercial publication whose staff included a supremely gifted writer who hadn't published anything since 1964. A decade on, one can readily imagine his patience privately fraying as year followed year with little true cause for hope. Even so, Shawn was "content to wait" on Mitchell, according to McGrath. Besides, as everyone knew, Shawn avoided confrontation as assiduously as he did confined spaces, and he would have considered it unseemly—this being *The New Yorker,* after all—to raise questions of productivity with Mitchell. But Mitchell knew full well his lack of production put Shawn in a difficult spot. "That was an embarrassment to me," Mitchell would say later on. "I didn't want people to think, 'What was Shawn doing?'" At the same time, he added, "There was a kind of favoritism involved. We had a great respect for each other. We'd grown up here at a time when the wages were very small. He realized that and, in effect, he was making it up to me. Those are rather subtle things to explain to people."

Despite that implicit quid pro quo, Mitchell's meager pay of late was increasingly preying on his mind. As his general outlook on life darkened and spiraling inflation ate into what little he took home, Mitchell had become obsessed to the point of bitterness about his compensation—not just in terms of what he was making at the time but over the course of his career. He wasn't a fool; Mitchell knew well the role he played in *The New Yorker*'s popularity and profitability, especially through the forties and fifties. Yet after all that work and critical praise, his weekly pay in 1970 was only one hundred seventy dollars, of which he netted only one hundred thirty. Perhaps emboldened by Shawn's positive response to the submission of his first original material in years, Mitchell decided to confront him about his salary. It wasn't enough for him to live on, he told the editor. Mitchell was uncharacteristically upset—and explicit about what had happened to his standard of living.

For instance, Mitchell said he was supposed to get medical checkups twice a year, including X-rays. But "that costs two hundred dollars each time I go and I can't afford it," he told Shawn, according to notes Mitchell made at the time. "I can't afford to buy books. I go to the theater maybe once a year. I eat lunch in a restaurant no more than twice a week, the rest of the time in the automat." He confided that Therese had recently gone to work to augment their income, but it still wasn't enough for them to make ends meet. While in the past his farm income would have bridged any gap, that was no longer true, because the federal government was reducing tobacco allotments.

Beyond the dollars-and-cents of the situation, Mitchell told Shawn, he no longer felt appreciated. When he was elected to the National Institute of Arts and Letters, he said, no one from the magazine's top management even mentioned it to him. He had remained quiet when younger reporters talked to other publications about *The New Yorker*'s low pay or its growing reputation for editorial stodginess after two decades under Shawn. "My policy has been to stay in my office and do my work and keep my mouth shut," Mitchell said, "but now I am desperate. Young people who are imitating Profiles I wrote and which I can no longer do because I don't want to do the same thing over and over are being paid many times the amounts I was paid and are being treated much better in many other ways," such as in their retirement packages and profit participation. Though Mitchell's agitation clearly had been building for years, it was a recent episode that had put him over the brink. A young writer at the magazine had sought his advice about whether to stay at *The New Yorker* because of its prestige or to jump to a rival and make more money. In the course of the conversation, he shared with Mitchell how much he was making—and it was a good bit more than Mitchell was. Mitchell was shocked by this, he told Shawn, and "I have been seething ever since."

By this point in his life, it was not that unusual for Mitchell to get worked up, but it was highly unusual for him—or any *New Yorker* employee, for that matter—to focus that ire directly on Shawn. Over the years, the editor had cultivated an aura of benevolent dictatorship at *The New Yorker*, exerting a courteous but unquestioned rule. The main lever of his control was his arbitrary but uniformly parsimonious pay scale. Shawn essentially held that it was a privilege to work for *The New Yorker*, and questions of appropriate remuneration were really no one's business but his. As Mitchell suggested, however, the younger staffers, with less fealty to Shawn, were beginning to compare salaries—among themselves and with colleagues at other magazines— and they were pressuring him to pay them with more than prestige. Within several years, in fact, the Newspaper Guild would threaten to organize *The New Yorker*'s editorial staff, the most serious challenge to his authority Shawn had faced. He would weather it, but only after promising to improve the salary structure, which he did.

As for Mitchell's own dilemma, Shawn pledged to do what he could, and not long afterward he raised Mitchell's weekly pay to just under three hundred dollars. He did this in part by incorporating the magazine's annual employee bonus into the writer's regular wage. This was a significant concession, because *The New Yorker*'s bonus participation by staff had traditionally been an unpredictable, on-again-off-again affair—another of Mitchell's bones of contention.

This gesture seemed to mollify Mitchell, who, as a writer who wasn't writing, knew he didn't have the strongest negotiating position. He and Shawn resumed their usual relationship and sporadic story meetings, which in time basically evolved into an annual session in which Mitchell updated him on what he was working on. If what Mitchell had been working on for a decade remained a mystery to most people at the magazine, Mitchell said it was not a mystery to Shawn. Mitchell was being "sidetracked" by a variety of things, he readily acknowledged to the editor, including the fact he was spending more time helping tend to the family's farms in North Carolina. But Shawn figured that "sooner or later" his patience would be rewarded.

After one of these meetings, in April of 1977, Shawn "was encouraging" about the progress Mitchell had reported, according to a note in the writer's journal. Shawn, as usual, didn't press Mitchell on a completion date. He did, however, offer some reassurance to Mitchell, who by now was worried about whether even Shawn might reach the point of exasperation. "He gave me the impression—I didn't bring the matter out in the open—that I can stay at *The New Yorker* and keep on trying to finish it as long as I want to—or as long as I can hold up," Mitchell wrote.

And he *was* making progress—slow progress, admittedly. From the copious notes he left from this period and from the three opening chapters that exist, it seems his intention was to toggle between his two worlds, North Carolina and New York, and that the familiar theme of exile would figure prominently. One journal note, for instance, recounts the day when, while walking in Brooklyn's historic Green-Wood Cemetery, he made the "discovery" that he was "not a New Yorker, never felt myself to be . . . I am a North Carolinian . . . Walking along the cemetery path, or up one of the hills, the vista, sudden realization: I am not going to be buried here. That is what cuts me off. I have always known it in the back of my mind. I don't belong here, I have not really thrown in my lot with these people."

At least through the first half of the seventies, Mitchell was pursuing this narrative as vigorously as he had anything in a long time. He maintained a folder of notes, clippings, and miscellany, which he always reviewed before going back to North Carolina; he used this material to construct lengthy "to do" lists for each trip, and they clearly were those of a writer reporting on the details of his own past: "Find out the year the old barn was torn down and the truck garage was put up"; "Try to find out the year I was baptized"; "Get photographs of the four sides of the house"; "Measure the circumference of the trunk of the black walnut tree at the Butler Place"; "Check on names of roads, such as White Pond Road, Old Rowland Road"; "Get a copy of the history of Ashpole church."

In the draft of Mitchell's personal narrative, the first chapter is a sweeping portrait of his adopted home, New York. It manages to convey a life's worth of impressions of the city, but with no sense at all of being rushed or overwrought. The opening paragraph sets the tone as only Mitchell can:

> In my time, I have visited and poked around in every one of the hundreds of neighborhoods of which this city is made up, and by the city I mean the whole city—Manhattan, Brooklyn, the Bronx, Queens, and Richmond. I have gone to some of these neighborhoods only once or twice, but I have gone to others—or to certain streets in them—over and over and over again, sometimes for reasons that I clearly understand and sometimes for reasons that I dimly understand and sometimes for reasons that I don't understand at all. Certain streets haunt me and certain blocks in certain streets haunt me and certain buildings in certain blocks in certain streets haunt me. At any hour of the day or night, I can shut my eyes and visualize in a swarm of detail

what is happening on scores of streets, some well-known and some obscure, from one end of the city to the other—on the upper part of Webster Avenue, up in the upper Bronx, for example, which has a history as a dumping-out place for underworld figures who have been taken for a ride and which I go to every now and then because I sometimes find a weed or a wild flower or a moss or a fern or a vine that is new to me growing along its edges or in the cracks in its pavements and also because there are pleasant views of the Bronx River and of the Central and the New Haven railroad tracks on one side of it and pleasant views of Woodlawn Cemetery on the other side of it, or on North Moore Street, down on the lower West Side of Manhattan, which used to be lined with spice warehouses and spice-grinding mills and still has enough of them left on it to make it the most aromatic street in the city (on ordinary days, it is so aromatic it is mildly and tantalizingly and elusively exciting; on windy days, particularly on warm, damp, windy days, it is so aromatic it is exhilarating), or on Birmingham Street, which is a tunnel-like alley that runs for one block alongside the Manhattan end of the Manhattan Bridge and is used by bums of the kind that Bellevue psychiatrists call loner winos as a place in which to sit in comparative seclusion and drink and doze and by drug addicts and drug pushers as a place in which to come into contact with each other and by old-timers in the neighborhood as a shortcut between East Broadway and the streets to the south, or on Emmons Avenue, which is the principal street of Sheepshead Bay, in Brooklyn, and along one side of which the party boats and charter boats and bait boats of the Sheepshead Bay fishing fleet tie up, or on Beach 116th Street, which, although only two blocks long, is the principal street of Rockaway Park, in Queens, and from one end of which there is a stirring view of the ocean, and from one end of which there is a stirring view of Jamaica Bay, or on Bloomingdale Road, which is the principal street of a quiet old settlement of Southern Negroes called Sandy Ground down in the rural part of Staten Island, the southernmost part of the city.

From that present tense, Mitchell in the second chapter immediately plunges into the past, to his beginnings in Fairmont. That opening passage:

It is odd, to begin with, that I ever had any connection with New York City at all. The great majority of my ancestors have been farmers or mixed up in some way with farming, and I come from a part of the country—Robeson County, North Carolina—where the people tend to stay put. One day recently I was in the Local History Room of the Public Library. While waiting for a book to be delivered from the stacks, I dawdled along the open shelves that line one side of the room, killing time by reading titles, and I came across a set of volumes on each of whose spines was lettered: "CENSUS 1790 / HEADS OF FAMILIES." I opened the first volume and saw that the full title was "Heads of Families at the First Census of the United States Taken in the Year 1790." I got down the volume for North Carolina and took it over to a reading table and looked up Robeson County and found it, and then I looked up the section in the lower part of the county in which I was born and grew up and in which most of the people in my family still live and found it, and then I started going down the columns of names. The names were not listed alphabetically but evidently in the order that they were taken down by the census taker as he made his rounds. I had not gone far before I began to smile with the pleasure of recognition, for many of the old names suddenly and unexpectedly come upon were very familiar and dear and magical to me, and I soon saw that a much higher proportion than I had ever realized of the names that are around in my section of Robeson County today were also around as far back as 1790. 1790 names are, in fact, with a few newer ones, the most numerous and the most characteristic names of the countryside today—Pitman, for example, although now generally spelled Pittman, and Lewis and Inman and Grimsley and Musslewight or Musslewhite (now spelled Musselwhite) and Hedgepath (now spelled Hedgepeth) and Griffin and Grantham and Thompson and Mitchell and Ashley and Townsend and Atkinson and Bullock and Purvis and Leggett and Jenkins and Page and Oliver and Barnes and Gaddy and Rogers and Strickland and Harding (now spelled Hardin) and McMillen (now spelled McMillan) and Ivey and Watson and Hunt and Hill and Stephens and Oxendine and Stone and Davis and Britt and Lockileer (now spelled Locklear) and Taylor and Turner and Lee and Lowry. When I go down to Robeson County for a visit, and ride around the countryside with my father or one of my brothers or sisters or brothers-in-law or sisters-in-law or nephews or nieces or cousins, these are the names that I see most frequently on the fronts of stores and filling stations and sawmills and cotton gins and tobacco warehouses and on the sides of trucks and on roadside mailboxes and on miscellaneous roadside signs.

Having set up this New York–North Carolina dichotomy, Mitchell then produced a much shorter third chapter, in which he discusses how he came to live in the past and what that means. He admits he's not altogether pleased to find himself in this position. "I am not entirely satisfied with the phrase living in the past as a description of my way of life," he writes; "it makes me sound like some kind of sad old recluse, but living in the past is the closest I can come to it. . . ." Then he tries to explain himself.

I should also say that when I say the past I mean a number of pasts, a hodgepodge of pasts, a spider's web of pasts, a jungle of pasts—my own past; my father's past; my mother's past; the pasts of my brothers and sisters . . . the pasts of a score or so of strange men and women—bohemians, visionaries, obsessives, impostors, fanatics, lost souls, gypsy kings and gypsy queens, and out-and-out freak-show freaks—whom I got to know and kept in touch with for years while working as a newspaper reporter and whom I thought of back then as being uniquely strange—only-one-of-a-kind-in-the-whole-world-strange— but whom, since almost everybody has come to seem strange to me, including myself, I now think of—without taking a thing away from them—as being strange, all right, no doubt about that, but also as being stereotypes—as being stereotypically strange, so to speak, or perhaps prototypically strange would be more exact or archetypically strange or even *Ur*-strange or maybe old-fashioned pre-Freudian-insight strange would be about right. . . .

This excerpt comes from a single labyrinthine sentence that accounts for more than half of the entire chapter. It sweeps across the decades from Fairmont to the Fulton Fish Market, with long digressions on three of Mitchell's "strange men and women": Lady Olga ("I was exiled by my own flesh and blood"); street preacher James Jefferson Davis Hall ("The end of the world is coming! Oh, yes! Any day now! Any night now!"); and gypsy Madame Mary, beneath whose kind, grandmotherly mien, Mitchell said, was a calculated genius for finding vulnerable people and a "mercilessness with which she could gradually get hold of [their] money." A twelve-hundred-word sentence, however virtuosic, can't help but come across as a kind of literary parlor trick. But Mitchell constructed it this way to establish that these many pasts of his were inseparable from one another, that they flowed from and into one another seamlessly, even inevitably—a virtual river of experiences. This third chapter was to function as the book's jumping-off point and provide the *raison d'être* for Mitchell to look back over his life and plumb the connections, as well as the tensions, between his real and adopted homes.

As it happens, all three chapters also represent excellent illustrations of another favorite Mitchell technique: the list. In such instances Mitchell pulled together example after example of what he was writing about, in almost staccato fashion, as seen in the Fairmont chapter's march of household names: ". . . and Griffin and Grantham and Thompson and Mitchell and Ashley and Townsend and Atkinson and Bullock and Purvis. . . ." In lesser hands this could be a mere writerly tic, but Mitchell used a list to accomplish a number of things at once. It subtly conveys authority—the narrator was on the scene and has an extraordinary grasp of the material he's writing about. It puts across his keen powers of observation—nothing, even the most seemingly insignificant detail, is beyond his seeing and interpreting. Finally, a Mitchell list always has a music to it; he labored to get its "sound" as right as its weight and pace. And so, when he visits the graveyard with Mr. Hunter, he doesn't merely indicate that the gravestones are being overtaken with weeds and unruly wildflowers. He tells us they are "ragweed, Jimson weed, pavement weed, catchfly, Jerusalem oak, bed-straw, goldenrod, cocklebur, butter-and-eggs, dandelion, bouncing Bet" and so on. If the reader has scant idea what most of these plants are, we know the author most assuredly does. As the writer Luc Sante observed, "Setting these objects side by side in a row has an effect that is both as plain as Shaker furniture and as expansive as a cinematic tracking shot."

The first chapter of Mitchell's memoir is essentially complete. The second chapter is largely complete, although near its close it stops mysteriously, mid-anecdote, and it's not clear from his notes how Mitchell intended to end it. The brief third chapter seems complete. But after drafting these opening sections—about twelve thousand words in all—Mitchell seems to have stopped the writing (if not the reporting), and he left no overt indication as to where he planned to take the story line. On the contrary, from his jumbled papers one gets the impression that he didn't know himself.

Nonetheless, several aspects of the book do seem clear. Given the effort Mitchell was making to reconstruct his own history and that of Fairmont, there is no question that the North Carolina part of his life was going to figure prominently; it was not just there for biographical context. On the other hand, it was still going to be essentially a New York story—*his* New York story. Since Mitchell had settled on autobi-ography, it wouldn't exactly be the book he'd sketched out in "Joe

Gould's Secret"; in spirit it was probably going to be closer to the idea he'd pitched, unsuccessfully, to St. Clair McKelway back in the mid-thirties, about the young arrival from the South trying to figure out New York even as he was trying to figure out himself. And without doubt the people and places that had helped Mitchell do just that—Joe Cantalupo and Ann Honeycutt and the gypsies and preachers and sideshow performers and McSorley's and the Fulton Fish Market—would all make appearances.

But how to write that? Obviously the two worlds, North Carolina and New York, were going to be held in some kind of juxtaposition. Yet it's not known if, from a structural standpoint, Mitchell planned to continue caroming back and forth or if the two worlds would some-how eventually merge in his narrative. Now confronted with that question, the writer seemed puzzled. Indeed, the third chapter drops him at a fork in the road, and not knowing which direction he wanted to take may be the reason he simply stopped where he was.

On the fortieth anniversary of their marriage—the 1931 elope-ment, that is, not the second, "formal" wedding a year later—Mitchell and Therese had decided to splurge by dining at Gage and Tollner, a Brooklyn establishment that since 1879 had kept alive the spirit of the gaslight age. They didn't go there often, because it was pricey and rather out of the way. But Mitchell thought it "the best restaurant in the city," which, given his sophisticated palate, was saying something. Much as he loved its seafood, the house specialty, what Mitchell val-ued most about Gage and Tollner was what it stood for—the "old furnishings and old Negro waiters and old ways of doing things." Therese had a crab dish with Lyonnaise potatoes and some wine; Mitchell had the striped bass with a baked potato and two bottles of Bass ale. The meals cost eighteen dollars; Mitchell tipped their waiter three dollars and sent over another dollar to the restaurant's head-waiter, a friend.

They passed a lovely evening reminiscing, about that fateful train ride out to Greenwich and about all the things, good and bad, that had transpired since. It was typical of Mitchell that in his cryptic journal notes about that night he recorded more about the cost of the food and tips than the substance of their conversation. In this instance, however, it's not difficult to surmise. They may have compared notes on what they had been reading; Mitchell's tastes were as eclectic as ever, but no more so than Therese's, who avidly consumed everything from popular novels to Thomas Hardy to the *New York Post*, all of which she liked to read sprawled on the couch while she smoked trim cigarillos and popped Good & Plenty candy. They may have talked about Mitchell's memoir in progress. They likely discussed their *New Yorker* friends and how, as they all became parents together, Therese began to make photographic portraits of their children. And certainly they talked of Nora and Elizabeth, the young women they had become, and the families of their own they were starting.

After dropping out of Vassar, Nora in time would obtain her college degree, as her father had predicted. Along the way she met a Princeton student named John Sanborn, who (much to Mitchell's delight) would become a tugboat captain. They married in 1962 and by now, a decade later, had two children, a boy and a girl. Meanwhile, Elizabeth's young adulthood, like Nora's, was not exactly a straight trajectory. She began college at Transylvania University in Kentucky but left after several years. She had recently met and married an Atlanta man named Hal Curtis, a development that relocated her to Georgia. In the next few years they would have three children—two girls and a boy—before eventually divorcing. In time Elizabeth, too, would obtain her college degree, by attending classes at Agnes Scott College and Oglethorpe University.

Throughout the first half of the seventies, Joseph and Therese tried to see their expanding family as often as possible—not too difficult in the case of Nora and John, who were only an hour away in New Jersey; more so with Elizabeth and Hal down in Georgia, though their (relative) proximity to Fairmont accommodated "piggyback" visits. At this professionally frustrating time in Mitchell's life, his daughters and grandchildren were a great comfort to him. At the same time, his counsel and unstinting support would prove equally comforting to his daughters as they navigated the challenges of marriage and inescapable setbacks of child-rearing. When Nora and John hit a difficult patch early in their relationship, for instance, Mitchell tried to be as available to them as possible without being judgmental. "He had strong feelings about it all, of course, and everything that hurt us, hurt him," Nora wrote. "When he gave advice he gave it in the least obtrusive way. Some of the best he ever gave me (after I was harrumphing and haranguing about some political or social episode) was, 'Honey, you don't have to have an opinion about *everything*.'"

On the other hand, to a writer, grandchildren were a tempting diversion, if the best kind. As Mitchell told Shawn, all sorts of things seemed to be conspiring now to keep him from his typewriter—and Mitchell, frankly, allowed them to do just that.

Some of the interruptions he could do nothing about, like the slow decline and death of his father. Others appeared unexpectedly. In late 1974, for instance, he was appointed to the advisory council of the South Street Seaport Museum. The museum was established in 1967 near the Fulton Market site, along the East River. Its purpose was to preserve the historic buildings there, threatened at the time by inattention and development, and to serve as an interactive educational facility by reproducing life along the waterfront during the bustling period of the mid-nineteenth century. Joe Cantalupo was one of the museum's founders and biggest advocates.

The appointment delighted Mitchell. It brought him full circle to his early days in the city when he discovered the Fulton Fish Market and the characters who would populate his Mr. Flood stories. At a time when New York was in thrall to the wrecking ball, here was an enterprise trying to save and celebrate an important part of its past. Almost from the museum's inception, Mitchell had done some volunteer work there; no doubt encouraged by Cantalupo, he was already a member of the project's Local History Committee, which was researching the history of the seaport and building a special collection for scholars and other interested parties—work that dovetailed nicely with Mitchell's own reporting.

At first his involvement in the advisory council was strictly in the preservation aspect. In time, though, he came to "believe wholeheartedly in the entire program of the seaport," Mitchell wrote upon his appointment. "I believe that the things we are doing down there, as foolish as some of them may seem to be at first glance, are beginning to have an effect for the good on the way many citizens feel about the city and about their links to the city . . . and I believe that this is of enormous importance to the future of the city. If I remember Gibbon correctly, the healthy growth as well as the decline and fall of great empires and great cities are directly related to just such matters." Though Mitchell would become decidedly less enthusiastic about the eventual commercialization and "malling" of the South Street Seaport area in general, he would stay connected to the Seaport Museum for the rest of his life.

Given his growing venerability as a New York "elder," Mitchell would continue to be approached about such worthwhile endeavors—for instance, the essay on his favorite saloon, when someone had the idea to get a "McSorley's Day" proclaimed in New York for its one hundred twenty-fifth anniversary, in February of 1979. Though apparently not written for publication, the essay, at fifteen hundred words, was one of the more substantial things Mitchell had actually written in a while. The undertaking also made him self-consciously aware of one ironic change: Largely because he had plucked the onetime neighborhood bar from obscurity, it now had a kind of international cachet. Stubbornly disdaining fashion, McSorley's had become . . . well, fashionable. As Mitchell wrote:

In 1970, James Cameron, the veteran English foreign correspondent, did a survey of the world's most famous bars for the Sunday Magazine of the London *Times,* and he put McSorley's high up on the list, along with such places as the downstairs bar at the Ritz Hotel in London, the Crillon Bar in Paris, Harry's Bar in Venice, the Excelsior Bar in Rome, the Regina Bar in Munich, and the Cosmopolitan Bar in Cairo. The owners of McSorley's and its bartenders have never been able to make up their minds how they feel about this sort of thing—whether, that is, they would prefer the place to be obscure and peaceful or famous and jumping. "Some nights there's only a dozen or so old-timers in McSorley's and they sit against the walls and read newspapers and doze and watch the stove get red hot, and I like it in here on those nights," one of the bartenders once said, "but I have to admit that I also like it on nights when it seems that every ale drinker in New York, New Jersey, and Connecticut and his brother had decided to drop into McSorley's for a couple of mugs of ale and all of a sudden there's standing room only and not much of that and we have to send a pot-boy to stand in the door and block the way and keep repeating over and over that nobody outside can come in until somebody inside goes out.

THOUGH THE DEATH OF his father still left Mitchell feeling bereft, in another sense it was a release. For the first time he really *could* imagine himself not just parachuting in and out of North Carolina but actually living much of his life there. Indeed, Fairmont became yet another impediment between Mitchell and his writing during this period, as he took on a more active role in the family business. His brother Jack had assumed the responsibilities A.N. once handled, and he looked out for his older brother's financial interests. But Joseph's personal involvement was keener than ever. He consulted on what stands to timber out from the large swaths of the farm that were forested, as well as on how best to reforest those same areas. Ditches had to be dug and kept clear for proper drainage and irrigation. Innumerable fire lanes were cut. Then there was the planting side of the operation. With the declining demand for cotton and with tobacco being notoriously hard on soil, the family experimented with year-round rotations, growing winter wheat and, in the spring, corn and soybeans. Mitchell threw himself into all this activity with such enthusiasm that one of his sisters took to teasing him, "Why don't you give up farming and take up writing?"

On the farm, Mitchell was in his element in a way that was no

Mitchell and daughter Nora inspect a family warehouse in Fairmont.

longer true in New York. Like many children of the land, he had a visceral connection to property and it could be rekindled by the simplest task, be it clearing brush or slathering skinned trees with gummy black paint to inhibit insects. Mitchell readily rediscovered the joy of his childhood here—living in the past, but in the best sense—and it was a place where he could channel his energies into things that were about growth, not decline. He confided to people that he and Therese were looking forward to the day—not far off now—when they could live half the year in New York and half in Fairmont. Mitchell cautiously allowed himself to dream.

Then, late in the evening of April 3, 1979, Therese suffered a stroke in their Greenwich Village apartment. Mitchell was also home and got an ambulance there quickly, but Therese suffered considerable loss of movement on her left side. After a month in the hospital and several additional months of rehabilitative therapy, she would largely recover her mobility, though she walked with a cane and had some

slurring of speech. In an effort to avoid a recurrence, doctors also operated to clear fatty deposits from her carotid arteries.

Just as Therese's life was returning to some semblance of normalcy,
it took an even more dire turn. In January of 1980, she began to experience severe pains accompanied by bleeding. Several weeks of increasingly targeted tests finally resulted in a diagnosis of renal cancer. Her
left kidney was removed, but in so doing the surgeons saw that the
cancer had metastasized to other organs, including the lungs. Further
surgery was deemed pointless.

Over the next months, as Therese steadily weakened, her husband
was her primary caregiver. He tended to her every need in the apartment, monitored her pain medication, scheduled her doctor's appointments, and got her there and back. Eventually he would carry her from
one room to another when it was necessary. As this essentially became
Mitchell's full-time job, all other activity—in New York or North
Carolina—was suspended indefinitely.

For an older generation in particular, cancer was considered such a
death sentence that it was spoken of in whispers, or code, if at all.
Mitchell had some firsthand experience with the affliction. By this
time one of his sisters had died of cancer, and another had been diagnosed with it. He himself had had an earlier episode of (benign) mel-
anoma, and Mitchell would always harbor a low dread that a graver
cancer would eventually catch up with him. In any case, at a time
when a doctor's complicity still made it possible for a husband to do
such things, Mitchell withheld Therese's true condition from her. To
tell her, he felt, would deprive his wife of hope and thus undermine her
will to persevere. Instead, he tried to rally her. "I'd be telling her it was
going to get better, it was going to get better. Trying to encourage her,
you know," Mitchell would remember near the end of his own life.
"And then I guess I got to believing it myself." According to a nephew,
David Crowley—the son of Therese's only sibling, Maude—Therese
at this time "sounded woozy [on the telephone] and told me she didn't
understand what was wrong with her."

With great effort, Mitchell arranged for his wife, by that point in a
wheelchair, to fly up to Marblehead, Massachusetts, that June to visit

Joseph and Therese on the porch in Fairmont,
which in time became as much her home as his.

Maude. Therese enjoyed the oceanside setting, and she had come here often over the years. Now she stayed for three weeks. Halfway through, she sent Mitchell a postcard saying that she and her sister were going to a seafood restaurant in nearby Salem that night for dinner and that she was looking forward to gaining back some weight. She missed him, she added, and wrote in Norwegian, "I love you, my little parrot." Therese had used such pet phrases when they were dating and early in their marriage, but as Joseph read the card he realized that she hadn't done so in years. "When she was in Marblehead she still believed without any doubts (except maybe in the middle of the night) that any day she would start regaining her strength and that after a while everything would be all right again," Mitchell would recall. "This card," he said, "broke my heart."

Of course, Therese wasn't going to get better, as Mitchell knew—and Therese almost certainly suspected. The family's agreed-upon fiction was that she was dealing primarily with a heart condition; all the while the cancer was doing its inexorable work. Early in July, with Therese rapidly reaching a point where she wouldn't be able to travel at all, the Mitchells flew to Fairmont so that Therese could spend her remaining time there, surrounded by extended family and the tranquillity she loved as much as her husband did. Mitchell set her up in the bedroom that had been empty since A.N.'s death four years earlier. There he read to her for hours on end, particularly from a recently published biography of Liebling. It diverted Therese with many memories, both pleasant and piquant. They spoke of their return to New York when she improved.

But it was in Fairmont that she died, on October 22, 1980. Therese, who for forty-nine years had been such a perfect philosophical match and emotional counterbalance to her husband, quietly slipped away from him. She was seventy years old.

At some point during his wife's illness, Mitchell had made a note to himself, apparently when contemplating her epitaph: "She had a loving heart. It saddened her to see anyone in trouble. She wanted everything good for everybody."

The depth of this final loss to Mitchell, after their half century of shared life and love, was profound. Therese had brought spontaneity to his orderly compulsion. Her sunny disposition helped offset his bouts of depression. When he railed about how the "goddamned sons of bitches" were ruining pretty much everything there was to ruin, her teasing neutralized his ire. Now that emotional ballast was gone; he was seventy-two years old, and a widower. A week after the funeral, Mitchell's daughter Elizabeth put him on a plane back to New York. "One of my most haunting memories is of him walking away from me at the Fayetteville airport," she recalled, "on his way back to the apartment, alone."

CHAPTER 15

A GHOST IN PLAIN VIEW

In my time, I have known quite a few of the worlds and the worlds within worlds of which New York City is made up, such as the world of the newspapers, the world of the criminal courts, the world of the museums, the world of the racetracks, the world of the tugboat fleets, the world of the old bookstores, the world of the old left-behind churches down in the financial district, the world of the old Irish saloons, the world of the old Staten Island oyster ports, the world of the party-boat piers at Sheepshead Bay, and the worlds of the city's two great botanical gardens, the Botanical one in the Bronx and the Botanic one in Brooklyn. As a reporter and as a curiosity seeker and as an architecture buff and as a Sunday walker and later on as a member of committees in a variety of Save-this and Save-that and Friends-of-this and Friends-of-that organizations and eventually as one of the commissioners in the Landmarks Preservation Commission, I have known some of these worlds from the inside. Even so, I have never really felt altogether at home in any of them. And I have always felt at home in Fulton Fish Market.

—*From Joseph Mitchell's unfinished memoir*

· ·

DESPITE THE EMBRACE OF MITCHELL'S FAMILY, THE AFTERMATH of Therese's death was impossibly dark and difficult for him. For Nora this was symbolized in heartbreaking fashion by her mother's photographic negatives. Years before, as Therese had stopped taking photographs, she had put the negatives into boxes and squirreled them away in various nooks of their apartment that her husband hadn't already filled with his esoteric collections. Once in a while Nora and Elizabeth would ask to see them, but Mitchell demurred. "After she died . . . my father was so bereft that he couldn't bear to look at anything that reminded him of their early life together," Nora said, "and we eventually stopped asking to see them."

Mitchell sought solace where he could. He talked informally about his grief to a psychologist whom he knew as a fellow parishioner at Grace Church in New York. Grace was a historic Episcopal church located a few blocks from his home in the Village—and for good measure, a spectacular example of French Gothic Revival architecture. Mitchell began regularly attending services sometime in the mid- to late seventies. Though never actually Episcopalian, he would spend six years as a vestryman there, which is to say he was one of the parishioners tasked with helping to oversee the church's administration. Colleague Brendan Gill recalled of Mitchell's membership at Grace that he held some "unease as a native of his Baptist and Presbyterian Low Country of North Carolina and finding himself in Episcopalian precincts. Joe complained gently that the Episcopals tended to go pretty damned easy on hellfire."

As he'd aged, and as he'd endured the mounting personal losses, Mitchell—at heart always a spiritual pilgrim—had resumed a more formal faith life. Then again, in all his years prowling the city he had made a special point of acquainting himself with services of almost every imaginable persuasion—Muslim, Catholic, Lutheran, Jewish, Greek Orthodox, Ukrainian Orthodox, Dutch Reformed. This ecclesiastical adventuring touched his passions for both architecture and anthropology. And churches revealed much of the city's character. This truth is evident in material he had written several years prior, in the opening chapter of his autobiography—much of which pivots around the churches of New York:

> I am not an Episcopalian . . . but I sometimes go to Holy Communion in an Episcopal Church. I particularly like to go to communion in one of the beautiful old Episcopal churches downtown in the financial district or a little farther up, in

Greenwich Village or on its outskirts—Trinity or St. Paul's or Grace or Ascension or St. Mark's or St. Luke's. And I especially like to go to one of these churches on a sunny Sunday morning in midsummer when the streets in the neighborhood are practically deserted and everything is peaceful and serene and far more birds than on weekdays it seems are moving around in the trees and bushes and ivy in the churchyard and the stained glass is blazing and the doors have been set ajar and the lower windows have been raised a little and somewhere or other an electric fan is whirring and prayer books and hymnals when opened in the warm air release the vinegary pungence of old books that have been handled a lot and only a sprinkling of people are present, a sprinkling of old reliables, among whom are always a few bony, stiff-backed, self-assured old women with Old New York sticking out all over them.

Comforting as he found such sacred spaces, Mitchell without Therese was an unsettled man whose spirits continued to ebb. Examples of despondence and a deepening general depression abound throughout this period. In various notes in his journals, Mitchell talks about being suspended in "worlds within worlds": "The city rooms of three newspapers, the *World*, the *Herald Tribune*, the *World-Telegram*, were worlds within worlds. Even smaller worlds: the match-game players from the HT at Bleeck's, the early-lunch crowd from the W-T at Nick's Bar and Grill (those who went to work at 6 or 7 or 8 and were ready for lunch at 11). The regulars at McSorley's, the regulars in almost any saloon. Of the many who once inhabited some of these worlds within worlds, I am the only one left." Mitchell began to meet regularly with other former staffers of the defunct *Herald Tribune;* they gathered to reminisce and provide mutual support. Mitchell enjoyed the klatches well enough, but he found they also provoked a strong melancholy, reminding him of the litany of old pals no longer around to reminisce with.

As discouraging as it was to Mitchell to be outliving his cohorts and loved ones, an even worse sensation began to take hold. He worried that he was surviving into reputational obscurity. Or, as he put it a little later on in his life, "I'm a ghost."

With his depression, Mitchell's fitful attempts to do creative work more or less ground to a halt. When people asked what he was doing

Mitchell was so passionate about the architectural history of New York City that his "volunteer" engagement became almost a full-time job.

with himself, he explained that he was still on staff at *The New Yorker* and was busy working on a book that he'd "had to postpone . . . a couple of times." He would add that he had every intention of picking it back up, and certainly he hoped he could. But he was beginning to wonder himself if he ever would.

——

THEN, IN 1982, NEW York mayor Ed Koch provided Mitchell yet another opportunity to avoid writing, for another indisputably noble cause. Koch appointed the writer to the city's Landmarks Preservation Commission, the municipal agency charged with identifying and protecting New York's historic buildings. The commission had been created in the mid-sixties by Mayor Robert Wagner in response to the rising concern by New York residents like Mitchell over the loss of so many landmark structures—the 1963 demolition of the old Pennsylvania Station being a particularly infamous example. By the time Koch reached out to Mitchell, the commission was at odds with a number of historic churches for denying or altering some of their controversial development projects. The chairman of the commission, Kent Barwick, was an acquaintance of Mitchell's from Grace Church, where he was also a member. He knew how much Mitchell prized the city's architectural heritage. He also figured that appointing a new commissioner with official connections to Grace might be read by the city's churches and clerical groups as a conciliatory gesture.

In fact, at one of Mitchell's first commission meetings, representatives of Trinity Church, the venerable Episcopal institution in the heart of the Wall Street district, were presenting early renderings of a pedestrian bridge they wanted to build to connect the church with its offices and ancillary space across Trinity Place. Several commissioners were clearly unimpressed with the draft design, however, and the tension in the room began to build. Barwick thought it might be a good time to ask the heretofore-silent Mitchell to weigh in. As he did so, Barwick conspicuously reminded the petitioners that Commissioner Mitchell was a respected vestryman at Grace Church. But if Barwick expected diplomacy, he got candor. Summoning his best Carolina drawl, Mitchell pronounced, "It's just like Trinity—so arrogant. They've always been so *arrogant!*" The room erupted.

For an antiquarian and building lover like Mitchell, serving on the Landmarks Preservation Commission was a dream assignment. Commissioners routinely found themselves in the field examining buildings under review for protection. Mitchell delighted in traversing old, sometimes filthy buildings and filling notepads with architectural observations. He was particularly taken with cast-iron buildings. "He knew the history of every goddamned building in Soho," said Philip Hamburger.

Barwick, who would go on to serve several stints as president of the Municipal Art Society, had seen that expertise up close. In a sense, it was Mitchell who led Barwick to his life's work in the first place.

As a college student, Barwick spent a dime to buy a used copy of *McSorley's Wonderful Saloon*, then consumed it in one sitting. That inspired him to begin frequenting McSorley's, which he fell in love with. This ardor, in turn, caused Barwick to learn about a proposed redevelopment of the Cooper Square neighborhood, which would, among other things, put the wrecking ball to McSorley's. In a panic and unsure of what to do, Barwick called Mitchell, out of the blue. The writer sympathized, to the point where he agreed to accompany his new young friend to testify against the project before Mayor Wagner and the Board of Estimate. Riding back uptown in a cab after the meeting, Mitchell pointed out to Barwick various real estate developments and went into detail about how they came about—often as not, in New York tradition, via political chicanery. The young activist never forgot how knowledgeable Mitchell was, both about the buildings and about the deals behind them. (After years of argument, the Cooper Square project was defeated.)

Mitchell's combination of knowledge and passion made him effective on the Landmarks Commission. "He was always very generous with his time, very thoughtful," Barwick said. "Joe's knowledge of New York was quite unusual. He knew the people so well. He knew the city from the pavement up. He was really respected." The two would also work closely on the South Street Seaport project, and Barwick recalled in particular a speech Mitchell once gave at the museum. He wanted to make a point about cultural awareness. "Joe was passionate that people understand where their food came from. It wasn't just that he had a passion for the fish market and the seaport as historic places to be saved. He wanted people to know about the fishermen, the business, the market. He really wanted people to understand their relationship with food."

Still, the landmarks role was often a grind for a man in his seventies. When he was invited, Mitchell was told that the commission's work would take only several hours a month. In reality the board met frequently, and its meetings were often emotional and marathon affairs. One year into his term, Mitchell complained to a colleague that a recent session "as usual" lasted from 9:30 A.M. until nearly midnight. (In the same letter he expressed bemusement at his newly exalted station. "I am now one of the Commissioners and get letters extremely puzzling to the people in the mail room here addressed to the Honorable Joseph Mitchell.")

Looked at another way, the Landmarks Commission became virtually a second job for Mitchell during his five-year appointment. This far exceeded the volunteer's avidity he had, say, for his work at the seaport. Between the commission's numerous and protracted meetings and Mitchell's own passion for preparation, the landmarks commitment became almost all-consuming.

While this civic obligation clearly impeded Mitchell's writing, no one who cared about him could begrudge him something that gave him so much pleasure. Preservation initiatives like the South Street Seaport and the Landmarks Commission ultimately vindicated his long-standing belief that something important is lost when a great city turns its back on its history. On a personal level, his passion for acquiring architectural curios never relented. In fact, as Mitchell aged, he even demonstrated a willingness to get a little reckless in their pursuit. In one journal note, Mitchell describes his fixation with trying to remove the number off the doorway of a building that was to be razed the next morning. It was night, and he was working furiously, trying to keep one eye out for the authorities. Prying at the numbers wasn't working; eventually he realized they were bolted into place and that he would need to get inside the building to free them. The building, of course, was locked up tight. So in a spontaneous and adrenaline-fueled moment, he took his hammer and hurled it through one of the painted-over windows adjacent to the door. Having thus gained entry,

Mitchell sawed at the bolts for fifteen minutes until he tapped the numbers free.

A friend who had tagged along was alarmed at how what began as an after-dinner lark suddenly escalated to breaking and entering. That went too far, even with a building on the eve of being torn down. He told Mitchell he was beginning to think he was crazy.

"And I know I am," Mitchell said.

THROUGH ALL THIS, JOSEPH MITCHELL, creature of routine, reported to work at *The New Yorker* most every day, like every other staffer at the magazine. Well into his seventies, his health remained generally sound. Once a two-pack-a-day smoker, he had given up cigarettes back in the late 1950s. As an older man it now irritated him that climbing the stairs out of the subway left him a little winded. When he was diagnosed with a touch of arthritis, the idea of it bothered him more than any actual discomfort. Still, when he began to have some nagging pain in his neck and shoulders, he was persuaded to swap out his ancient wooden office chair for a modern, adjustable, ergonomically correct one. After trying it out for several days, Mitchell relegated the old chair to the corner of his office. This was an uncomplaining companion of more than four decades, over the years following him around *The New Yorker* "from office to office and floor to floor," a partner in some of the most significant stories he'd written. But as it became apparent that the new chair did in fact make him feel better, Mitchell decided to make the switch permanent, and one day while he was at lunch, a workman removed the old one. On his return, "I glanced over in the corner, and I had a sharp, intensely painful feeling of sadness," Mitchell said, "a feeling of disloyalty toward a discarded inanimate object." He recognized the sensation as precisely the same one he'd experienced many years before, when a mechanic informed him the family car was so far gone that it would cost more to repair than to replace with a new one. Mitchell reluctantly agreed and let it go for twenty-five dollars. He felt as if he'd just sold a child. "As we were leaving the garage," he remembered, "I turned and looked at the shabby, beat-up old car in which we had driven up and down the [North Carolina] roads with great enjoyment for three summers knowing that I would never see it again and I collapsed inside with shame and with pure, unadulterated gazing-down-into-the-open-grave-as-the-coffin-is-lowered bitter choked-up scalding grief."

All in all, however, Mitchell was holding up rather well. His life-long regimen of walking no doubt was paying dividends. He was still quite trim, if fighting a bit of the gentleman's paunch. He dressed as smartly as ever, his bald pate invariably covered with a fedora when he was out. The hair that still grew at each side was closely cropped and mostly gray. His blues eyes could still dance, twinkle, or pierce, on cue.

Mitchell still tended to take his lunch with coworkers, most often from his own cohort but not infrequently with younger ones. He preferred the humble yet reliable eateries in the vicinity of the magazine. Like many of the veteran *New Yorker* writers, Mitchell belonged to the Century Club, but, unlike them, he seldom went there. As he once quipped, "I'm saloonable, I'm even bar-and-grillable, but I have found out to my sorrow that I'm really not very clubbable." One long day that *did* begin at the Century, however, was especially memorable for one of those younger colleagues, writer Ian Frazier.

Frazier had come to *The New Yorker* from Chicago in 1974. At the time he didn't know Joseph Mitchell or even his work. But someone introduced him to Edmund Wilson's *Apologies to the Iroquois,* and he recalled being stunned by Mitchell's opening piece on the steelworking Mohawks and by the fact that a magazine article could pack that much sheer power and poignancy. Frazier was so moved that it sparked his own interest in the plight and culture of Native American communities, which he would go on to write about in such acclaimed works as *Great Plains.*

Frazier began to acquaint himself with Mitchell, who he said struck him like "someone from mythology" or a *Front Page* figure. "He just had this look about him, with his fedora and his suit and his raincoat," Frazier said. "He managed to combine real elegance with just the *possibility* that he could be a bum." He was also taken with Mitchell's occasional crankiness, especially concerning the inescapable march of technology. When the magazine updated its telephone system, Frazier and Mitchell attended an orientation session together concerning what the newfangled machines could do. Frazier was amazed at how openly disdainful Mitchell was of the woman leading the training, almost to the point of heckling her. When she was done, Mitchell asked, "Now, will these changes affect the phones down in the lobby?" The instructor, somewhat baffled by the question, said no, the lobby phones would be left alone. Replied Mitchell, "Then *those* are the phones I'm going to use."

One day Mitchell invited Frazier to lunch at the Century, where they talked for hours as the other diners came and went. Eventually they decided to move on to a bar, continuing their conversation. Then it was off to another bar, and then, finally, to McSorley's, where afternoon pleasantly passed into evening. Frazier was so entranced by Mitchell and their conversation that he forgot his wife was waiting for him at home—and that she was due any moment with their first child. In that pre-cellphone age, she'd had no way of tracking down a moving target. When Frazier finally got back to his Brooklyn home after "lunch," at around 8:00 P.M., he found not only his wife but his mother-in-law and sister-in-law waiting for him. By this point, he recalled, he was as intoxicated as they were irritated. After an awkward silence, Frazier finally blurted out the only thing he could think to say: "I was drinking all day with Joe Mitchell." With that simple declaration, all was forgiven; the three women, it turned out, were as much Mitchell fans as he was. (Some days later, Mitchell stopped Frazier at work and said, "You mean your wife was at home about to have a baby, and you were out all afternoon and evening drinking with me?" He paused. "Why, that was *irresponsible!*")

People did relish Mitchell's company; as Chip McGrath put it, "Every day you had a Joe sighting was a great day." Because their offices were on the same floor, McGrath said he often seemed to bump into Mitchell in the men's room, where they might engage in lengthy, impromptu conversations—Mitchell doing most of the talking—about James Joyce or more-contemporary writers or religion or the latest issue of *The New Yorker*. Mitchell seldom failed to surprise. In one such exchange, McGrath happened to mention that he felt the poet Elizabeth Bishop, who had recently died, was rather underappreciated. "And Joe blew me away by just standing there in the men's room, wadding up paper towels and reciting Bishop's poems. Holy shit; he did that. Whether he was writing or not, he was reading all the time. He knew everything." (After Jonathan Schell published the first of his "Fate of the Earth" articles in the magazine in 1982, Mitchell sent him a rare fan note, calling it "the most impressive article *The New Yorker* has ever published, including Hersey's *Hiroshima*. The predicament you are writing about, and dealing with so powerfully on so many levels—the so-called practical, the political, the philosophical, the religious, etc.—makes the predicaments that Gibbon and Spengler and Toynbee wrote about seem like Sunday school picnics.")

Nevertheless, where it came to Joseph Mitchell, most *New Yorker* people had one burning question: What was he doing? What were once whispers grew louder with each passing year—he seemed to be trapped in what was becoming the longest case of writer's block in history. There were all the signs that he was writing *something;* that's what he told people, and indeed his outward routine was essentially the same as it had been when he was producing stories. He would arrive, go into his office, remove his coat and hang it, shut the door, and go to work. Colleagues often purposefully cocked an ear as they passed that door, and they might well hear Mitchell inside, typing. But typing what? What was he working *on?* With the possible exception of what hermitic J. D. Salinger might be doing up there in New Hampshire, Mitchell was becoming the literary circle's biggest mystery. If anything, Mitchell's mystery was all the more fascinating because he was being (professionally) hermitic right there at work, under everyone's nose.

McGrath, Hamburger, and others confirm that the Mitchell fixation reached the point where some staffers were known to rummage in Mitchell's trash can, in a vain search for clues. But this curiosity was driven strictly out of respect, McGrath said, "it was not bemusement at all." In fact, it was precisely because Mitchell *was* such a revered writer that this compulsion to know what he was working on existed;

had he been a lesser figure, the question would have been of no consequence. Then again, a lesser figure never would have been extended the open-ended courtesy in the first place.

None of this was easy for Mitchell, of course. He was acutely aware not only of the internal curiosity but also of the growing number of people outside the magazine who wondered why on earth *The New Yorker* continued to pay a writer, his past accomplishments notwithstanding, who was not writing. "Joe had a hyperintelligence," said Hamburger. "I'm sure he was aware of [what was being said]. Nobody ever stopped to think of the pain, how painful it must have been for him not to be writing."

Others close to Mitchell acknowledged that. His daughter Elizabeth said that for a number of years after the publication of *Joe Gould's Secret*, the family wasn't especially cognizant of any particular "block" in his productivity, because the intervals between his later stories had become so protracted already and because he was continuing to pursue story ideas and conduct interviews much as he had before. They also appreciated the time he was committing to North Carolina. His brother Jack had died in 1983; that meant the farm supervision transferred to Joseph's surviving brother, Harry, and Joseph tried to help out as he could. One way was with the management of the properties' considerable woodlands. By this time Mitchell had become increasingly passionate about the many benefits of reforestation. He had seen the debilitating cycles of fire and disease; he became expert in discerning when trees had passed their maturity and should be timbered. "I am afraid [I am] almost obsessively interested in the subject," Mitchell admitted to a friend.

Nonetheless, Mitchell's daughters did gradually realize that something had changed about their father's writing work, that none of it was coming together as Mitchell wished, and in his later years he would sometimes talk to them about his inability to finish a story. Mitchell expressed guilt and anger about the situation, on occasion even apologizing for it—"a jumble of emotions," Elizabeth said. Her father, she concluded, had become a prisoner of his own expectations. In the same vein, Janet Groth, a *New Yorker* receptionist who knew

Mitchell well at this time, recalled that on the few occasions over lunch when Mitchell tried to talk about his writing difficulties, she caught "the note of suppressed panic in [his] voice." In conversations with friends like Roy Wilder, Mitchell also lowered his guard on the subject. "Sometimes I just wish they'd fire me and I would go home to North Carolina," Mitchell remarked in one such call.

But it remained the case that, taking Shawn's cue, no one in authority at the magazine really pressed Mitchell about the situation. They assumed—or at least hoped—that eventually this long-aborning work would simply materialize and that it would be so self-evidently wonderful that it would justify their indulgence.

Shawn's patience was an extension of the unorthodox philosophy the magazine always had about its writers—all flowing from founder Harold Ross. Writers were a different, difficult, balky, and inexplicable breed, Ross maintained, speaking from hard experience. Beyond that, different writers produced at different speeds and were motivated by different impulses. It was all very mysterious. Talent could perhaps be nudged, but it couldn't be stampeded. Thus, according to Brendan Gill, "lack of productivity [at *The New Yorker*] is neither rebuked nor deplored. On the contrary, it may be sneakingly admired, as proof that the magazine considers writing an occupation often difficult and sometimes, for the best writers, impossible."

Another of Mitchell's admirers at the magazine was the writer Calvin Trillin, who came a generation after Mitchell. In trying to explain the enigma of Mitchell's last fallow period, he said it was important to remember that *The New Yorker* was unusual in *many* regards—including the fact that it had so many full-time writers on the premises in the first place, when most magazines relied almost exclusively on contributors who typically worked from their homes. Since most *New Yorker* writers were paid by the piece, Trillin continued, no one really knew what anyone was up to—or cared all that much. "*Not* writing was not that unusual at *The New Yorker*," he said. "A lot of people forget that. It was always hard to tell what people were doing, exactly. At one point when I first got there, there were people on salary—very small salary—to write Talk of the Town, and as far as

I could tell none of them wrote Talk of the Town. They worked on fiction; I don't know what they did. It was like having a little fellowship."

At bottom, then, why wasn't Joseph Mitchell finishing anything? There is, unsurprisingly, no "magic bullet" answer. But in hindsight, one truth does emerge with an almost startling clarity. Even allowing for all the external factors that impeded his writing expectations, it was Mitchell himself who'd set things up so that there could be, in essence, only one outcome—failure.

That setup for failure occurred early on, in the wake of "Joe Gould's Secret," when Mitchell decided that his next project would be a full-blown book rather than simply another story.

In one of the rare instances where Mitchell tried to explain the long slump, he would write, "A number of years ago, after brooding off and on . . . about the fact that I have never actually written a book (all my books, as you know, are collections), I decided I would stop writing Profiles and Reporter at Large pieces for a while and go ahead and write a real book—as a matter of fact, I decided that I would write the unwritten book that I described in 'Joe Gould's Secret.'" Yet as straightforward as that sounds, it represented a huge challenge for Mitchell—because, as he acknowledged, that was something he had never done before, and he didn't quite know how to go about it. As complex as his stories were, books have their own structure and pace. Narrative threads and characters must be established and interwoven over a much longer arc, as the writer builds both his story and the tension to drive it. Just as many accomplished newspaper journalists stumbled with the transition to magazine writing at *The New Yorker*, the shift from short (nonfiction) story to book was no easy task, even for someone as deft as Joseph Mitchell.

That challenge becomes even taller when a writer isn't absolutely certain what story he wants to tell and what characters will tell it. In Mitchell's case, as has been seen, that was all something of a jumble. He knew the basic notions and themes he wanted to put across, but he never really figured out what to focus on or how to integrate the various themes into the operatic tale of New York he envisaged. In part to compensate for that indecision and inaction—and to show the rest of the world that he was still busy—Mitchell simply kept reporting, accumulating information and family histories and anecdotes about all these people and institutions: Ann Honeycutt, Joe Cantalupo, McSorley's, the Fulton Fish Market, himself. He felt—hoped—that in that activity the solution to his problem eventually would reveal itself, a *deus ex machina*. In the end, however, he merely wound up with overflowing file drawers full of paper, a ragged trove that, upon encountering it, one can imagine almost literally burying Mitchell and his book.

In time, then, Mitchell's inability to move forward preyed on his deep capacity for guilt, which in turn compounded his growing stress over the situation. And stress always could block Mitchell, especially when combined with discouragement—which, of course, the stress only exacerbated. As early as the mid-forties, Mitchell himself had taken note of this tendency. In a letter to friend John McNulty, he discusses having undertaken the reporting on what was planned as a two-part Profile—what would become "Dragger Captain." Mitchell was enthusiastic about the project, but he hit a snag, he says, and came to a hard stop for several months. "It drove me into the worst slump I've ever been in, and I got to feeling that if I didn't finish it, and finish it to my satisfaction, I'd never be able to write another word." If Mitchell had such an adverse reaction to a temporary obstruction, one can appreciate his being genuinely stymied by all these mounting pressures three decades later.

So it was that Mitchell was psychologically set up to struggle. Add to that the convergence of the other realities of his life: advancing old age and its attendant inertia; the personal tragedies and family obligations; the proliferating outside activities and diversions, such as his role with the city's historic preservation efforts—and in time the mere idea of writing a new, sustained work became essentially impossible. He was too weighed down with, as he described it, "that bleak and hollow remoteness that a writer who hasn't published anything for a long time is bound to feel. . . ." Mitchell had stepped into a trap, one largely of his own device.

By this point, whatever others thought he was up to, Mitchell himself was beginning to face up to the reality that his great "New York story" might never get written. He was tired in every respect, losing energy and losing heart.

On the other hand, he was beginning to think seriously about what he perhaps might do with the great New York story he had, in effect, already written.

CHAPTER 16

UP IN THE OLD HOTEL

Your letter is one of the first I am really answering because it has meant so much to me. If you remember, in your letter you said you had thought of writing to me about missing my stories in *The New Yorker* but had decided not to do so until you read in the Author's Note of my book that graveyard humor exemplified the cast of my mind—"so," you continued in your letter, "you will appreciate this: I thought you were dead." Well, Mrs. Edwards, I don't know why, but that delighted me. It filled me with cheerfulness. I keep the letter in the tray drawer of my desk and anytime one of those strange, sudden attacks of depression that many of us have hits me, I get it out and reread it, and it never fails to cheer me up.

—From a letter to a fan of Up in the Old Hotel, *1993*

. .

WITHIN A YEAR OF THERESE'S DEATH, A STILL-GRIEVING MITCHell determined he needed to resume a semblance of social life, and he began dating. One of the first people he saw was a fellow writer—Marie Winn, a New York City journalist, author, and urban naturalist who, among other things, was (and remains) an authority on the wildlife of Central Park. She is also the sister of *New Yorker* writer Janet Malcolm and sister-in-law of longtime *New Yorker* editor Gardner Botsford (who died in 2004), both good friends of Mitchell's. Over the years Winn and Mitchell, though not particularly close, had many overlapping acquaintances and so sometimes found themselves guests at the same dinners and cocktail parties. In the period after Therese's death, Winn, then formally separated from her husband, happened to be spending some time working in her sister's *New Yorker* office—giving herself, as she described it, a professional "change of scenery." Mitchell began dropping by when he saw her there, and before long they were keeping steady company.

The two had many shared interests, not least being New York City itself. Both also happened to be in emotional turmoil at this time and were feeling vulnerable. Winn had long been an enthusiast of Mitchell's work, and they would often make pilgrimages to sites of special significance to him, such as the Sandy Ground cemetery with George Hunter's grave. As their relationship deepened, Mitchell sometimes shared with her stray pages of work in progress, such as sketches from his journal, but Winn said she never saw anything that looked remotely "finished." In social settings, she became accustomed to people asking Mitchell what he was working on. "He was horribly tormented by that question," she recalled, and he invariably replied that he was hard at work on pieces about Joe Cantalupo or Ann Honeycutt. But in Winn's estimation that was essentially a stock response, "the party line—and then he would look at me and sort of wink."

Their relationship grew serious enough that the subject of marriage did arise, but in Winn's view it was always an unlikely prospect. Mitchell held the institution of marriage in such sober regard, she explained, that he would not have been comfortable feeling he had helped bring hers to an end. In fact, Mitchell over time subtly encouraged Winn to give her marriage another chance, and she and her husband eventually reconciled.

Even before Therese's death, Mitchell had maintained a regular Friday lunch engagement with Janet Groth, who while working at *The New Yorker* began doctoral studies at New York University. She would go on to a respected career as a university professor and author, with particular expertise in the life and work of yet another *New Yorker* figure, Edmund Wilson. After Therese's death, Mitchell apparently made a point of seeing even more of Groth, according to her published memoir. But while Groth was young and beautiful and Mitchell certainly had a flirtatious streak, the serial luncheon was a platonic one, she reported, their shared passion being literature—especially the works of Joyce, which had brought her to Mitchell's attention in the first place. The lunches came to a gradual end as Groth left the city to begin her academic career.

In time, Mitchell began to see a *New Yorker* colleague named Sheila McGrath, who was the executive administrator of the magazine's editorial department. She oversaw much of the behind-the-scenes mechanics of producing a weekly publication—getting staffers on the payroll, securing advances for writers, making travel arrangements, and so forth. Most important of all, she was a key liaison between the editorial staff and William Shawn in regard to the business aspects of his fiefdom. McGrath (no relation to fellow staffer Chip McGrath; a native of Newfoundland, she pronounced her name "McGraw") had an office on the magazine's twentieth floor, as did Mitchell, Brendan Gill, Philip Hamburger, Emily Hahn, and many other writers—and because of that proximity, she recalled, she met Mitchell on her very first day of work at *The New Yorker* in 1967. While she and Mitchell had been friendly through the years, they were not really close.

It was only after Therese's death, and almost by chance, that their relationship took a more intimate turn. One afternoon McGrath realized that several workdays had passed with no sign of or word from Mitchell, which, even allowing for his city wanderings, was uncharacteristic. Calling his apartment, she got no answer, so McGrath decided to go see for herself if everything was all right. When she arrived she banged on Mitchell's door, and after an uncomfortably long time with no response he finally answered—looking haggard and so weakened by flu that he'd barely been able to get off the couch. McGrath went off to restock his empty cupboard and helped get him through that illness. From that point they began going out, and they would remain a couple until Mitchell's death.

An actress as a young woman, McGrath shared Mitchell's love of literature, poetry, and the arts, and her temperament was as steely as Mitchell's was stubborn. Her sense of order—after all, keeping the magazine's internal affairs on track was essentially her job—nicely complemented Mitchell's *need* for order. And because she, too, had been reading Mitchell's writing almost all her life (McGrath's widely traveled parents in Newfoundland were early subscribers to *The New Yorker*), she had a deep appreciation for his life and work. Though she was some three decades his junior, they proved to be a good match.

McGrath took it upon herself to try to bring the vulnerable Mitchell back to emotional life. As part of that, they joined a mutual friend, Mary Painter—Shawn's longtime personal assistant—for a two-week vacation in Paris in the summer of 1984. Mitchell had always wanted to go to Paris; Liebling, the great Francophile, had urged him to make the trip for as long as they knew each other. Painter secured a large apartment near the Luxembourg Gardens, where she had stayed on previous visits, and the three of them happily explored the city's cafés, museums, bookstores, and side streets. Mitchell—no surprise—was enchanted. He and McGrath made their return by way of another great walker's city, London, and the entire adventure left Mitchell revitalized.

As McGrath had hoped, it also helped jump-start his thinking about that long-delayed book.

DIEHARD FANS, WHO HAD grown impatient waiting for a new Mitchell story that never arrived, and younger ones, who'd stumbled onto his work only through word of mouth, had to make do with his previously published books. But as time passed, those volumes became nearly as scarce as *new* Mitchell material. A veritable Mitchell cult gradually coalesced, with devotees who scoured secondhand bookstores for dog-eared copies of *McSorley's Wonderful Saloon,* or *Old Mr. Flood,* or even his first book, the collection of newspaper matter, *My Ears Are Bent.*

In the sixties, Calvin Trillin was working at *Time* magazine and didn't really know about Joseph Mitchell until a friend at *The New Yorker* lent him a copy of *McSorley's.* "I read it and I was just astonished by it," he says of the discovery. "I just think that [Mitchell] seems to get the marks of writing off of his prose so that it looked like it just appeared. You didn't feel him working on it. It was as if you were just looking at what he wanted you to look at without any interference, and that's a great art."

Not long after his initiation to Mitchell, Trillin went to work for *The New Yorker* himself. A fellow tenant in his building was Mitchell's close friend Robert MacMillan, a *New Yorker* editor, and "Bob agreed to let me borrow *My Ears Are Bent* if I promised not to take it out of the building." From that point on, Trillin, like so many others, sought all Mitchell's volumes in a kind of a quest. This was no small challenge; when Mitchell's books *did* turn up in stores, they were quickly snatched up by equally determined aficionados. In those pre-Internet days, Mitchell collectors would compare tactics and share accounts of how they came to win particular titles. Being the oldest of Mitchell's books, *Ears* was a genuine rarity. Trillin remembers coming across it at a bookstore in Seattle; the price tag said it was a mere three dollars. Knowing how scarce the book was, Trillin thought the listed price might be a mistake, and in fact, when he was checking out, the sales clerk examined the volume and said rather gruffly, "Where'd you get that book?" Trillin was anxious: "I had this irrational fear he was going to take it away from me," he recalled. When Trillin pointed to the shelf he had taken it from, the clerk informed him that there *had* in fact been a mistake: The books from that section were half off. So Trillin got his original copy of *My Ears Are Bent* for one dollar and fifty cents.

In truth, the Mitchell scarcity was a manufactured one, engineered by Mitchell himself. Over the years, publishers had implored him, practically pleaded with him, to permit the reissue of his books in paperback. But Mitchell resolutely declined. He felt strongly that paperback reprints, such as those of Liebling's work, seldom garnered serious attention or had much impact. Besides, he had another idea in mind— that one day all his books would be reissued in a kind of master anthology. But the notion had remained lodged in his head, while Mitchell ostensibly pursued his great New York tale like Ahab chasing the white whale.

In the end his quarry proved too elusive. By the late eighties, it had become clear even to Mitchell that he was not going to write a retrospective profile of Ann Honeycutt, his female doppelgänger; he was not going to be able to marshal the story of his mentor Joe Cantalupo as the centerpiece for his sweeping narrative of New York City; he was not going to compile another installment of the gypsies of the city—and it was increasingly unlikely he would be turning out any more chapters detailing his *own* life and experiences. Now an octogenarian, Mitchell knew in his heart that his writing life was done. If he didn't like that truth, he could at least live with it. But it saddened him to the marrow that as the manic modern world whizzed by him, it also seemed to be leaving behind his hard-earned reputation as a writer. By this point, Joseph Mitchell had come to grasp the dreadful irony: If he was known by a modern audience at all, it was for *not* writing.

As it happened, however, he wasn't quite correct about that. If Mitchell was done writing, he was not altogether finished publishing.

In the mid-eighties, Dan Frank was a talented young editor at Viking Books, where he was introduced to Mitchell via *Joe Gould's Secret*, which Viking had published. He was smitten. He went back and read all Mitchell's books, coming away with the idea to reprint each of them—upon which he learned that many editors before him, including at his own imprint, had had the same idea and failed. Frank, however, was undeterred. He was convinced there was still an appreciative audience out there for Mitchell's kind of stories. "I have in common with Joe a deeply elegiac sense of the transience of our lives coupled with the permanence of the past, a sense of being haunted by first and last things," Frank would later write. "And I of course wanted to succeed where all of my editorial colleagues else failed."

In 1986 he first reached out to Mitchell, suggesting that if they could meet for lunch, he promised *not* to discuss Mitchell's work—which Frank in fact honored. But as they became better acquainted, they did of course start talking about the past books, and Frank began to ascertain the obstacles he was up against. Mitchell believed the old books should be published together, not separately, and that omnibus volume should be hardcover. Unlike other editors Mitchell had spoken with, Frank thought both those ideas "made perfect sense." For him, the true hurdles lay elsewhere. For starters, Mitchell talked about including new, as yet unwritten pieces to freshen the anthology, in particular portraits of Honeycutt and Cantalupo. Frank's larger concern was that the idea of the new pieces was a tidy vehicle for further procrastination—how could you publish the book without all the material in hand?—and as such had proved quite useful to Mitchell. Frank could sense how torn the writer was about actually seeing the anthology into print. On one level Mitchell was eager about the idea, clearly, but on the other he dreaded the inevitable and uncomfortable questions he knew such a book would raise about what he had been doing since 1965.

Beyond that, Frank also grew to fear that Mitchell's pursuit of Cantalupo and Honeycutt was, at bottom, quixotic and ultimately unwinnable. "I felt that he knew that those pieces were embedded in a time and a place that was no more," Frank explained. "Whatever notes he may have assembled toward those pieces, the fact is that he was a reporter, and one of the conditions that allowed him to write was to return obsessively to the subject for one further detail, one further insight, observation, or clue—and that was no longer possible. [Cantalupo died in 1979; Honeycutt in 1989.] In some sense he became his subjects, and whatever that act of impersonation was required the person he was writing about to be available to him."

Still, as he courted Mitchell, Frank rode along with this prospect of incorporating new matter into the anthology. While the editor had no real objection to additions, neither did he think them essential. Mitchell's past work by itself—pulled together in a logical fashion, handsomely packaged, and intelligently promoted—would stand up well enough to sell, he felt. He thought the book would generate a lot of publicity. It would remind the long-ago fans of why they had waited so expectantly for the next Mitchell piece in *The New Yorker*, searching each week's issue like an Easter egg hunt. And, Frank hoped, it might bring an entirely new audience to Mitchell—readers born since his last published story.

Frank gained an influential ally in Sheila McGrath, who also believed there were still Joseph Mitchell readers out there. She quietly lobbied for the project, getting Mitchell to reread his stories and think about how they might be arranged and presented.

With Frank subtly pulling and McGrath subtly pushing, Mitchell began to warm to the idea. When a reporter for *New York* magazine called in early 1987 and inquired what his plans were, Mitchell replied that he had been working on an "omnibus" collection that would have old and new material and would also explain what he'd been up to all these years. Mitchell added that the book would be published within a year—but he characteristically and politely declined to say anything further about it, adding, "I'd like it to be a kind of surprise."

NOT LONG BEFORE THAT INTERVIEW, Mitchell received a surprise of his own—in fact, the most jolting piece of *New Yorker* news he'd had since the unexpected death of Harold Ross some thirty-five years earlier. Late one afternoon, Sheila McGrath poked her head into Mitchell's office, with "an expression of shock on her face," Mitchell would note in his journal. She had just learned that the owner of *The New Yorker*, media magnate S. I. Newhouse, was prying Shawn from the editorship of the magazine. This was January 12, 1987, and Shawn's final day was to be March 1.

The unthinkable news—Shawn no longer running *The New Yorker* was the cultural equivalent of the Dodgers no longer playing in Brooklyn—stunned not only the magazine's staff but the wider literary world, making the front page of *The New York Times*. Yet in retrospect the only truly surprising aspects were the timing and the manner in which it was done. Two years earlier, in equally stunning fashion, Newhouse—who had built his fortune on a string of newspapers around the country—had purchased *The New Yorker* from the Fleischmann family. That news had not gone down well with the staff or, in particular, with Shawn. Shawn issued a rare but pointed memo on the development, saying that "the editorial staff was not a party to these negotiations. Nor were the views of the editorial staff solicited during these negotiations. We were not asked for our approval, and we did not give our approval." Even though Newhouse at the time promised that Shawn would remain in charge and keep his independence, it was not an auspicious start. Newhouse and Shawn were every bit the other's equal for stubbornness. Beyond that, Shawn at the time of the sale was seventy-seven years old and had conveyed little credible evidence that he was thinking about leaving anytime soon.

Now he was essentially being fired. Taking his place would be the highly respected book editor Robert Gottlieb, who ran another iconic Newhouse property, Knopf. Mitchell and McGrath spent much of the rest of that day spreading the news to their colleagues and discussing possible responses. The next day there was a meeting of the entire editorial staff at the *New Yorker* offices, where Shawn told them that, contrary to what Newhouse had announced, he had had no intention of quitting on March 1; the decision had been made for him.

To a staff that had long prided itself and counted on its editorial freedom from the business side, the whole affair felt like a coup. And the assemblage responded in a way that would only happen at *The New Yorker*. A committee composed a letter to Gottlieb, politely but firmly imploring him to change his mind and turn down Newhouse. Mitchell and McGrath signed the petition, along with about one hundred fifty of their colleagues. These included almost all the leading staff writers and contributors—even the reclusive J. D. Salinger.

Gottlieb graciously declined the staff's offer to resign before he'd even begun, and a few weeks later he was making rounds in the *New Yorker* offices, starting to build relationships. One of the staffers he made a point of seeing was Mitchell. The two men talked for maybe fifteen minutes. They compared notes about their shared taste for idiosyncratic collecting—Mitchell with his pickle forks and handmade bricks, Gottlieb his kitsch purses from the city's flea markets. Mitchell then turned the talk to what he had been working on. "I tried to explain to him why I haven't finished anything in a long time, and I think I was able to. In other words, I think he understood me," Mitchell noted after the conversation. "I told him I have a deadline of my own—an inner deadline."

Though little more than a get-acquainted chat, the meeting left Mitchell a bit more hopeful about the editorial change he had been dreading. "I have a feeling things are going to turn out much better than I thought they would," he wrote.

The next day was Shawn's last at the office. It was a poignant and bittersweet occasion, especially for those few, like Mitchell, who had known the editor for his entire tenure at *The New Yorker*. There was to be a party for Shawn at day's end, but a melancholy Mitchell slipped out of the building early. When even William Shawn was seen to be expendable, the modern world had truly overtaken Joseph Mitchell.

A few months after Gottlieb took office, he picked up again with Mitchell, who went into more detail about having tried to work on "the most ambitious piece of my life" for a number of years, only to be tripped up by innumerable and painful "interruptions"—most especially the passing of his father and its various complications with the farm in North Carolina, followed by the long, agonizing death of Therese. Meeting yet again that October, Mitchell asked his editor, "Can you take another year [of me] working on this?" To which Gottlieb replied, "I'm not worrying about you if you're not worrying about us."

Years later, for a *New Yorker* retrospective on Mitchell's career, Gottlieb characterized these visits as "very pleasant," saying that he didn't press for details on Mitchell's work in progress and the writer didn't volunteer them. "I liked him, liked his work, and I wanted to be respectful without being demanding," the editor said. "I just showed, I hoped, a continuing affectionate interest without being exigent. It quickly became apparent to me that we were going through some ritual."

IN EARLY 1991, MITCHELL's "other" editor, Dan Frank, moved to Pantheon. Though he had continued to nudge Mitchell along for the past few years, he had yet to secure a commitment from him. That May, after yet another inconclusive conversation, Frank in frustration wrote to Mitchell:

Joe, I don't know how to persuade you to allow your work back into print. At lunch, we spoke briefly of how what the truth might look like would be little like what scientists or ministers have in mind. I recalled this on seeing some words of Eudora

Welty who, in talking of Walker Percy, said "only a judicious portion of this truth is the factual kind; much of it is truth about human nature, and more of it is spiritual." Your books possess that truth, and those fortunate to read your books, today or years hence, will recognize it and be enriched by it.

This entreaty must have done the trick, as soon after, the two came to a formal agreement that Pantheon would bring out the long-aborning Mitchell anthology, and by early summer they were deep into the logistical details. The book would pull together the material originally published in *McSorley's, Old Mr. Flood, The Bottom of the Harbor,* and *Joe Gould's Secret,* plus seven previously uncollected stories. These last would include some of his earlier North Carolina–based fictional pieces for *The New Yorker,* as well as such important later stories as "The Mohawks in High Steel" and "The Gypsy Women."

Mitchell continued to talk to Frank, as he had to his *New Yorker* editors, about the "new material" he'd been working on. Indeed, for the rest of his days Mitchell would reference these pieces as living things, works in process, albeit ones that were never forthcoming. This was not disingenuousness; there's no question that a part of Mitchell truly did hope he would be able to set the new stories down one day, even as another part knew he could not. According to Chip McGrath, who in his role as deputy editor of *The New Yorker* got updates from Mitchell, it always sounded as if he was "writing it in his mind."

Having the Pantheon contract and an actual plan energized Mitchell. "I haven't had a book published in so long, this feels like my first one," he told the *Times.* The book would be called *Up in the Old Hotel,* after the Profile of his old friend Louie Morino and doubtless because Mitchell appreciated the aptness of that story's theme—that, in the end, rummaging around for the past will get you dirty but little else. (Like every other aspect of the project, arriving at an acceptable title proved something of an ordeal. Initially, Mitchell pitched *Born Again: Four Unavailable Works of Joseph Mitchell,* but Frank persuaded him that would put the emphasis on the mere fact of publication rather than the material itself. Mischievously, Mitchell also suggested some part of "the worms crawl in" children's song from "The Rivermen." Frank demurred but indicated that pulling *some* phrase from Mitchell's oeuvre did make sense, which ultimately they did.)

Mitchell became keenly focused. He wrote his own flap copy for the book's jacket. With Sheila McGrath's help, he read over every scrap of the previously published material, making small edits here and there (as a confirmed technophobe, he was disconcertingly amazed how easy this was once his drafts were put into a computer) and trying to decide whether the story order should be shuffled around to make more sense in the omnibus format. For the most part, Mitchell kept the story lineup consistent with the original books. His goal was, in the main, to have related material appear together while still keeping the overall arc of the stories largely in chronological order. Thus, the new stories were all inserted into the *McSorley's* section. He left the first Joe Gould Profile in *McSorley's*, where it had originally appeared, but kept the long sequel by itself at the end of the anthology. This vetting process was painstaking, in one sense literally. About this time Mitchell was dealing with complications from cataract surgery, including a detached retina that hospitalized him for several days. The situation for many months made reading most uncomfortable for Mitchell, and writing difficult.

Still, he was gratified to be assaying his life's work all at once. He was especially delighted, he wrote, to find "how often a kind of humor that I can only call graveyard humor turned up in them," he wrote in the "Author's Note" for the collection. He goes on to recount some of his Fairmont childhood and explains how the family's tradition of communing in cemeteries had ultimately caused him to connect the folly and futility of life with our final resting places.

Then, in a vivid end note, Mitchell ties his own sardonic outlook to his discovery as a young man of a late Mexican artist who, it turned out, was a kindred soul:

Another influence on my cast of mind has been a Mexican artist named Posada. I first heard of him in 1933, during the worst days of the Depression, when I was a reporter on the *World-*

Telegram. I had gone up to the Barbizon-Plaza Hotel to interview Frida Kahlo, who was the wife of Diego Rivera and a great painter herself, a sort of demonic surrealist. That was when Rivera was doing those Rockefeller Center murals. Thumb-tacked all along the walls of the hotel suite were some very odd engravings printed on the cheapest kind of newsprint. "José Guadalupe Posada," Kahlo said, almost reverentially. "Mexican. 1852–1913." She told me that she had put the pictures up herself so she could glance at them now and then and keep her sanity while living in New York City. Some were broadsides. "They show sensational happenings that took place in Mexico City—in streets and in markets and in churches and in bedrooms," Kahlo said, "and they were sold on the streets by peddlers for pennies." One broadside showed a streetcar that had struck a hearse and had knocked the coffin onto the tracks. A distinguished-looking man lay in the ruins of the coffin, flat on his back, his hands folded. One showed a priest who had hung himself in a cathedral. One showed a man on his deathbed at the moment his soul was separating from his body. But the majority of the engravings were of animated skeletons mimicking living human beings engaged in many kinds of human activities, mimicking them and mocking them: a skeleton man on bended knee singing a love song to a skeleton woman, a skeleton man stepping into a confession box, skeletons at a wedding, skeletons at a funeral, skeletons making speeches, skeleton gentlemen in top hats, skeleton ladies in fashionable bonnets. I was astonished by these pictures, and what I found most astonishing about them was that all of them were humorous, even the most morbid of them, even the busted coffin on the streetcar tracks. That is, they had a strong undercurrent of humor. It was the kind of humor that the old Dutch masters caught in those prints that show a miser locked in his room counting his money and Death is standing just outside the door. It was Old Testament humor, particularly the humor in Proverbs and Ecclesiastes. Gogolian humor. Brueghelian humor. I am thinking of that painting by

Brueghel showing the halt leading the blind, which, as I see it, is graveyard humor. Anyway, ever since that afternoon in Frida Kahlo's hotel suite, I have been looking for books showing Posada engravings. I never pass a bookstore or a junk store in a Spanish neighborhood of the city without going in and seeing if I can find a Posada book. My respect for him grows all the time.

Up in the Old Hotel was published in August of 1992. As the date neared, Mitchell's anxiety grew. Would anyone want it? Would anyone even remember who he was?

He needn't have worried. *Hotel* came out to tremendous critical acclaim. (The cover of the paperback edition, still in print almost a quarter-century later, features the same iconic Mitchell photograph as the frontispiece of this book.) It was as if a long-lost treasure had been retrieved from the ocean floor for people to appreciate all over again.

The critical response was unalloyed joy tinged with reverence. The *Times* typified this admiring tone, calling the book in essence a gift to New York: "That city, the one in which Joseph Mitchell finds his gloom lifted by the smoke [of the Fulton market] itself, no longer exists. But a book like *Up in the Old Hotel*—in print forever, one hopes—will cause another melancholy soul . . . to look in the waste places of the present city, listen to its lunatic ravings and report back to us, as amply and as sympathetically as Mr. Mitchell has done. 'STAND AT THE BAR AND JUST LISTEN.'"

Beyond the reviews—maybe even more important than the reviews—was the personal attention *Hotel* prompted for Mitchell. Suddenly he seemed to be everywhere. There were television interviews, newspaper feature stories, profiles, photographs—most of the latter showing the same well-dressed, trim man, carrying a little more wear and tear but no less dapper than before. He looked younger than his eighty-four years; he was still walking the city, still vigorous, still mischievous. He had to juggle several pairs of glasses to contend with his lingering eye problems, but, other than that, about his only concession to old age was switching from regular leather shoes to black "dress" Reeboks. More than flattering, the stories all reminded people of Mitchell's substantial body of work and planted him firmly in the American literary pantheon. His decades-long spell in the wilderness was scarcely mentioned.

Mitchell's joy is evident at a book party celebrating the publication of Up in the Old Hotel.

A touching bonus came in the hundreds of fan letters that arrived, many from friends and acquaintances he hadn't heard from in decades. Mitchell was delighted by the turn of affairs—delighted, stunned, and humbled. He had not been forgotten after all, it turned out, merely misplaced.

All the attention also rekindled his enthusiasm. In one of the 1992 interviews he gave in conjunction with the publication of *Hotel*, Mitchell refers—in the present tense—to still wanting to finish the autobiographical history of the fish market. "I just hope I can hold on long enough to write about these things," he said. "At the end of your life, you are the only one who knows how far short you fell from what you intended. And that doesn't help, because at the end of your life you don't always know what you intended."

CHAPTER 17

HOMECOMING

[I] GOT IN THE habit of looking at people—people sitting across
from me on a bus, for example—and speculating on how much time
they had left on Earth. A vigorous young girl—she may have seventy-
five years ahead of her. An old woman—she won't be here this time
next year, lying in some cemetery somewhere. A thin, wiry, sharp-
eyed old man—not an ounce of excess fat on him—he's the kind
who'll live forever. He's many years older than I am, but long after
I'm dead and gone, he'll be around.

—*From Joseph Mitchell's journal, circa early seventies*

. .

ONE AFTERNOON MITCHELL AND SHEILA McGRATH WERE RETURN-
ing to Manhattan on the ferry after a day trip to Staten Island.
Seated out in the open air, they noticed a yellow piece of paper scut-
tling along the deck toward them, when it suddenly swept up onto
their bench as if being delivered. McGrath grabbed the sheet, which
had writing on it, and as she read the message she was taken aback:
"My name is Mitchell," it said. "Please take me home." She handed it
over, and she saw the writer blanch as he in turn took in the words.
McGrath thought Mitchell might even faint, so clearly unsettled was
he by something she took for an enigmatic coincidence but he inter-
preted as anything but.

"Joe was a great believer in talismans, charms . . . he believed in evil
spirits," Philip Hamburger said of his friend. "He knew damn well
that there *were* evil spirits out there." For much of his life, in fact,
Mitchell carried with him a handmade iron nail that had passed down

to him from his grandfather's cotton mill, Hamburger pointed out. "He thought this was good at warding off whoever these spirits were."

For Mitchell, one would have to say the talisman, in the main, did its work well. He led a long and lovely life—in many ways, yes, even a charmed one. He had a satisfying and mutually gratifying marriage of half a century's duration. It was a union that produced two children, five grandchildren, and a great-granddaughter, all of whom adored Mitchell, and vice versa. He grew up with the privileges and culture afforded a Southern planter's son yet came of age in New York City at its most magical and captivating, where he met countless of the era's leading figures. For six decades he worked for a magazine that writers respected more than any other, under not one but two of the most influential editors in the history of American letters—both of whom let Mitchell do precisely as he pleased. And near the end of his life he capped that career with a triumphant professional rebirth.

If his life's journey had its share of sorrows, too, no one knew better than Mitchell that that was the way of things, and at the end of the day not even the most potent talisman was going to prevent that. Let the dead bury the dead.

Only a month after *Up in the Old Hotel* was published, Robert Gottlieb left *The New Yorker* and was replaced by an even more controversial appointment, the young British editor Tina Brown, fresh from her rehabilitation of one of *The New Yorker*'s sister imprints, *Vanity Fair*. It was true that Brown had a taste for the sensational and a genius for publicity-grabbing provocation, but those qualities often caused people to overlook her substantial editorial gifts—not least being her appreciation of writing talent. Brown, like Gottlieb, arrived with an immense respect for Mitchell and his past work. And like Gottlieb, she hoped he could be coaxed from his writing slump. Telling him "it is still my dream" to publish some new Mitchell material, no matter how modest, Brown tried a number of inducements. She prevailed on him to weigh in when there was a major fire at the Fulton Fish Market. On the occasion of *The New Yorker*'s seventieth anniversary, in February of 1995, she asked if he might write a short memoir. When Shawn died in December of 1992, and the magazine was preparing its tribute to him, she solicited a contribution from Mitchell, who had worked for Shawn for about as long as anyone on the premises. But each time approached, Mitchell said that he couldn't oblige, much as he might wish to. He liked Brown well enough and appreciated her ministrations, even if, like many of *The New Yorker's* veteran guard, he was discouraged by "old colleagues retiring or dying or being fired or having to vacate their offices to make way for the incoming Brits, and all that." But creatively he seemed spent.

Physically, though, he was still just fine—to most who encountered him, in fact, he appeared nearly age-resistant. A full medical workup in November of 1994 confirmed that. While Mitchell had put on a little more weight than he liked in recent years and on occasion experienced an irregular heartbeat, there seemed to be nothing of any real consequence ailing him. Meanwhile, he and McGrath were continuing to enjoy their relationship. She often accompanied him on his trips back to North Carolina, and in the summer of 1994 they took an extended vacation to England and Ireland. They lingered especially in Dublin, where Mitchell happily retraced the footsteps of the Joycean characters he knew like old friends.

In part because he still felt spry, Mitchell, even at this late juncture, was quietly contemplating one final writerly overture for the magazine. His enthusiasm still elevated from the warm reception for *Hotel,* Mitchell turned up at McGrath's apartment one day with a grocery sack full of typewritten pages and plopped it on a table. The unorganized pile represented much of the start-and-stop work he had occupied himself with for the previous three decades, including many of the sketches, notes, and anecdotes from his irregular journal. He had never shared this material with her before. He invited McGrath to look it over and to let him know if she saw anything that, with some rewriting, might be suitable for *The New Yorker.* McGrath excitedly waded into the pile and immediately latched on to the three essentially complete chapters of autobiographical matter. She consolidated the typewritten pages and entered them into her computer. McGrath felt that with very little additional work, these forays into Mitchell's personal history could be put into publishable condition.

Had Mitchell been granted but a little more time, McGrath said, he would have done just that, for he gave all evidence of preparing to tackle this new project with the same enthusiasm he had brought to *Hotel*.

Curious about the natural world even as an old man,
Mitchell studies the flora near his Fairmont home.

In the waning months of 1995, however, things came to an abrupt stop. Mitchell began to experience bouts of back pain, of mystifying origin, and the discomfort became severe enough that it began to affect his gait. Through that winter and into spring Mitchell went to a number of doctors, including internists and orthopedists, and underwent a lengthy series of tests for everything from disk issues to tuberculosis. He and McGrath became increasingly frustrated as they heard an assortment of potential diagnoses about the cause, even as the symptoms worsened. Finally, a doctor diagnosed lung cancer, which was subsequently confirmed—but which, by that time, had metastasized to his brain. A lingering Mitchell premonition had come true.

Mitchell was admitted to Columbia-Presbyterian Medical Center in New York, but the cancer was beyond cure. In those final days, his family and loved ones gathered around him. At one point, as the end neared, he quietly said, "There was so much I still wanted to do."

Joseph Mitchell died on May 24, 1996. He was eighty-seven years old.

The family returned him to Fairmont for his funeral and burial, ending a tug-of-war for Mitchell's affection that began his first week in New York City almost seven decades earlier. Several dozen people attended the funeral, which was presided over by the pastor emeritus of Fairmont's First Baptist Church. His eulogy naturally recounted Mitchell's literary achievements, but as the writer's hometown pastor, he used the occasion to figuratively return Mitchell to his roots. He noted how appreciative the Fairmont community was that Mitchell had seen fit to come back so often in the latter years of his life, helping with the farm and in particular reforesting the family properties. At the end, turning to Nora and Elizabeth, he added that the daughters were "grateful most of all for his goodness as a person, and his love and faithfulness as a father. I feel that Joseph Mitchell treasured this more than all the other honors combined."

Then Mitchell, who throughout his life had found so much beauty and comfort in graveyards, was laid to rest in the Floyd Memorial Cemetery, next to Therese. As he once wrote in his journal: "An old man walking alone down a cemetery path, [you] can tell by the way he walks that he knows exactly where he is going: among all these graves, he has a certain one in mind." The tombstone awaiting Mitchell bore an epitaph from Shakespeare's elegiac seventy-third sonnet, a favorite line of his selected by his daughters: "Bare ruined choirs, where late the sweet birds sang."

THE PASSING OF JOSEPH Mitchell was marked by obituaries and appreciations from all over the English-speaking world. Unsurprisingly, the most expansive of these was produced by Mitchell's colleagues at *The New Yorker*, which gave over six pages of the June 10, 1996, edition to his life and literary import—a tribute comparable only to what they had done a few years earlier at Shawn's passing. "Joseph Mitchell, who died May 24th, at the age of eighty-seven, was a staff writer at *The New Yorker* for fifty-eight years and was one of its dearest and most irreplaceable friends," the piece began. "But his death is not merely a personal loss to his colleagues, or a loss to the magazine. He was an essential figure in modern writing and in the history of the city."

The man who had outlasted Ross, Shawn, E. B. and Katharine White, Wolcott Gibbs, James Thurber, his friend Liebling—and so many others who had forged the magazine—was remembered by such contemporaries as Brendan Gill, William Maxwell, Roger Angell, and Philip Hamburger. Lillian Ross recalled the first time she read *The New Yorker*, in 1944, and discovered Mitchell by encountering the indelible figure of Hugh G. Flood. "As I read, I knew immediately that I wanted to report and to write in a way that would be worthy of Joe Mitchell," Ross wrote. "When I joined the magazine—Joe used to call it 'our paper'—I discovered that everybody else here also wanted to write in a way that would be worthy of Joe Mitchell. Nobody ever tried to imitate him, but everybody learned from him. Mystically, he gave us the key to finding our own original ways of working."

Calvin Trillin testified similarly of Mitchell as an inspiration. Once, while promoting a book in the seventies, Trillin was asked about writers he admired. He replied that he'd be willing "to trade pretty much everything I'd written for a paragraph of 'Old Mr. Flood' or 'Joe

Gould's Secret.'" Reading his own quote later in the newspaper, Trillin said it hit him as so overly "flowery" that it might embarrass Mitchell. As it happened, *The New Yorker*'s in-house newsletter reprinted the interview, and one day Mitchell turned up at Trillin's office with a copy in hand. He thanked Trillin for the compliment. "I guess I sort of got carried away," Trillin said sheepishly. Mitchell smiled and said, "You're not going to take it back, are you?"

Two decades after he brought out *Up in the Old Hotel,* editor Dan Frank still marvels at the unique transit that was Mitchell's career—from journeyman journalist to a literary writer of the first rank. It was a rare and inspirational achievement in American letters. "When you look at his work as a daily beat reporter during the 1930s, you realize how quick he was, how adept he was at the type of copy a newspaper—especially one whose editions were appearing three or four times a day—demanded," Frank explained. "And [you see] how skilled he was at listening. But when you move from his early work to the compositions of the 1950s, you realize that his purpose [then] stood at direct cross-purposes to his original goal: the desire to find ways to record in more lasting form what was in danger of disappearing, to find a way in words to preserve what would otherwise be unnoticed, lost sight of, disappear. . . . Novelists create fictional characters that may be based in part on people they knew; Joe did the opposite—he took the Sloppy Louies and Mr. Hunters and 'represented' them with all the imagination, depth, and complexity that a novelist employed in the creation of his characters. Only Joe's characters were real, and his 'representation' of them placed them in a context, a community, a history, a past that was larger than them, so that one could see how they were shaped, from whence their outlooks and attitudes came."

For many contemporary journalists and writers of nonfiction, Mitchell *still* inspires. And it's likely that as long as human beings are laid low by life's trials and humiliations, and as long as they somehow manage to overcome or outlast these indignities, Joseph Mitchell's work will endure.

In 1982, a political science professor from California sent Mitchell a note that, as smartly as anything he'd ever received, summed up what his life's work had meant to countless appreciative readers over the years. "I do not know of anyone whose writing so happily combines the qualities of purity, simplicity and unaffectedness, of kindness, sweetness and serenity, as does yours," he told Mitchell. "At least they are its qualities that, for me, over and over again are present in it and are the source of the great pleasure I take in it. I always glow with a gentle cheerfulness, feel somehow cleaner, more contented, and more appreciative, after I have read even a few pages from one of your books." The fact that Mitchell kept this particular letter close at hand and often returned to it, especially in those final years when he wandered in the professional wilderness, suggests that the effects his writing had on this particular reader were precisely the ones he'd hoped to achieve all along, from the earliest days of his apprenticeship to his ultimate mastery.

Would it have been wonderful to have some fresh Mitchell in the final trimester of his life? Without question. But *Up in the Old Hotel* alone comprises thirty-seven stories and almost three hundred thousand words, and that reckoning doesn't take into account Mitchell's grinding decade of newspaper work, which produced at least several million more. By any fair measure he was not only productive but, in his day, prolific. More to the point, everything he *did* write mattered. As Philip Hamburger would say when asked about his friend's output, "Why didn't he write more? Well, he wrote enough."

In the end, maybe it was Mitchell himself who set forth the most exacting measure of a writer's enduring worth—and, in typical fashion, he did so by channeling the wisdom of another. In the eulogy he delivered many years before for A. J. Liebling, Mitchell related a conversation he had with a longtime owner of a secondhand bookstore, who talked about the steady demand that remained for Liebling's out-of-print books. "Literary critics don't know which books will last," the bookseller told Mitchell. "And literary historians don't know, and those nine-day immortals up at the Institute of Arts and Letters don't know. *We* are the ones who know. We know which books can be read only once, if that, and we know the ones that can be read and re-read and re-read."

In early 1996, just three months before Mitchell died, the Modern Library published an elegant new edition of *Joe Gould's Secret*. Though Mitchell was battling his still-undiagnosed cancer, he rallied enough to do a reading from the book at an event that February at Books & Co. in Manhattan.

His Modern Library editor, Susan DiSesa, recalled that Mitchell was unusually nervous about the appearance. He was unaccustomed to such readings, and he asked her, "Do you think anyone will come?" The reading was set for 6:00 P.M., and to calm himself Mitchell came by the bookstore an hour early to practice at the microphone. But when he arrived, a small crowd had already gathered. Before long the presentation area was packed, and by six the audience filled the store's staircase and stretched out the front door. "Joe glowed," DiSesa said. "He read beautifully for thirty minutes. At the end, he signed books, new ones and old out-of-print ones. . . . He talked, posed for pictures, laughed. The scene became a wonderful party."

Among the crowd were family members, friends, and *New Yorker* colleagues. But so, too, were a waitress from his beloved Oyster Bar at Grand Central; the owner of McSorley's; a union janitor with a strike placard; lawyers; editors; secretaries—and a stripper.

Mitchell people.

ACKNOWLEDGMENTS, AND A NOTE ON THE SOURCES

· ·

I T WAS MY HAPPY FORTUNE TO GET TO KNOW JOSEPH MITCHELL, LATE in his life, as I was reporting a biography of a person he revered, *New Yorker* founding editor Harold Ross. I talked to Joe about Ross on a number of occasions, sometimes in his small, spotless office and at other times on the phone. He could not have been more gracious or helpful. He was also personally at peace at that time, as *Up in the Old Hotel* had just appeared and the world was rediscovering what those of us in journalism had never forgotten—here was the master.

Some years later, when I was a new dean at the University of Maryland's Philip Merrill College of Journalism and looking for a creative project in my discipline, I hit on the idea of a biography of Joe himself, who had died in 1996. Even allowing for the triumph of *Hotel*, I still felt he was remembered too much for what he hadn't written—the wilderness years of his late career—instead of for what he had. Alas, I badly underestimated the extent to which academic administration monopolizes body, soul, and calendar. And I certainly never foresaw actually running an entire school, which I have done since 2008 as president of St. Norbert College, a remarkable liberal arts institution just outside Green Bay, Wisconsin.

Thus this portrait of Joseph Mitchell took much longer than I expected. At times along the way, as one interruption after another slowed my progress, I began to think that Joe's decades-long writer's block wasn't so mystifying after all! Nonetheless, I wish to thank Joe's family and friends for their unfailing patience with me. I am grateful as well to my colleagues both at Maryland and St. Norbert for their understanding as I pursued this book.

I owe special thanks to Joe's two daughters, Nora Mitchell Sanborn and Elizabeth Mitchell, who shared so much with me about their father but also, importantly, about their mother, Therese. In addition to sharing their memories, they gave me hundreds of documents, letters, photographs, and other family treasures. And Nora in particular must be acknowledged for writing some years ago an extensive and colorful family history, from which I have drawn liberally.

Joe's lone surviving sibling, Harry Mitchell, was welcoming to me from the outset. So, too, was Joe's nephew Jack Mitchell, who still lives in Fairmont in the house adjacent to where Joe grew up. Jack helped me understand not only the family history but the rhythms and routines of farm life in that part of North Carolina. Another of Joe's nephews, David Crowley, was generous as well with family details and photographs.

Sheila McGrath was Joe's literary executor, and another *New Yorker* person I got to know when I was working on the Ross biography. This book would not have been possible without her encouragement and support. Sheila died after a three-year battle with cancer, and her daughter, Ashley Fraser, was very helpful to me as I was bringing the book to a conclusion.

I am deeply grateful to the distinguished critic Norman Sims, a professor in the Commonwealth Honors College at the University of Massachusetts at Amherst. Norman is an expert on literary journalism, and in 1988 and 1989 he conducted three interviews with Joe, in which he talked expansively about his writing techniques, theories, and motivations. Norman drew on these interviews for several important publications of his own. But he graciously provided me full transcripts of the Mitchell interviews, which I have mined extensively here. Likewise, another colleague, Ben Yagoda, professor of English and journalism at the University of Delaware, interviewed Joe for his sweeping *New Yorker* history, *About Town: The New Yorker and the World It Made*, and made the full transcript available to me.

An old friend, Clint Williams, was a lifesaver; he kept me moving with his reporting assistance and copious editorial suggestions and hunches. It was Clint, for instance, who realized that Joe almost certainly suffered from a condition called dyscalculia, the mathematics analog to dyslexia.

Another friend, the late *New Yorker* writer Philip Hamburger, got me on my way by spending hours remembering Joe and their days together at the magazine. Phil loved Joe and provided great insight into his friend's quirky and sometimes contradictory personality. I thank as well those other *New Yorker* friends and colleagues of Joe's who were especially helpful to me—including, but not limited to, Chip McGrath, Calvin Trillin, Ian Frazier, Roger Angell, Gardner Botsford, Mary Painter, and David Remnick. Thanks also to the specialists at the New York Public Library's Rare Books and Manuscripts division and to the Center for Oral History at Columbia University.

I'm grateful to Marie Winn, David Britt, Ken Koyen, Roy Wilder, Jr., Kent Barwick, Jack Sargent Harris, and others who spoke to me about Joe. And to Jim Rogers for his expertise on Joe's writing, Mike Capuzzo for his encouragement and suggestions, and Gene Roberts—like Joe, a treasured son of North Carolina—for his local knowledge, mentoring, and friendship. And as for Amy Sorenson and Jamie McGuire, they make all things possible.

I owe much to Dan Frank, not only for his help with this book but because it was Dan's tenacity and good judgment that made *Up in the Old Hotel* a reality and thus introduced Joseph Mitchell to a new generation of fans.

At Random House, David Ebershoff and his associate Caitlin McKenna oversaw this project with acuity and sensitivity, and copy editor Kathleen Lord applied her keen eye and ear. I also want to thank the legendary Bob Loomis. I'm sorry I outlasted you into your well-deserved retirement, Bob, but I'll be forever grateful to you for signing up this project and believing in it so fervently.

Peter Matson—so patient and discerning and supportive—you're the best.

Finally, to my wife, Deb, and our family: So many wonderful and momentous things have happened to us in the years this book was aborning. Thank you for your constant support and understanding as I was sharing so much of that time with Joe Mitchell.

—Thomas Kunkel
Summer 2014

NOTES

ABBREVIATIONS

JM is Joseph Mitchell

MEAB is *My Ears Are Bent*

NMS is Nora Mitchell Sanborn

NS is Norman Sims

UITOH is *Up in the Old Hotel*

CHAPTER 1: THE WONDERFUL SALOON

6 "As in [Old John's] time, fresh sawdust": JM unpublished essay on McSorley's, January 1979.

6 "find a chair at one of the round tables": JM journal note, undated.

6 "most of the NYC that I knew": Ibid.

6 one of the few places left where Mitchell could "escape for a while": Ibid.

9 "He is a reporter only in the sense": Stanley Edgar Hyman, "The Art of Joseph Mitchell," *The New Leader*, 12/6/65.

9 His characters "might have come straight out of Dickens": Malcolm Cowley, "The Grammar of Facts," *The New Republic*, 7/26/43.

CHAPTER 2: THE CENTER OF GRAVITY

14 "I spent a large part of my childhood": JM unfinished autobiography.

14 "From the time I was old enough": Ibid.

15 "happens to be a remarkably inexact": JM, *UITOH*, p. xvi.

15 "I used to climb a tremendous white oak": JM unfinished autobiography.

16 In early spring of 1896: Interview with David Britt.

18 "I don't know if she expected": NMS family memoir.

21 "I wasn't worried about my father": JM journal note, undated.

21 A.N. "was very smart and a good businessman": NMS family memoir.

22 "A lot of men made their career decision": Interview with David Britt.

22 "Know a little something": JM journal note, undated.

23 She was "one of the finest women": Interview with David Britt.

24 "she must have had a pretty hard life": NMS family memoir.

24 "Averette, did your ox fall in the ditch?": Interview with Sheila McGrath.

25 "This is for me": Thomas L. Rich, Jr., JM funeral eulogy, 5/28/96.

26 the "irritation in his voice": JM journal note, undated.

27 "Let the dead bury the dead": JM interview with NS.

27 "I never heard my own father": JM journal note, 1977.

27 "I'm not in favor of people taking": Ibid.

28 "Friend, I have resigned": JM, "The Downfall of Fascism in Black Ankle County," *UITOH,* p. 355.

29 "They were just little one-ring circuses": (Raleigh, N.C.) *News & Observer,* 8/16/92.

29 "a veritable carnival": NMS family memoir.

29 "My father was very proud": JM interview with NS.

31 "God is everywhere": JM journal note, undated.

33 He grasped "the significance and provenance": NMS family memoir.

33 he "developed an interest in it": JM journal note, undated.

34 "How wonderful it was to find them": JM interview with NS.

34 "Here and there she would pause": JM, *UITOH,* p. xi.

35 "It was the first time I ever heard" and dynamite story: JM journal note, undated.

35 "He never said so in so many words": Ibid.

36 "You have to be extremely good at arithmetic": JM interview with NS.

36 "deliberately or inadvertently": JM journal note, undated.

36 "He would ruin meals": NMS family memoir.

38 "Go to the board": JM journal note, 1986.

CHAPTER 3: CHAPEL HILL

39 "I dimly recollect one day": JM to Francis Hayes, 9/3/85.

40 "his paralysis over mathematics": NMS family memoir.

40 "It became obvious": JM to Rex Stout, 5/9/44.

42 "I probably learned more about writing": JM to Jim Kelly, 8/6/76.

42 "I remember our meetings": John Armstrong Crow to JM, 9/22/92.

43 "I knew I had to get some other way": JM interview with NS.

43 "I stumbled up the stairs": JM, "Friday Night," *The Carolina Magazine,* June 1928.

44 "Yuh can trust a good horse": JM, "The Man Who Liked Horses Better Than Women," *The Carolina Magazine,* April 1928.

44 "He holds out his hand": JM, "Three Field Sketches," *The Carolina Magazine,* March 1928.

45 "They sat on the porch quietly": JM, "Cool Swamp and Field Woman," *The New American Caravan,* 1929, p. 138.

47 "I call it deadly determination": Interview with Jack Mitchell.

47 "Son, is that the best you can do": (Raleigh, N.C.) *News & Observer,* 8/16/92.

47 "Well, son, do the best you can": JM journal note, undated.

CHAPTER 4: DISTRICT MAN

48 "New York in the thirties": Interview with Philip Hamburger.
49 "A great many New Yorkers": JM interview with NS.
50 "Half the soda jerks": (Raleigh, N.C.) *News & Observer,* 8/16/92.
50 "He did not actually say so": JM journal note, undated.
51 "one of the most exciting periods of my life": JM to Thomas Waring, 6/4/81.
52 "We used to sit in the doorway": JM, *MEAB,* p. 4.
53 "Everyone was watching the tall": JM, *MEAB,* p. 142.
54 lived in a series of "furnished-room houses": JM unfinished autobiography.
54 "I started walking, all day": JM journal note, undated.
56 "Lost my shyness—would approach anyone": Ibid.
57 "Well, I own a horse": David Crowley to author, 8/18/05.
58 "She . . . had a benign view": NMS family memoir.
59 "You made your bed": Ibid.
59 Therese considered it "inevitable" that her talented husband would outshine her as a writer: Ibid.
60 "decided the story was too hot": Richard Kluger, *The Paper: The Life and Death of the New York Herald Tribune,* p. 250.
61 Mitchell nursed his grudge for months: The account of Mitchell's tantrum in Ogden Reid's office is drawn from various sources, including recollections of Stanley Walker, Joan Walker Iams, and Mitchell himself, in his journal notes.
63 "I got tired of hoofing after": JM, *MEAB,* p. 7.
63 "This was no career for anyone": Interview with Jack Sargent Harris.
64 "There were very few words in Joe": Ibid.
64 "even the winch-drivers": JM, *MEAB,* p. 7.
65 "It is south of Leningrad": Ibid.
65 "the smell of sacrifice in the streets": JM op-ed piece in *New York Herald Tribune,* 1931 (specific date uncertain).
66 "Looking back on it": JM journal notes, undated.

CHAPTER 5: ASSIGNMENT: NEW YORK

68 "my oldest friend in New York": JM journal note, undated.
68 "He ate too much just like Joe Liebling": JM interview with Ben Yagoda, 1995.
69 Cantalupo "was so involved in the fish market": Ibid.
69 he became a "fish market buff": JM to E. Virgil Conway, 12/11/74.
69 "I got a feeling for New York speech": (Raleigh, N.C.) *News & Observer,* 8/16/92.
70 "There would be a whole lot of wreaths": JM interview with Nora Sayre.
70 "Get out of it": JM, *MEAB,* p. 280.
70 "[A]nother visitor was Mickey Welch": Ibid., p. 119.
72 "After painfully interviewing one of those gentlemen": Ibid., p. 15.
73 "The best talk is artless": Ibid., p 11.
74 "Persons whose names are in the *Social Registers*": JM, "They Got Married in Elkton," *The New Yorker,* 11/11/33.

75 "She decided to sing": JM, "Home Girl," *The New Yorker*, 3/3/34.

76 "The relatives were waiting": JM, *MEAB*, p. 211.

76 "It takes ten beers to quench one's thirst": Ibid., p. 183.

78 "There was a peculiar journalistic world": JM interview with Nora Sayre.

80 "compared with our competitors": JM, *MEAB*, p. 20.

80 "The questioning of Mrs. Anne Morrow Lindbergh": *New York World-Telegram*, 1/3/35.

81 "We used to go down there at night": JM, *MEAB*, p. 21.

82 "In the morning all the ashtrays": Ibid., p. 23.

83 "Be more debonair": Thomas Kunkel, *Genius in Disguise: Harold Ross of The New Yorker*, p. 260.

84 "When the Lindbergh trial is over": St. Clair McKelway to JM, 1/9/35.

85 "Outside the leaves on the maples": JM, *MEAB*, p. 173.

86 "It was a hell of a lot better to know": Richard Gehman, "Jack Bleeck and The Formerly Club," *True* magazine, January 1953.

87 "My memories of that period": Ann Honeycutt interview with Nora Sayre.

88 called Honeycutt "a Molly Bloom figure": *The New York Times*, 12/29/96.

88 Thurber "slapped me from across the table": Burton Bernstein, *Thurber: A Biography*, p. 174.

90 "She was naked": JM, "Mr. Grover A. Whalen and the Midway," *The New Yorker*, 7/3/37.

91 "Frankly, we are a little puzzled by it": St. Clair McKelway to JM, 11/30/36.

91 "The essential trouble with these stories": Ibid., 10/1/37.

93 and he "began telling me how to look at the world": JM interview with author.

93 "I began to see that I had written": Ibid.

96 "Perhaps no other city in the world": *New York Herald Tribune*, 1/23/38.

CHAPTER 6: A REPORTER AT LARGE

102 something "very unusual" for the editor: St. Clair McKelway to JM, 7/22/38.

102 "Look, Mitchell, if you'd like to come up here": JM interview with author.

103 "This formality being over": Harold Ross to JM, 9/8/38.

103 "Half the people here were always in debt": JM interview with author.

104 "Mitchell, who has been working for us": William Shawn to Harold Ross, August 1943.

105 Mitchell asserted that Maryland-style terrapin stew: The Mitchell–H. L. Mencken anecdote about terrapin stew comes from a series of exchanges among JM, Mencken, and St. Clair McKelway in 1939.

112 "For quite a while, the people I wrote about": JM interview with NS.

112 Mazie "ran a movie theater": JM interview with author.

112 "In *My Ears Are Bent* Mazie is indeed": Noel Perrin, "Paragon of Reporters: Joseph Mitchell," *The Sewanee Review*, Spring 1983.

113 "Sometimes a bum" and "Now and then, in the Venice": JM in *MEAB*, p. 100, for the first; and JM in *UITOH*, p. 25, for the second.

114 Ross "had a view of those people": JM interview with NS.

115 Mitchell "looked at freaks with love and affection": Interview with Philip Hamburger.

115 "I urged Diane not to romanticize freaks": Patricia Bosworth: *Diane Arbus: A Biography*, p. 177.

115 "The difference between Joe Mitchell's portrait": Interview with Philip Hamburger.

116 "Liebling had read a story I'd written": JM interview with NS.

116 Borrow was "a forerunner of Joe's and my interest": Raymond Sokolov, *Wayward Reporter: The Life of A. J. Liebling*, p. 98.

117 Colonel Robert R. McCormick "daily assures Chicagoans": A. J. Liebling, "Cassandra on Lake Michigan," *The New Yorker*, 1/14/50.

117 "In the light of what Proust wrote": A. J. Liebling, "Memoirs of a Feeder in France: A Good Appetite," *The New Yorker*, 4/11/59.

117 it "liberated me to talk to Joe": JM interview with NS.

118 "Pecker bone of a young": Interview with Roger Angell.

118 Mitchell "understood the complicated importance": Sokolov, *Wayward Reporter*, p. 232.

119 "The Joes often went to the Red Devil": Brendan Gill at JM memorial tribute, 10/7/96.

119 "Therese Mitchell took photographs of them": Sokolov, *Wayward Reporter*, p. 123.

124 Joe Gould "wasn't just a bum": Ross Wetzsteon, *Republic of Dreams: Greenwich Village: The American Bohemia, 1910-1960*, p. 419.

124 take off in "awkward, headlong skips": JM, "Professor Sea Gull," *UITOH*, p. 64.

125 "I remember telling [my] editor": JM, "Joe Gould's Secret," *UITOH*, p. 633.

125 "I understand you want to write something": JM, Ibid., p. 635.

128 "Look," he said. "You're the one": Ibid., p. 680.

CHAPTER 7: THERE ARE NO LITTLE PEOPLE

130 "They lived in this cramped little apartment": Interview with Philip Hamburger.

131 "Look at the bosom": Interview with NMS.

136 "the purpose of this interview": This and subsequent particulars are from the report of the Civil Service Commission interview.

139 "For years he has been studying": *Time*, 8/2/43.

140 "He is a remarkably competent, careful": *New York Herald Tribune*, 8/1/43.

140 "Mitchell's collection of portraits": Cowley, "The Grammar of Facts."

CHAPTER 8: MR. MITCHELL AND MR. FLOOD

149 "Tell the mayor of the fish market": M. Lincoln Schuster to JM, 11/24/44.

149 "Thank you ever so much for your telegram": JM to M. Lincoln Schuster, 11/27/44.

150 "I had been trying to write this thing": JM interview with NS.

153 "Insofar as the principal character is concerned": JM to Milton Greenstein, 9/28/61.

154 "ten or twelve people have spoken of": Harold Ross to JM, 11/28/44.

155 "People, throngs of people, went down there": JM interview with NS.

155 "When I first read ['Old Mr. Flood'], I took it": Interview with Philip Hamburger.

156 "Joe has been working hard at being an old man": Brendan Gill, *Here at The New Yorker*, p. 318.

156 "On his ambivalence about strong drink": JM, "Mr. Flood's Party," *UITOH*, p. 428.

156 "On pretentiousness": JM, "The Black Clams," *UITOH*, p. 408.

157 "On 'new and improved' foods": JM, Ibid., p. 397.

157 "On religion and the hereafter": JM, "Old Mr. Flood," *UITOH*, p. 375.

157 "On life": JM, "The Black Clams," *UITOH*, p. 408.

157 "All the things I said in there about eating fish": JM interview with NS.

157 "Joe was a man who dwelt at great length": Interview with Philip Hamburger.

157 "Sometimes facts don't tell the truth": JM interview with NS.

158 was "appalled" by the idea of continuing: Ibid.

158 "As a reporter of the New York scene": *New York Herald Tribune*, 10/24/48.

159 the Mr. Flood pieces "fiction of the highest": Interview with Philip Hamburger.

CHAPTER 9: THE BOTTOM OF THE HARBOR

165 "I'm enclosing a clipping": JM to Ellery Thompson, 5/13/48.

167 "a fascinating book to anyone interested": JM to Daniel deNoyelles, 6/12/78.

167 "Books, so many books": Interview with NMS.

167 "I [wrote] with a kind of shorthand": JM interview with NS.

168 "If you're going to have lunch with him": Interview with Philip Hamburger.

169 "He butchered according to Leviticus": JM journal note, April 1989.

170 "Mitchell invented a temporal dimension": *Village Voice*, 4/29/05.

171 His desk held a glass full of "needle-sharp pencils": Gardner Botsford, *A Life of Privilege, Mostly*, p. 149.

171 Nonfiction writing "has to have a lyricism": JM interview with NS.

172 "I'd insert maybe three commas": Interview with Gardner Botsford.

172 "[He] took forever to write a piece": Botsford: *A Life of Privilege, Mostly*, p. 196.

174 "I would report that I've read": Harold Ross to JM, 7/26/49.

182 "This climax is a tremendous letdown": Perrin, "Paragon of Reporters: Joseph Mitchell."

182 "articles about old restaurants were getting to be": JM journal note, 6/27/78.

183 "remember conversations word for word": JM journal, undated.

184 "Something that Louie said after we came down": JM interview with NS.

CHAPTER 10: MR. HUNTER

186   "You had to make every edge cut": JM reporting notes for "Mr. Hunter's Grave."

187   "[E]very time I read the Anna Livia Plurabelle section": JM, *UITOH*, p. xii.

194   "He knew that everything had fallen apart": *The New York Times*, 7/22/92.

194   "The revelations that keep coming": JM interview with NS.

195   "I couldn't really write about anybody": Ibid.

198   "At *The New Yorker*, and in nonfiction writing": Ben Yagoda, *About Town: The New Yorker and the World It Made*, p. 401.

199   it was difficult to say "how much . . . is gospel and how much": Ibid.

199   "[This] manifestly is not quote at all": Ibid.

200   "Yes, there was something literary": Interview with Dan Frank.

201   "If you find [a subject]": JM interview with NS.

201   "We don't know what the hell is going on": JM interview with NS.

202   "I've been reading your pieces": John Davenport to JM, 10/19/56.

203   "We are observing": George Hunter to JM, 12/10/56.

CHAPTER 11: A RIVER IN A DREAM

205   "I really don't know how they did it": Interview with NMS.

205   Therese would "saunter down the street": NMS, in an introduction to an exhibition of Therese Mitchell photographs, July 2006.

206   "He was so canonical": NMS family memoir.

208   "He . . . spoke to his family every Sunday": Ibid.

208   "He generally thought people were pretty horrible": Interview with NMS.

208   "I told him . . . how that traumatized me": Ibid.

208   "As I said, either 'harbour' or 'harbor'": JM to Ivan Von Auw, Jr., 10/14/61.

209   "Listen, Nick," Mitchell snapped, "when I feel like": (Fredericksburg, Va.) *Free Lance-Star*, 11/17/41.

209   could "suddenly become a different person": Interview with Philip Hamburger.

210   "is generally the way he reacted": NMS family memoir.

211   his "genius for finding real-life metaphors": *The Washington Post*, 7/21/85.

213   "The memorable things in *The Bottom of the Harbor*": *The New York Times*, 4/24/60.

214   "One day [Ross] put his head in my office": JM to James Thurber, 8/24/57.

214   "When I first came to *The New Yorker*": Ibid.

215   "Mr. Liebling, if you're expecting": JM journal note, undated.

218   "someone had beaten [us] to the punch": JM interview with NS.

218   "If [Mitchell] ever disappears": Gill, *Here at The New Yorker*, p. 319.

218   His "antiquarianism was obsessive": Interview with Philip Hamburger.

218   "He had enormous collections of old bricks": Ibid.

CHAPTER 12: JOE GOULD REVISITED

221 "In this state," Mitchell wrote: JM, "Joe Gould's Secret," *UITOH*, p. 681.

223 "I was exasperated": Ibid., p. 687.

226 "I have been working on [it]": JM to Clayton Hoagland, 5/1/63.

227 "a *New Yorker* Profile that I've been working on": JM to Roy Wilder, Jr., 11/17/63.

227 "You'd love London, I think": St. Clair McKelway to JM, 8/6/57.

229 "You could hear Liebling": Interview with Philip Hamburger.

229 "Every Christmas since 1963": JM to Jean Stafford, 1/23/78.

230 "Everybody sat for a while": JM eulogy for A. J. Liebling, January 1964.

233 "Then we realize that Gould has been Mitchell": Hyman, "The Art of Joseph Mitchell."

233 Gould "is Mitchell's nightmare vision of himself": Christopher Carduff, "Fish-eating, Whiskey, Death & Rebirth," *The New Criterion*, November 1992.

233 "To me a very tragic thing": JM interview with NS.

233 "bolsters rather than contradicts Mitchell's suspicions": *Village Voice*, 4/7/00.

CHAPTER 13: INTO THE PAST

236 "My share in the proceeds": JM to A. N. Mitchell, 7/23/64.

237 "One day the producer called me up": JM to Rose Wharton, 10/21/64.

237 "Afterwards, we went over to the Ritz-Carlton": Ibid.

238 "No one on the eighteenth floor": Susan Sheehan to JM, 9/24/64.

238 "Joseph Mitchell is one of our finest journalists": *The Washington Post*, 9/19/65.

238 "Mitchell is a formidable prose stylist": Hyman, "The Art of Joseph Mitchell."

240 "When the New Journalists came ashore": Norman Sims, *True Stories: A Century of Literary Journalism*, p. 165.

240 "We never thought of ourselves as experimenting": JM interview with author.

241 "I was a reporter, and then I became a magazine writer": JM journal note, undated.

241 "I didn't have a whole lot of interest": JM to Evan Elliot, 10/10/90.

243 "he fed that alligator everything he could think of": JM interview for the North Carolina Awards, 1984.

244 *The Robesonian*—"a novel I have been reading": JM unfinished autobiography.

245 "I especially liked it because it linked me": JM to Roy Parker, October 1983.

245 "After I'm down in North Carolina": JM interview with NS.

245 "a town in which I grew up": JM unfinished autobiography.

246 "We always thought Joe would come back": Interview with Harry Mitchell.

246 "I have offered to give [Joseph] the McCall farm": Interview with David Britt.

246 wielding a "long carving knife": JM journal note, 7/28/74.

247 "See if the commode will flush": Ibid.

248   "One of the reasons I got so depressed": Ibid., 1974.

249   "I very rarely feel altogether at ease": Ibid., 7/29/74.

251   "I no longer have much enthusiasm for New York City": JM to Roy Wilder, Jr., 8/12/72.

252   "I know the exact day that I began living in the past": JM unfinished autobiography.

253   "I was very sure that he was seeing": JM journal notes, undated.

254   "In other words": JM to Ellery Thompson, 12/18/75.

254   "The reason I have hesitated to write to you": JM to K. C. Butler, 9/22/76.

257   "I am only now beginning to realize": JM journal note, undated.

257   "I wanted his respect": (Raleigh, N.C.) *News & Observer*, 8/16/92.

257   "No matter how boring it may sound": JM to Ann Honeycutt, 3/14/77.

CHAPTER 14: INTO THE WILDERNESS

258   "Except for Maron Simon": JM to Thomas Waring, 6/4/81.

260   "they simply weren't representative": JM journal note, undated.

260   He was "distinctly a New Yorker": JM interview with Ben Yagoda.

262   "What I must establish as quickly as possible": JM journal note, undated.

263   "Well, take it easy": Ibid.

263   "I got to be like the younger brother": JM interview with Ben Yagoda.

263   "Listening to Joe talk about her": *The New York Times*, 12/29/96.

264   "We had without ever talking about it": JM journal note, undated.

264   "I went back into the kitchen": Ibid.

265   "I began to be oppressed": JM unfinished autobiography.

265   "use myself as the center": JM journal note, undated.

266   Shawn called it "some of the best writing": Ibid., 5/14/70.

267   Shawn was "content to wait": Interview with Charles McGrath.

267   "That was an embarrassment to me": JM interview with NS.

268   "that costs two hundred dollars each time": This and subsequent comments about his finances from JM's journal notes, circa 1970.

270   Mitchell was being "sidetracked" by a variety of things: JM interview with NS.

270   "He gave me the impression": JM journal note, 4/6/77.

271   "Find out the year the old barn": JM journal notes, undated.

276   they are "ragweed, Jimson weed, pavement weed": JM, "Mr. Hunter's Grave," *UITOH*, p. 529.

276   "Setting these objects side by side": Luc Sante in foreword to reissue of JM's *The Bottom of the Harbor*, 2008.

277   Mitchell thought it "the best restaurant in the city": JM to Linda Mitchell Lamm, 1/20/64.

279   "He had strong feelings about it": NMS family memoir.

280   he came to "believe wholeheartedly": JM to E. Virgil Conway, 12/11/74.

280   "In 1970, James Cameron": JM unpublished essay on McSorley's, January 1979.

281   "Why don't you give up farming": JM to Francis Hayes, 9/3/85.

283 "I'd be telling her it was going to get better": (Raleigh, N.C.) *News & Observer,* 8/16/92.

283 Therese at this time "sounded woozy": Interview with David Crowley.

284 "When she was in Marblehead": JM journal note, undated.

285 "She had a loving heart": Ibid., circa autumn 1980.

285 "One of my most haunting memories": Interview with Elizabeth Mitchell.

CHAPTER 15: A GHOST IN PLAIN VIEW

287 "After she died": NMS in an undated essay on her mother.

287 he held some "unease as a native of his Baptist": Brendan Gill at JM memorial tribute, 10/7/96.

289 "I'm a ghost": *The New York Times,* 5/25/96.

289 a book that he'd "had to postpone": JM to Thomas Waring, 6/4/81.

290 "It's just like Trinity—so arrogant": Interview with Kent Barwick.

291 "He knew the history of every": Interview with Philip Hamburger.

291 "He was always very generous": Interview with Kent Barwick.

292 "I am now one of the Commissioners": JM to Noel Perrin, 9/28/83.

293 "I glanced over in the corner": JM journal note, 1/21/88.

294 "I'm saloonable": Ibid., undated.

294 "He just had this look about him": This and subsequent story from an interview with Ian Frazier.

295 "Every day you had a Joe sighting": Interview with Charles McGrath.

296 calling it "the most impressive article": JM to Jonathan Schell, 2/8/82.

296 "it was not bemusement at all": Interview with Charles McGrath.

297 "Joe had a hyperintelligence": Interview with Philip Hamburger.

297 "I am afraid [I am] almost obsessively": JM to Shelagh and John Metcalf, 12/18/90.

297 "a jumble of emotions": Interview with Elizabeth Mitchell.

298 she caught "the note of suppressed panic": Janet Groth, *The Receptionist: An Education at The New Yorker,* p. 38.

298 "Sometimes I just wish they'd fire me": Remarks by Roy Wilder, Jr., on JM's induction into the North Carolina Literary Hall of Fame, 5/17/97.

298 "lack of productivity [at *The New Yorker*] is neither": Gill, *Here at The New Yorker,* p. 314.

298 "*Not* writing was not that unusual": Interview with Calvin Trillin.

299 "A number of years ago, after brooding": JM to Addison Potter, 6/23/82.

300 "It drove me into the worst slump": JM to John McNulty, 12/30/45.

300 "that bleak and hollow remoteness": JM to Addison Potter, 6/23/82.

CHAPTER 16: UP IN THE OLD HOTEL

302 "Your letter is one of the first": JM to Lucretia Edwards, 7/29/93.

303 "He was horribly tormented": Interview with Marie Winn.

305 "I read it and I was just astonished": This and subsequent story from interview with Calvin Trillin.

307 "I have in common with Joe": Interview with Dan Frank.

309 "I'd like it to be a kind of surprise": *New York,* 2/9/87.

309 "the editorial staff was not a party": William Shawn note to *The New Yorker* staff, 3/8/85.

310 "I tried to explain to him": JM journal note, 2/12/87.

311 "Can you take another year": Ibid., 10/16/87.

311 "I liked him, liked his work": Mark Singer, "Joe Mitchell's Secret," *The New Yorker,* 2/22/99.

311 "Joe, I don't know how to persuade": Dan Frank to JM, 5/22/91.

312 he was "writing it in his mind": Interview with Charles McGrath.

312 "I haven't had a book published": *The New York Times,* 7/22/92.

315 "That city, the one in which": *The New York Times,* 8/16/92.

317 "I just hope I can hold on": (Raleigh, N.C.) *News & Observer,* 8/16/92.

CHAPTER 17: HOMECOMING

318 "My name is Mitchell" story: Interview with Sheila McGrath.

318 "Joe was a great believer in talismans": Interview with Philip Hamburger.

319 Telling him "it is still my dream": Tina Brown to JM, 4/28/94.

320 discouraged by "old colleagues retiring": JM to Peter Shepherd, 12/31/92.

322 "There was so much I still wanted": Singer, "Joe Mitchell's Secret."

322 the daughters were "grateful most of all": JM funeral eulogy by Thomas L. Rich Jr., 5/28/96.

324 "When you look at his work": Interview with Dan Frank.

325 "I do not know of anyone whose writing": Addison Potter to JM, 6/17/82.

325 "Why didn't he write more": Interview with Philip Hamburger.

326 "Joe glowed": Susan DiSesa at JM memorial tribute, 10/7/96.

SELECTED BIBLIOGRAPHY

American Caravan IV, Alfred Kreymborg, Lewis Mumford, and Paul Rosenfeld, eds. New York: Macauley, 1931.

"An Appreciation of Joseph Mitchell," Raymond J. Rundus, ed. *Pembroke Magazine,* No. 26, 1994.

The Art of Fact: A Historical Anthology of Literary Journalism, Kevin Kerrane and Ben Yagoda, eds. New York: Touchstone, 1997.

Baker, Russell. "Out of Step with the World." *The New York Review of Books,* 9/20/01.

Beller, Thomas. "The Old Man and the Seafood." *The Village Voice,* 4/29/05.

Bernstein, Burton. *Thurber: A Biography.* New York: Dodd, Mead, 1975.

Blount, Roy, Jr. "Joe Mitchell's Secret." *The Atlantic Monthly,* August 1992.

Bosworth, Patricia. *Diane Arbus: A Biography.* New York: Alfred A. Knopf, 1984.

Botsford, Gardner. *A Life of Privilege, Mostly: A Memoir.* New York: St. Martin's, 2003.

Bourke, Angela. *Maeve Brennan: Homesick at The New Yorker.* New York: Counterpoint, 2004.

Carduff, Christopher. "Fish-eating, Whiskey, Death & Rebirth." *The New Criterion,* November 1992.

Carrington, Tucker. "The Grammar of Hard Facts: Joseph Mitchell's *Up in the Old Hotel." Virginia Quarterly Review,* Winter 1996.

Corey, Mary F. *The World Through a Monocle: The New Yorker at Midcentury.* Cambridge: Harvard, 1999.

Cowley, Malcolm. "The Grammar of Facts." *The New Republic,* 7/26/43.

Emery, Edwin. *The Press and America: An Interpretive History of the Mass Media,* 3rd ed. Englewood Cliffs: Prentice-Hall, 1972.

Gill, Brendan. *Here at The New Yorker.* New York: Random House, 1975.

Groth, Janet. *The Receptionist: An Education at The New Yorker.* Chapel Hill: Algonquin, 2012.

Hyman, Stanley Edgar. "The Art of Joseph Mitchell." *The New Leader,* 12/6/65.

"Joseph Mitchell." Reminiscences by various *New Yorker* writers. *The New Yorker,* 6/10/96.

Kinney, Harrison. *James Thurber: His Life and Times.* New York: Henry Holt, 1995.

Kluger, Richard. *The Paper: The Life and Death of the New York Herald Tribune.* New York: Alfred A. Knopf, 1986.

Life Stories: Profiles From The New Yorker, David Remnick, ed. New York: Random House, 2000.

Literary Journalism in the Twentieth Century, Norman Sims, ed. New York: Oxford, 1990.

Kunkel, Thomas. *Genius in Disguise: Harold Ross of The New Yorker.* New York: Random House, 1995.

Mehta, Ved. *Remembering Mr. Shawn's New Yorker: The Invisible Art of Editing.* Woodstock, N.Y.: Overlook, 1998.

Mitchell, Joseph. *My Ears Are Bent.* New York: Sheridan, 1938.

———. *McSorley's Wonderful Saloon.* New York: Duell, Sloan and Pearce, 1943.

———. *Old Mr. Flood.* New York: Duell, Sloan and Pearce, 1948.

———. *The Bottom of the Harbor.* Boston: Little, Brown, 1960.

———. *Joe Gould's Secret.* New York: Viking, 1965.

———. *Up in the Old Hotel, and Other Stories.* New York: Pantheon, 1992.

The New American Caravan, Alfred Kreymborg, Lewis Mumford, and Paul Rosenfeld, eds. New York: Macauley, 1929.

Perrin, Noel. "Paragon of Reporters: Joseph Mitchell." *The Sewanee Review,* Spring 1983.

Rogers, James. "Old Men in Graveyards: Joseph Mitchell's Dialogue with Seumas O'Kelly." *Canadian Journal of Irish Studies,* Spring 2009.

Ross, Lillian. *Here But Not Here: A Love Story.* New York: Random House, 1998.

———. *Reporting Back: Notes on Journalism.* Washington: Counterpoint, 2002.

Rundus, Raymond J. *Joseph Mitchell: A Reader and Writer's Guide.* New York: iUniverse, 2003.

Severo, Richard. "Joseph Mitchell, Chronicler of the Unsung and the Unconventional, Dies at 87." *The New York Times,* 5/25/96.

Singer, Mark. "Joe Mitchell's Secret." *The New Yorker,* 2/22/99.

Sokolov, Raymond. *Wayward Reporter: The Life of A. J. Liebling.* New York: Harper & Row, 1980.

True Stories: A Century of Literary Journalism, Norman Sims, ed. Evanston: Northwestern, 2008.

Wetzsteon, Ross. *Republic of Dreams: Greenwich Village: The American Bohemia, 1910–1960.* New York: Simon & Schuster, 2002.

Yagoda, Ben. *About Town: The New Yorker and the World It Made.* New York: Charles Scribner's Sons, 2000.

Zinsser, William. "Journeys with Joseph Mitchell." *The American Scholar,* Winter 1993.

PHOTO CREDITS

INDEX

Page numbers in *italics* refer to illustrations.

THOMAS KUNKEL is the author of *Genius in Disguise: Harold Ross of The New Yorker*, and he also edited a collection of Ross's letters. He has written or edited four other books. He is president of St. Norbert College in De Pere, Wisconsin, and prior to that he served eight years as dean of the Philip Merrill College of Journalism and president of *American Journalism Review* at the University of Maryland. Before moving into higher education, he worked as a reporter and editor at several of the nation's most respected newspapers. He and his wife, Debra, live in De Pere.

ABOUT THE TYPE

This book was set in Caslon, a typeface first designed in 1722 by William Caslon (1692–1766). Its widespread use by most English printers in the early eighteenth century soon supplanted the Dutch typefaces that had formerly prevailed. The roman is considered a "workhorse" typeface due to its pleasant, open appearance, while the italic is exceedingly decorative.